KW-483-338

Contents

BRITISH POETRY SINCE THE SIXTEENTH CENTURY

A Students' Guide

John Garrett
Associate Professor of English
University of Qatar

MACMILLAN

HERTFORDSHIRE
LIBRARY SERVICE

No.
H22 802 1106

Class
821.009

Supplier	Price	Date
DN	5.95	8/88

© John Garrett 1986

All rights reserved. No reproduction, copy or transmission
of this publication may be made without written permission.

No paragraph of this publication may be reproduced, copied
or transmitted save with written permission or in accordance
with the provisions of the Copyright Act 1956 (as amended).

Any person who does any unauthorised act in relation to
this publication may be liable to criminal prosecution and
civil claims for damages.

First published 1986

Published by
MACMILLAN EDUCATION LTD
Houndmills, Basingstoke, Hampshire RG21 2XS
and London
Companies and representatives
throughout the world

Typeset by
Wessex Typesetters
(Division of The Eastern Press Ltd)
Frome, Somerset

Printed in Hong Kong

British Library Cataloguing in Publication Data
Garrett, John
British poetry since the sixteenth century:
a students' guide.
1. English poetry–History and
criticism
I. Title
821'.009   PR502

ISBN 0–333–41370–9
ISBN 0–333–41371–7 Pbk

Acknowledgements

I wish to thank my colleagues Professor Alexander Kinghorn and Dr Neil McEwan for their valuable advice in the preparation of this text for publication.

The author and publishers wish to thank the following who have kindly given permission for the use of copyright material: Jonathan Cape Ltd for 'Fire and Ice' by Robert Frost from *The Poetry of Robert Frost* edited by Edward Connery Lathem; Chatto & Windus Ltd for 'Anthem for Doomed Youth and extract from 'Strange Meeting' by Wilfred Owen from *The Collected Poems of Wilfred Owen* edited by C. Day Lewis; Faber and Faber Ltd for 'Mūsee des Beaux Arts' and extracts from 'Their Lonely Betters' from *Collected Poems* by W. H. Auden and 'A Childish Prank' and extracts from 'That Moment' and 'Crow and the Birds' from *Crow* by Ted Hughes; Grafton Books for 'Buffalo Bill's' from *The Complete Poems* 1913–1962 by e e cummings; A. P. Watt Ltd on behalf of Michael B. Yeats for 'Politics', 'The Lake Isle of Innisfree' and 'Sailing to Byzantium' by W. B. Yeats from *The Collected Poems of W. B. Yeats*, Macmillan, London Ltd and Macmillan Publishing Co for 'The Lake Isle of Innisfree', 'Politics', ©1940, 1968 and 'Sailing to Byzantium', ©1928, 1956 by W. B. Yeats from *The Poems of W. B. Yeats* edited by Richard J. Finneran.

Every effort has been made to trace all the copyright holders but if any have been inadvertently overlooked the publishers will be pleased to make the necessary arrangement at the first opportunity.

This book is dedicated to my wife, Leila.

Introduction

It is the aim of this book to open up some of the gates that may appear to be unassailable or unscalable to the student whose familiarity with the literature of the British Isles is at present rudimentary. Ease of access is what is required and this is what will, it is hoped, be facilitated by the pages that follow. Some students have grown accustomed to thinking of William Shakespeare as an ogre or of Alexander Pope as a dry old bachelor, both of them writing in an English as archaic as it is incomprehensible. If this book can conquer prejudices like these and reveal that the works of such authors are as alive and informative today as ever they were, it will have achieved its goal.

In the following chapters selected poems will be presented for study, in chronological order, so that the book as a whole may provide the basis for an intensive course in British poetry for sixth-formers and first-year college and university students. Occasionally works by American poets are quoted, in illustration of points not conditioned by geography; but in the main the poetry dealt with here comes from native-born or naturalised British writers. The book sets out initially to demonstrate some of the methods by which poetry works – the means by which it gains its effects and accomplishes its end of absolute communication. From this the book moves on to a survey of the last four hundred years, a period during which poetry has been written in a relatively stable and 'modern' English language. The whole object is to alert readers to what has been going on in British poetry over the last four centuries: to introduce them to some illustrious people and to prepare them to meet others for whom room could not be found in these pages.

What characteristics, if any, are peculiar to British poetry? Which features are more accentuated than in the poetry of other nations? Britain's poetic wealth has been accumulating through the centuries gradually but inexorably, like the growth towards magnificence of a coral reef. When the Old English wordsmiths – the makers of *Beowulf*, 'The Seafarer' and 'The Wanderer' – were hewing their ringing, alliterative lines from the unwieldy granite of the Anglo-Saxon language, they were not only producing the first primitive examples in their culture of the power of poetry to survive time, but giving voice to themes and motifs that have continued to inform the matter and spirit of British poetry ever since. These were the pioneers of poetry in the British Isles, and perhaps they foresaw for their endeavours a no less perishable end than that encountered by the haunted individuals, ever aware of death's imminence and ubiquity, of their verses. As yet there was no certainty of permanence for what they had made, for there was no existing body of literature to which their works could be attached. All might vanish, like the companions of the disconsolate 'Wanderer',

In the night of the past, as if they had never been.

('The Wanderer', 88)

Even when Geoffrey Chaucer, several centuries later and in a language closer to the English of our own times, was embedding his poetry in parchment – a surer guarantee of survival than the earlier practice of oral recitation and transmission from memory – there is no sign that he regarded himself as part of a burgeoning poetic tradition. In fact, despite his confident use of vernacular English to convey an entire emotional range,' he was more indebted to Continental influences than to the patrimony of his native island. Besides, like his Anglo-Saxon predecessors, he could not have seen himself as contributing to a 'national' heritage, which was nonetheless unobtrusively consolidating. There was as yet no binding factor, either in history or geography, linking one British poet to another. Chaucer's English contemporary William Langland was writing in a western dialect far removed from the London dialect of Chaucer's verse. Langland's English was as foreign to Chaucer as that of the Old English poets. Yet Chaucer's poetry shares some of the same preoccupations of his Anglo-Saxon forbears and establishes a closer kinship with them than he was aware of.

Just as Chaucer saw himself as a courtlier, more sophisticated poet than his rustic precursors, later generations were to consider him crude, in both the form and the content of his verses. The 17th-century writer John Dryden, while admiring the vitality of Chaucer's work, considered it 'rude' from a technical point of view and set about refining and rewriting it in accordance with the canons of 'polished' poetry then current. Chaucer seemed to have existed in isolation, separated in space and time from other members of the confraternity and rejected by Renaissance and later poets as an inconsiderable part of the national heritage. Only with the Romantic reappraisal begun by William Blake – who recognised 'God's plenty' amid the shrewd characterisations of Chaucer's Canterbury pilgrims – and with the subsequent phonological discovery of the metrical laws governing Chaucer's lines was Chaucer admitted to be an essential thread in the poetic tapestry of Britain. His more immediate successors would not have adjudged him thus; and the English sonneteers – the first poets to write in an English which approximates to that of our own day – acknowledged horizontal connections with their Continental brethren rather than vertical ties to a British genealogy, much as Chaucer himself had done two centuries earlier.

Yet despite these recurrent eschewals of a continuing 'British' tradition by the poets themselves, despite the rejection by one era of an earlier era and the pledge of a new start, the same ideas and obsessions keep emerging from poets of different epochs, demonstrating that there are, after all, common bonds that help to define British poetry. What are these? They may be summed up in two substantives: the seasons and the sea.

All British poetry is imbued with an awareness that nature is in a continual flux, moving from winter through spring to high summer, followed by a decline into autumn and beyond until winter comes along and wraps up everything in a cocoon of snow and ice. The poet of 'The Wanderer' comments on the 'blowing snow and the blast of winter' that 'enfold the earth . . . raging wrath upon men', in harsh sympathy with his melancholic mood; while Chaucer, in lighter vein at the start of his pilgrimage in *The Canterbury Tales*, finds himself in the midst of a season appropriate to his gaiety and optimism,

Whan that Aprille with hise shoures sote	(showers/sweet)
The droghte of March hath perced to the	(drought/pierced/
rote.	root)

('General Prologue', 1–2)

Four centuries later John Keats caught the lethargy of autumn after the year's labours have been brought to a fruitful conclusion, the harvest safely gathered in:

> Drowsed with the fume of poppies, while thy hook
> Spares the next swath and all its twined flowers.

('To Autumn')

The consciousness that things are continually changing, that life is becoming alternately stronger and weaker, that some men are ageing while others are simultaneously growing towards their prime, supplies much of British literature with an underlying rhythm. One senses that what is light may become dark (as in Shakespeare's *King Lear*) and, conversely, that what is dark will eventually lighten (as in Jane Austen's *Pride and Prejudice*). But the shortness of the British summer means that the emphasis in the nation's literature is often on the brevity of the period during which nature attains to fullness. So there is a latent awareness that darkness and sorrow are dominant in human affairs and that pleasure, youth and vitality must be snatched and enjoyed to the full for the few brief hours that they appear in this world. 'Youth's a stuff will not endure', sings Feste in Shakespeare's *Twelfth Night*, and it is a sentiment that runs like a melancholic undercurrent beneath the mainstream of the literature of the British Isles.

The other aspect of Britain that is an essential characteristic of its literature results from a geographical accident that has been both the strength and the weakness of its people: its insularity. From being separated by twenty miles of sea from the European continent, Britain has developed a feeling of 'separateness' from its neighbours. This separateness has manifested itself quite often as a feeling of national pride and superiority over its Continental cousins. In Shakespeare's *Henry V* twenty-nine Englishmen are killed during a battle in which ten thousand Frenchmen die. The playwright's feeling is that this makes the score about even. In William Wycherley's 17th-century play *The Country Wife*, and many other dramas of the Restoration period, the French are blamed for exporting venereal disease to the British Isles. At the end of the 18th century France, Italy, Spain and Germany supply the exotic settings and decadent characters for the English Gothic novels, in which anything indecorous and ungentlemanly can happen – and usually does.

Unspeakable crimes, in the general assumption, could only be fathered abroad, by the detested 'foreigner' – until Charles Dickens came along to reveal that London, too, nursed in its bosom a nest of vipers as loathsome as anything bred on alien soil.

Britons prided themselves on their 'difference' from the rabble across the Channel. This slim stretch of water has become the emblem of Britain's uniqueness. In the Second World War it was set alight to discourage German invaders. The sea is a recurrent, and very emotive, image in British literature. 'The unplumbed, salt, estranging sea', Matthew Arnold onomatopoeically called it, suggesting that mixture of dread and gratitude with which the British have traditionally beheld this barrier severing them from close contact with the rest of the world. John of Gaunt in Shakespeare's *Richard II* encomiastically refers to England as 'this precious stone set in a silver sea', a valuation in which the worth of the country is somehow enhanced by its isolation. The sea – like the seasons – shows many moods. Sometimes it is placid and brings calm or even melancholy to the spirit of the person who contemplates it (in Arnold's 'Dover Beach', for example); at other times it is a furious and vengeful god before whom the puny British native can only cower and grovel (this aspect of the sea is manifest in Coleridge's poem 'The Rime of the Ancient Mariner' and in Dickens's novel *David Copperfield*). The sea is an element that both buoys man up and bears him down, sometimes bringing him life, sometimes death. But like the varying seasons themselves – which can range overnight from balminess to cataclysm – the sea has impregnated the British character and is constantly lapping in the background of its literature.

This was so from the beginning. *Beowulf* opens with the sea burial of a warrior lord, in 'a ship put out on the unknown deep', where the sea provokes a tremor of fear at the prospect of the last voyage, Death. Chaucer, for all his metropolitan urbanity, returns to the sea time and again, seeing in it an emblem both of the ease of trade by which a man might become rich and of the threat of death that might swallow him whole in an instant:

> casuelly the shippes botme rente,   (the ship's bottom split)
> And ship and man under the water wente
> In sighte of othere shippes it byside.   (in full view of other ships)
> ('The Nun's Priest's Tale', 335–37)

The seasons and the sea are the means through which British literature has consistently expressed its deepest concerns: they are the distinctive imprint of its island character.

1 Approaching Poetry

Poetry is a compressed form of expression and seeks a response which is simultaneously emotional and intellectual. It thus tries to reach its audience by as many means, or through as many channels, as possible. The poet uses many poetic devices (rhyme, rhythm, alliteration, imagery and so on) to convey his general theme, or particular aspects of that theme, as efficiently and emphatically as possible. The patterns a poem makes – its music and its metaphors – all serve the imperatives of its theme.

Theme

When confronting a poem one seeks to discover as soon as possible what is its 'gist'. The best way to divine this is, first of all, to look at the title of the poem, since this will provide an early clue to the labyrinth. Here, for example, is a poem by the First World War poet Wilfred Owen:

Anthem for Doomed Youth

What passing bells for these who die as cattle?
    Only the monstrous anger of the guns.
    Only the stuttering rifles' rapid rattle
Can patter out their hasty orisons.
No mockeries for them; no prayers nor bells,
    Nor any voice of mourning save the choirs, –
The shrill, demented choirs of wailing shells;
    And bugles calling for them from sad shires.

What candles may be held to speed them all?
  Not in the hands of boys, but in their eyes
Shall shine the holy glimmer of good-byes.
  The pallor of girls' brows shall be their pall;
Their flowers the tenderness of patient minds,
  And each slow dusk a drawing-down of blinds.

The title alone should lead one to expect certain contradictions in the poem itself. An anthem is a religious song, a hymn of praise and glorification, sung at moments of gladness. Yet what is being praised here? It is an anthem 'for doomed youth': a song of praise for young people condemned to die. The contradiction implicit in it suggests that the title does not exactly mean what it appears to mean: it is *ironic*. The word 'anthem' is used ironically, for it is in fact not an anthem but its opposite, a *dirge* (or funeral lament), that is the appropriate mode for such sombre subject-matter. Thus in the title of the poem the tensions and ironies on which the poem itself is based are already indicated.

Owen's poem soon demonstrates this fundamental opposition between the ethereality of a world of spiritual values (the Church) and the reality of a world in which men are slaughtered like beasts (the field of war). If the poem is read through two or three times, its theme can be developed a little further. Then a prose paraphrase might be made of it, as follows:

The conventional ceremonies of the Church are inappropriately applied to men who have been killed senselessly. The world of religion and the world of the modern war-machine are poles apart and can have nothing to do with each other. Religion is unable to cope with or comprehend this inane sacrifice; only in the minds of those who have loved them will the full horror and the ineffable tragedy of these young soldiers' deaths be realised.

It is not a bad idea to attempt such a paraphrase of any poem that one wishes to study. Such a practice will lay bare the theme of the poem; and once the theme is determined, it is a simple matter to examine all the other facets (tone, imagery, diction and so forth) by and through which this theme is communicated. In the example above, this task has been facilitated by the title, which indicates the ironic stance that the poet is adopting towards his subject-matter. Many longer poems not only indicate their theme by their title but also give a summary in their opening lines of what is to follow. Thus John Milton's *Paradise Lost* is, as its title indicates, concerned with the ejection of man from the Garden of Eden and the first few lines of the poem elaborate this theme in what amounts to an extended subtitle:

> Of man's first disobedience, and the fruit
> Of that forbidden tree, whose mortal taste
> Brought death into the world, and all our woe,
> With loss of Eden, till one greater Man
> Restore us, and regain the blissful seat.

On the other hand many a shorter poem has been left untitled, and its meaning has to be deduced from the body of the poem itself without the aid of an initial guidepost.

Tone

Having discovered what the subject of a poem is, the reader should consider the question of what the poet's attitude towards his topic is. What tone does his 'speaking voice' convey? Is he angry, placid, bitter, ironic, indifferent or what? The poet is usually personally involved in what he is writing about, which is why he chooses to write in verse, a medium suggestive of emotional utterance. In other words poetry very often involves the poet *subjectively* in his material whereas a prose version of the same material would seem detached, and even scientifically *objective*, by comparison.

To illustrate this point here are two people's expressions of the same experience. In 1802 William Wordsworth and his sister Dorothy travelled across London's Westminster Bridge in the early morning. William wrote a poem about what he saw, while Dorothy recorded it in her journal. Here are the two versions:

a) *Composed upon Westminster Bridge, September 3, 1802*
   Earth has not anything to show more fair:
   Dull would he be of soul who could pass by
   A sight so touching in its majesty:
   This city now doth, like a garment, wear
   The beauty of the morning; silent, bare,

Ships, towers, domes, theatres, and temples lie
Open unto the fields, and to the sky;
All bright and glittering in the smokeless air.
Never did sun more beautifully steep
In his first splendour, valley, rock, or hill;
Ne'er saw I, never felt, a calm so deep!
The river glideth at his own sweet will:
Dear God! the very houses seem asleep;
And all that mighty heart is lying still!

b) It was a beautiful morning. The City, St. Paul's, with the river
and a multitude of little boats, made a most beautiful sight as we
crossed Westminster Bridge. The houses were not overhung by
their cloud of smoke, and they were spread out endlessly, yet the
sun shone so brightly, with such a fierce light, that there was
even something like the purity of one of nature's own grand
spectacles.

The 'poetic' version suggests involvement on the part of the writer
with the scene he is describing. 'Earth has not anything to show more
fair' indicates that he is making a judgement on what he sees. His
heart goes out to meet the beauty of the scene. The city is described in
terms of an elegant woman, wearing the clarity of the morning
sunlight 'like a garment'. It is a sight, however, that surpasses even
the beauty of women, the poet tells us: anyone who does not respond
in a similar manner to the sight before him must be 'dull of soul'.
Wordsworth's poem is an anthem in praise of the city of London; his
sister's 'prosaic' response seems cold and remote by comparison, her
reference to 'one of nature's own grand spectacles' suggesting the
detached attitude of a spectator in the gallery of a theatre.

Evidently in Wordsworth's poem the 'theme' is not confined to
description, to depicting the outlines of London in the manner of a
sketch or a photograph. The poet's enthusiastic response to the
sprawl of the city – his hyperbolical 'tone' of praise – is a part of the
theme, transforming the grey perimeters of the urban mass into
something radiant and sparkling. Often in a poem the tone of the poet
is inseparable from the theme of the poem. This is evident in Wilfred
Owen's poem. 'Anthem for Doomed Youth' does not merely convey
an apocalyptic picture of the carnage of the Great War, but it
demonstrates the poet's anger at it, his impatience with and derision

of traditional religion in its evasion of the horrific aspects of a conflict which, in all likelihood, it condoned and goes on condoning. Tone is indicated to the reader largely by the selection of *diction*. For instance, near the end of Wordsworth's poem the poet's ebullient reaction to the beauty he sees before him bursts out in the apostrophe, 'Dear God!' He can no longer contain himself; he calls on God to share in this experience and take delight in one of the beauties of His creation. The poet's attitude is also conveyed by his choice of epithets. The poem is liberally sprinkled with adjectives such as 'bright' and 'glittering', to show the gladness in the poet's response. However, in the Owen poem the adjectives chosen convey an opposite effect to Wordsworth's. 'Monstrous', 'shrill', 'demented', 'wailing' describe a world that has gone mad: the poet's attitude towards what he describes is that of a rage that feels itself futile and impotent before such large-scale, indescribable slaughter.

The following poem by the American poet Robert Frost shows how theme and tone are intertwined:

Fire and Ice

Some say the world will end in fire,
Some say in ice.
From what I've tasted of desire
I hold with those who favour fire.
But if it had to perish twice,
I think I know enough of hate
To say that for destruction ice
Is also great
And would suffice.

The theme of this short poem is the destruction of the world. The world, according to the Old Testament has already been annihilated once: by flood. The poet is here conjecturing the manner in which it will be destroyed the next time. Will it be by fire, or by ice? His linking of these two opposed forces with the two contrary emotions of desire and hate suggests that he foresees that the end of the world will not result from a geophysical accident but from man's own excesses. Mankind will perish either from too much desire (perhaps sexual desire, the 'fire' of liberated passion) or too much loathing. In either case the rational faculty would be swamped by an excess of unrefined feeling. Man would act from instinct alone and thus precipitate the catastrophe.

Frost's poem is short and deceptively simple; but the meaning, notwithstanding the poem's brevity, is hard to fathom. Very often in poetry there is a meaning – almost a mystery – which eludes capture; and any attempt to paraphrase the poem in prose will fail to seize this shadowy substance. Nevertheless, an explanation must be attempted, for only in articulating a response to a poem can the understanding of it be stretched to the fullest possible extent. It will always be evident, though, that the poem itself is the most perfect 'medium' for the poet's 'message'.

Robert Frost's poem is a contemplation of the end of the world, and its tone is established from the first words, as poetic tone nearly always is: 'Some say the world will end in fire, / Some say in ice'. This is not a scientific disquisition on the impending catastrophe, backed up by facts, figures and statistical analysis. The approach is almost casual, 'homely'. The poem unfolds in 'cozy' domestic idioms ('I hold with those', 'I think I know') suggestive of a down-to-earth speaker, not having much truck with intellectuals, quietly offering his opinions on a topic. The 'I' of the poem is an insistent presence, making known that his conclusions are based on personal experiences ('From what I've tasted of desire', 'I think I know enough of hate') rather than on any abstract intellectualising. The very shortness of the poem suggests that here is a speaker not much given to words. His style is laconic, almost casual, providing an effective contrast with the cataclysmic nature of the events he is chatting about. His apparent nonchalance towards the threat of universal death suggests that he has distanced himself from it. He has undergone enough desire and hate to be immune against any further onslaughts from them. He seems almost amused by the prospect of a possibly imminent disaster, even though such an event would encompass his own end along with everyone else's.

The whole tone of pithy understatement culminates in the last word of the poem. He does not say that the human race could produce enough hatred to destroy the world many times over, which is the approach that a Nonconformist 'fire and brimstone' preacher might adopt. He simply states that what human passions there are will 'suffice', or be adequate, for the complete destruction of this world. There is a sense of satisfaction, almost of complacency, in his concluding word. It is the full stop to the whole poem. It is this tension between the ostensible subject-matter of the poem – its vision of the end of the world – and the homespun, matter-of-fact delivery of the speaker that gives the poem its power to disturb. Again, the poet's tone or 'speaking voice' is an integral part of the theme of the poem.

Imagery

Imagery refers collectively to the whole body of individual images contained in a poem. An image is a picture. Like the images of saints in churches the poetic image appeals to the emotions and tries to elicit a response that is independent of reason or judgement. An image works emotively, whereas the argument of a poem, operating at 'head level', makes its appeal to the rational faculty. The argument of *Paradise Lost* is explained in the poem's opening lines, while the 'feeling' of the poem is evoked by several crucial images scattered throughout the poem: Satan in the form of a toad whispering in the ear of Eve and subduing her moral resistance, the glistening fruit representing the lustre and gloss of all earthly temptations and turning to ashes as soon as tasted and the sword of the angel at the gates of Paradise directing the hapless couple out of the garden and into the world's wastes. Thus on the verbal level Milton presents an argument for our mental approval: if man disobeys the edicts of God he will be punished. On the imagistic level, on the other hand, he conveys a sensual impression of Adam's and Eve's fall from grace, so that we sympathise with them in their distress even while intellectually conceding that their doom is just.

The use of imagery enriches the reader's response. His experience of the poem becomes more vivid. If a poet is trying to convey a state of mind, he is far likelier to catch his reader's attention by the use of an image. Thus when the speaker in T. S. Eliot's 'Love Song of J. Alfred Prufrock' is endeavouring to express his feeling that any form of mere instinctive and animal life would be purposeful in comparison to his own vacuous existence, he remarks:

> I should have been a pair of ragged claws
> Scuttling across the floors of silent seas.

The image of a crab is here used to suggest with clarity a complex emotional state. It is, moreover, not simply the crab that is settled on as a suitable image for this state but one particular aspect of this crab: its 'pair of ragged claws'. In the first line of the couplet Eliot presents a static image, like a photograph; in the second line this image acquires motion and becomes animated, like a film.

The image enables us – as the poet wishes – to bypass the tortuous reasoning processes and arrive instantly at what he wants to show us: we can sense what he means before we can comprehend it. This is the way that imagery very often works – subliminally, beneath the threshold of consciousness. Prufrock is trying to say that he would have preferred a life of brute instinct, free from the responsibilities entailed by conscious thought: a bestial rather than a human existence. The attraction of the 'silent seas' suggests the desire of the unheroic man to sink back into the primordial ooze of unconsciousness and death. The strength of this particular image – and of all powerful images – is that it conveys instantaneously a complex of feelings or ideas that would lose much of its effect if it were unfolded laboriously, unwound at length, without the aid of imagery.

An image elicits a sensory response, and its strongest appeal – though by no means its only appeal – is visual. When William Blake opens his poem 'The Tiger' with the line,

Tiger! Tiger! burning bright,

he does not mean that the tiger is literally on fire. He is using this image to suggest the intensity of the animal's inborn energy: an energy so powerful that it can be felt and seen (by the imagination) as heat and light. The poet has combined the literal subject of his description (the tiger) with the image of something that the powerful beast reminds him of (a fire), and the two concepts are fused in the vision of the burning tiger. If an image becomes common currency, however, it runs the risk of turning into a *cliché*: a figure of speech that has become so familiar as to have lost all its sharpness and become dull. Blake's image of the tiger 'burning bright' is original enough to strike the reader with all the force of a new impression.

John Keats, in 'Ode to a Nightingale', wishing to give a picture of the effervescent and revivifying quality of wine, describes it thus:

beaded bubbles winking at the brim.

The wine is made to seem alive: it is 'winking'. The bubbles ascend from the bottom of the glass in a continual stream, like a string of beads. Not only is this an image that is vividly present to the sight but the liquid seems to rise straight to the palate. The wine is not only seen but tasted; the poet has transmitted his image via the media of two senses. Keats is well-known for the 'sensuousness' of his imagery. In 'The Eve of St Agnes' he describes a feast prepared by Porphyro for his mistress Madeline in the seclusion of her bedchamber. Among the items of this sumptuous banquet are

> candied apple, quince, and plum, and gourd;
> With jellies soother than the creamy curd,
> And lucent syrups, tinct with cinnamon.

The reader is compelled to slow down, partly because of the punctuation and extra conjunctions ('quince, and plum, and gourd'), partly because of the long 'ū' sounds in 'gourd', 'soother' and 'lucent'. The poet makes us savour the delicacies he is presenting. Furthermore, in articulating many of the phrases ('jellies soother', 'lucent syrups') the tongue adopts the position of sucking something sweet; and the profusion of 's' sounds encourages the production of saliva, as if in anticipation of digesting foodstuffs. The long vowels in 'creamy curd' depict the slowness with which the rich liquid is poured, and the short 'ĭ' sounds in 'syrups tinct with cinnamon' suggest the spiciness or piquancy of the dishes described.

Keats's poetry also offers examples of images that appeal to the other three senses. In this line from 'Ode to a Nightingale' Keats again uses the image of wine to stimulate a multi-sensual response:

> The coming musk rose, full of dewy wine.

The rose is heavily-scented ('musk'), it is about to burst into bloom ('coming') and all its hoard of perfume appears to the poet's imagination as a cask of unbroached wine. Here it is the scent of wine – an indispensable part of its flavour, its 'bouquet' – that is the point of similarity between the two objects (rose and wine) but further correspondences are also latent in the image. The wine is 'dewy': cool and refreshing. There is also a colour link: both the rose and the wine have a deep red hue, aesthetically satisfying to the beholder. In this image Keats engages the reader's approval for the rose by presenting it in terms that are gratifying to three of the five senses: smell, taste and sight. He proffers the musk rose as if it were a glass of wine, ready to be absorbed into the bloodstream.

In the same poem he uses the device of onomatopoeia to present an image that can be heard as plainly as seen. A patch of exuberant natural growth is referred to as

The murmurous haunt of flies on summer eves.

Here the *assonance* and *alliteration* of the 'ŭ' vowel sounds and the 's' consonant sounds effectively reproduce the 'buzzing' noises of the insects. This is a frequent technique in poetry, where, as Alexander Pope declared, 'The sound must seem an Echo to the sense': the reader should hear, as well as see, what he is reading about. Keats has chosen words that add an unobtrusive soundtrack to the visual image of the evening.

As for the tactile sense, in 'Lamia' Keats describes the preliminaries to the wedding feast, one of which is the ritual ablution before sitting down to eat:

When in an antichamber every guest
Had felt the cold full sponge to pleasure pressed.

Here he is trying to make his reader feel, with his guests, the sensation of the washing process. He does this by a combination of metrical and alliterative techniques in the second line. This line has one extra stress than usual ('Hăd félt thĕ cóld fúll spónge tŏ pléasŭre préssed') because Keats qualifies the noun 'sponge' with two monosyllabic adjectives, each of which must be fully emphasised. Whenever an additional stress occurs in a line the metre of that line is retarded, in order to accommodate the extra emphasis. The speed of Keats's line is slowed down to emphasise the process of ablution. This is a service that would be performed by slaves, holding a sponge that is both 'cold' and 'full' and then squeezing it over the guest's torso. The release stage of this process is indicated by the resumption of the normal iambic rhythm ('tŏ pléasŭre préssed') and the restoration of the guest's sense of well-being is emphasised by the alliteration in this final phrase. The whole image has been presented in such a way as subtly to remind one of the experience of undergoing a cold shower: the initial shock of the cold water trickling down the spine, followed by a feeling of returning warmth as the body soon accustoms itself to the new sensation.

In a poem both *metaphor* and *simile* are used to convey images. The first involves a somewhat more forceful thrusting of the image upon the attention than the second does. A simile concedes that while there are similarities between the subject and the thing it is compared with (the image) there are also differences. A metaphor makes no such concession. The difference of degree of assertion is evident if one compares a simile such as 'the king was like a lion' with its metaphorical equivalent, 'the king was a lion'. In the former expression the subject and its image are kept separate; in the latter they have become fused. The distinction between these two devices is easily discernible, since the simile almost invariably begins with 'like' or 'as', the metaphor never. Blake's line 'Tiger! Tiger! burning bright' is a metaphorical image. The tiger is depicted as a fire or a beacon; it is God's burning bush, eternally aflame with the indestructible energy of its Creator. To say that the tiger is '*like* a fire, burning bright' would irreparably weaken the image.

A simile, on the other hand, allows the subject and its image to be more detached from each other. They can intermingle for a while, during which period the poet can elucidate the points of similarity that will enhance his theme, and then they can separate and go their own ways with no hard feelings. A simile presents an image that is *incidental* to the theme of the poem; but a metaphor provides an image that is *integral* to the presentation of the theme. Blake's tiger could not be separated from the fire that informs the animal; if it could, there would be no poem left. An example of the comparatively 'uninvolved' way in which a simile functions appears in the first four lines of one of Wordsworth's poems:

> I wandered lonely as a cloud
>> That floats on high o'er vales and hills,
> When all at once I saw a crowd,
>> A host of golden daffodils.

('I Wandered Lonely as a Cloud')

Here the simile begins at 'as' and ends at 'hills'; it exists for a line and a half and is then dispensed with. The poet is comparing his condition to that of a cloud floating over the hills and valleys. He sees in the clouds above him an image of his own aimlessness. He is 'wandering' without a goal, just as the clouds are blown wherever chance or nature propels them. Evidently the image of the cloud is an appropriate illustration of two aspects of the poet's condition: his lack of direction ('I wandered') and his isolation ('lonely'). There is a third point to be considered. The essential nature of a cloud is its ephemeralness: it will not 'float' forever but will soon either precipitate as rain or evaporate altogether. The poet feels that, like the cloud, he too is not long for this world.

Having described his initial state of mind by comparison with a cloud, the poet then goes on to explain how his attention was called back to earth by the sight of one of its more beautiful natural displays. The daffodils intrude on his sense of purposelessness and establish a connection between himself and his environment that furnishes him with both a feeling of consolation and a sense of renewed purpose. The image of the cloud is henceforth dismissed, as his state of mind changes from aloofness and isolation to a feeling of relationship with the products of the soil. The simile has been used to illustrate a mental state that is transitory. Unlike Blake's tiger, which is eternally afire, Wordsworth's 'wanderer' resembles a cloud only temporarily. The simile has a less intimate, less intrinsic connection with the subject than the metaphor.

Diction

Diction is the words or phrases that the poet chooses to use. It is the style in which he expresses himself. He may use long words of Latin or Greek derivation to give dignity to his theme (as Milton does) or he may employ the colloquial, or even 'cult', language of his day to stress the contemporaneity of his poem (as the American Allen Ginsberg does). Diction consists of the *choice* of words, quite apart from their use in creating images. The 18th-century poet might refer to birds as 'the plumy race'. He is giving an image of birds but his way of 'drawing' this image may suggest to modern readers something slightly pompous, or supercilious, in his attitude. Why does he not call a bird a bird? To find out the answer to this, his diction has to be examined in the context of his whole poem and of 18th-century attitudes. Diction has a cumulative effect: it conveys the tone of the poem.

John Milton is a poet who chose the sublimest of all themes: the justification of the ways of God to man. This was a theme calling for the maximum dignity of treatment. Milton could not write about heaven in the same way that he might have written about his wife or his dog. Even to mention a dog in the same context Milton would have to dignify it by a circumlocution of the 'plumy race' sort (perhaps 'canine tribe'?). Distance and decorum must be preserved at all times with such subject-matter and all familiarity banished. The tone must be ever solemn and serious. Milton not only achieved such a solemnity of tone but succeeded in sustaining it through one of the longest poems in the English language. He managed this largely through his choice of a preponderantly Latin diction, which, because of its 'impersonality', elevated its subject-matter and kept the reader at a respectful distance. For example, Milton's description of the ejection of Satan from heaven is Latinised in both vocabulary and word order:

> Him the Almighty Power
> Hurled headlong flaming from the ethereal sky
> With hideous ruin and combustion down
> To bottomless perdition, there to dwell
> In adamantine chains and penal fire.

> (*Paradise Lost*, I,44–48)

Here the long words lend dignity to the topic. Something epic is taking place. Milton uses 'combustion' and 'perdition' to express the concepts of fire and loss. Arcane adjectives such as 'ethereal' and 'adamantine' suggest the metaphysical plane on which the poem's events occur. Milton, furthermore, selects adjectives that express extreme states ('headlong', 'hideous', 'bottomless') to emphasise the grand scale of his drama. There is no call for half measures here. Milton can pull out all the stops, for he is 'singing' about an event of mythological significance: the rebellion of Satan and the subsequent history of the creation and fall of man.

Milton was writing during the 17th century, a time of great religious ferment in Britain. The style, or diction, of his poem indicates the high seriousness of the poet's attitude towards his Christian material. In contrast, the 20th-century American poet E. E. Cummings has written a poem which obliquely suggests the demise of all religions, and the level of his diction is lowered accordingly:

Portrait

Buffalo Bill's
defunct
          who used to
          ride a watersmooth-silver
                              stallion
and break onetwothreefourfive pigeonsjustlikethat
                                                  Jesus
he was a handsome man
                    and what i want to know is
how do you like your blueeyed boy
Mister Death

The difference in tone between this and Milton's poem is at once apparent. Whereas for Milton God retains all His immense and fearsome energy and is 'the Almighty Power' whom the poet dare not approach or even name directly, the speaker in Cummings's poem has lost all respect for God. The Son of God, for him, merely supplies the material for a mild oath ('Jesus / he was a handsome man'). The style of Cummings's poem is colloquial, while Milton's is formal or 'epic'. In Milton's poem we hear all the faith and fervour of a man whose life is lent meaning by the Christian doctrines of Creation and Life Everlasting. In Cummings's poem we hear the voice of the American barroom *habitué* for whom all heroic myths, whether they be of the Passion of Christ or of the opening up of the Wild West, have become flabby, desiccated and useless. This impression is made by the poet's use of such words as 'defunct', to suggest that the hero-myth (the 'blueeyed' cowboy) is no longer serviceable, like a worn-out machine. The conversational, humdrum tone of phrases such as 'and what i want to know is' adds to the overall effect of demoralised apathy. The banality of the speaker's diction almost reduces Cummings's poem to prose, threatening to remove it from the sphere of poetry altogether. This is not slipshod writing on the poet's part: he is deliberately conveying a sense of the lack of poetry in the speaker's life through a lack of poetry in his diction. It could be said that, in turning from Milton to Cummings, we are going from the 'sublime' to the 'ridiculous' in terms of tone and subject-matter. One is the poetry of great expectation, the other is the poetry of jaded illusion. And it is the diction that registers immediately the different tones and attitudes of the respective speakers.

A word is not a counter or an algebraic symbol. Each word is unique: it is not interchangeable. And it reaches the reader charged with a richness of suggestion. Keats, for example, is drawing upon common memories of early childhood – a time when the world was a perpetual adventure – when he writes in 'Ode to a Nightingale' about

> magic casements opening on the foam
> Of perilous seas, in faery lands forlorn.

By choosing the word 'casements' rather than the commoner word 'windows' and by combining this word with 'magic', 'perilous' and 'forlorn' – words which will inevitably call to mind romantic tales of knights questing on behalf of silken-haired damsels – Keats elicits the response that he wants. He seeks to 'charm' his reader, to weave a fairy spell around him. The fragile delicacy of such a spell is discernible if it is realised how easily it could have been broken had the poet written 'suds' instead of 'foam'. The poet selects words that are consistent with the tone he wishes to convey. In the opening of Samuel Taylor Coleridge's 'Kubla Khan' the diction establishes the mood that will predominate:

> In Xanadu did Kubla Khan
> A stately pleasure-dome decree.

Not 'command', which would have fitted in metrically just as smoothly, but 'decree', in order to indicate exactly the absolute authority of the monarch whose word was law.

The associations of a word – its 'connotations' – differ slightly each time the word is used, depending on the context in which it occurs. For example, to a man suffering from thirst water will have life-giving qualities, as it does in Coleridge's 'Rime of the Ancient Mariner':

> Water, water, everywhere,
> Nor any drop to drink.

But in Shakespeare's *Hamlet* the heroine, Ophelia, drowns herself, whereupon her brother Laertes laments:

> Too much of water hast thou, poor Ophelia.

In one context the word calls forth 'good' associations, in the other context 'bad' ones. Discussion of the associations contained within diction brings us into the proximity of imagery once more. The boundary between them can be drawn by saying that *diction* refers to the words used, *imagery* to the pictures which some of those words evoke. Diction does not have to be ornate or elaborate to be effective. A profusion of 'flowery' words can blur the intended meaning. Some of the deepest emotions are most effectively expressed in the plainest language, as Wordsworth was well aware:

> She lived unknown, and few could know
>   When Lucy ceased to be;
> But she is in her grave, and, oh,
>   The difference to me!
>
>   ('She Dwelt Among the Untrodden Ways')

The diction here is simple and unpretentious. No superfluous image is laid atop the bare 'grave'. No adjectives are brought in to qualify or moderate the statement of stark, unadorned grief. Nothing intrudes on the expression of this sorrow: even the rhythm is unobtrusive.

Rhythm

Rhythm works in coordination with imagery and diction, reinforcing the theme and tone of the poem. The commonest rhythm in English poetry is *iambic pentameter*, in which the pattern of one unstressed followed by a stressed syllable (˘ ´) occurs five times in a line of verse:

> Ĭ stóod tĭp-tóe ŭpón ă líttlĕ híll.
>
>   (John Keats, 'I Stood Tip-toe')

One may further *scan* the poem – or dissect it for its rhythm – by dividing it into its metrical units, or *feet*:

> Ĭ stóod| tĭp-tóe| ŭpón| ă lí|ttlĕ híll.

Five feet of the unstressed/stressed (˘ ´) pattern – five *iambs*, in other words – show this to be a line of iambic pentameter verse. If the stress were reversed, so that the emphasised syllable occurred first (ˊ ˇ), the feet would be *trochees*, and if there were four of them in a line, the verse would be *trochaic tetrameter*, another common rhythm in English poetry:

Bý thĕ| Ísăr,| ín thĕ| twíliğht.
(D. H. Lawrence, 'River Roses')

Within each line of four or more feet there is generally a pause – or *caesura* – in the rhythmic flow, usually coinciding with a pause in the sense or the punctuation of the line:

Ĭ stóod| tŭp-tóe|| ŭpón| ă lĭ|ttlĕ híll;
Bý thĕ| Ísăr,|| ín thĕ| twílĭght.

By varying the location of the caesura the poet can avoid the danger of monotony creeping into his verse.

Other metrical feet that occur, with less frequency, in English verse are *dactyls* (ˊ ˇ ˇ), *anapaests* (ˇ ˇ ˊ), *amphibrachs* (ˇ ˊ ˇ) and *spondees* (ˊ ˊ). Other line lengths, also of less frequent appearance, are *dimeter* (two feet), *trimeter* (three feet), *hexameter* (six feet) and *heptameter* (seven feet). Here, unusually, is a line of trochaic octameter:

Cómrădes,| léave mĕ| hére ă| líttlĕ,| whíle ăs| yét 'tĭs| éarly̆| mórn.
(Alfred, Lord Tennyson, 'Locksley Hall')

Rarer rhythms like this one are sometimes used for their novelty effect. The 'standard' rhythm remains that of iambic pentameter, a multi-purpose metre capable of conveying the profoundest sentiments –

Ĭ wáke ănd féel thĕ féll ŏf dárk, nŏt dáy –
(Gerard Manley Hopkins, 'I Wake and Feel the Fell of Dark')

as well as the most prosaic activities:

Ĭ wáitĕd fŏr thĕ tráin ăt Cóvĕntrý.
(Alfred, Lord Tennyson, 'Godiva')

In fact, its closeness to normal English speech rhythms probably accounts in large measure for the popularity of the iambic pentameter line. When it occurs in unrhymed verse – as it does, for instance, in the plays of Shakespeare and in Milton's *Paradise Lost* – it is known as *blank verse*. In this form the iambic pentameter line loses its *end-stopped* character: the sense spills over into the subsequent line or lines and the poetry more closely resembles conversation, though of a heightened emotional quality –

> I'll have some proof. Her name, that was as fresh
> As Dian's visage, is now begrim'd and black
> As mine own face.
> (W. Shakespeare, Othello, III.iii.390–92)

The rhythm of such lines is looser, less compulsory and, within certain limits, its scansion may be as much a matter of individual choice as of mandatory sanction.

But, whether it obtrudes or remains hidden, the rhythm of a poem should always assist the transmission of the subject-matter, as it evidently does in 'The Charge of the Light Brigade' by Alfred, Lord Tennyson:

> Hálf ă lĕague, hálf ă lĕague,
> Hálf ă lĕague ónwărd.
> Áll ĭn thĕ vállĕy ŏf Déath
> Róde thĕ sĭx húndrĕd.

The rhythm of one stressed syllable followed by two unstressed (the dactylic foot) echoes the sound of the hoofbeats of galloping horses. Furthermore, the phrase 'half a league' is twice repeated, to suggest the regularity of these hoofbeats and to give the cavalry charge some 'duration' in time. At this point in the poem sound matters more than sense: it is the tumult of the charging steeds that attracts the attention, rather than any definite conceptualisation of how much land is covered in 'half a league'.

The use of rhythm generally operates on a subtler level than it does in Tennyson's thundering horses; but it affects the reader nonetheless, in spite of his unawareness of its exploitation. The poet's ear for rhythm is the most delicate of his abilities. The greater his aptitude, the more readily the words seem to flow from his pen with an inborn ease, and, ironically, the more reluctantly is credit given him for writing so fluently. If the rhythm is fluid it suggests a sense of harmony, of conflicts resolved. In the Wordsworth quatrain, 'She lived unknown . . .', even though the subject is mournful, the rhythm insinuates the poet's acquiescence, his acceptance that death has its part in the tempo of universal nature. Rhythm, if regular, gives a sense of order. A beat recurring with predictable regularity soothes one with a sense that

Gód's ǐn hǐs héavěn –
Áll's ríght wǐth thě wórld!

In these lines from Robert Browning's 'Pippa Passes' the rhythmic repetition of one stressed syllable followed by two unstressed reinforces the sense that there is a divine hand guiding the apparently random and chaotic events of everyday life, a universal harmony with which man is ultimately in accord.

Rhythm does not always suggest order. In a poem about disorder the rhythm will tend to be disordered too. The two opening lines of one of John Donne's sonnets express the speaker's spiritual crisis:

Báttěr mỹ héart, thrée-pérsŏned Gód, fŏr yóu
Ǎs yét bǔt knóck, bréathe, shíne, ǎnd séek tŏ ménd.

(‘Holy Sonnet’, X)

These lines have an underlying pattern of iambic feet but the poet varies it considerably, beginning with a trochaic foot and inserting several extra stresses, to give an indication of the mental 'stress' he is undergoing as a result of his fears about his spiritual shortcomings. The more stressed syllables there are in a line of poetry, the 'jerkier' will be the rhythm of that line, particularly if the stresses clash with a metric foundation of alternate unstressed and stressed syllables. An example from *Paradise Lost* shows how the flow of regular iambic lines may be broken up by a line of stressed syllables for special effect:

Nŏ rést. Thrŏugh mány ǎ dárk ǎnd dréarỹ vále
Thěy pássed, ǎnd mány ǎ régǐon dólŏróus,
Ŏ'er mány ǎ frózěn, mány ǎ fierỹ Álp,
Rócks, cáves, lákes, féns, bógs, déns, ǎnd shádes ŏf déath.

(II.618–21)

It is hard to credit that this last line has no more than the ten syllables contined in each of the preceding lines. Yet so it has. Each word bears emphasis, compelling the reader to slow down and give it full weight, a mental process which duplicates the slow-going physical progress of Milton's fallen angels.

Rhythmic devices are deployed not only to retard the progress of a poem; they may also accelerate it. A line with many monosyllables will take longer to 'say' than one composed mainly of polysyllables.

And ten low words oft creep in one dull line,

as Pope's line from 'An Essay on Criticism' here demonstrates. Such a line seems longer and more laboured than one such as Milton's

    To undergo eternal punishment.
                                        (*Paradise Lost*, I.155)

Each of these lines contains ten syllables and has a basic iambic metre, yet Milton's polysyllabic line can be read with much more expedition than Pope's monosyllabic one. Knowledge of this phenomenon helps a poet create the effect that he wants.

Rhythm assists or promotes the theme of a poem with a subtlety which often escapes detection. A too-regular rhythm becomes monotonous and risks sending the reader to sleep. Some 18th-century verse could be criticised on these grounds. The 18th century prided itself on having banished all disorder and confusion from its social and mental life. It conceived of God as an artisan who had cunningly contrived a mechanical universe and the rhythm of its poetry, as these lines from Pope's 'Epistle to Burlington' indicate, tends to imitate the neatness of the Creator:

    His gardens next your admiration call,
    On every side you look, behold the wall!
    No pleasing intricacies intervene,
    No artful wildness to perplex the scene;
    Grove nods at grove, each alley has a brother,
    And half the platform just reflects the other.

Here the mesmeric swing of the iambic pendulum is ideally suited to the subject-matter. Pope is describing the landscaped symmetry of a country-house garden; each of his couplets is a self-contained unit, reflecting the self-containment of the garden described, bound in as it is and immunised against the outside wilderness by a circumferential 'wall'.

Pope, however, is somewhat critical of such excessive tidiness. The garden is perfectly balanced: each clump of trees has an identical clump planted opposite. The couplet form itself mimics this symmetrical structure in its counterpoised lines and parallel syntax:

No pleasing intricacies intervene,
No artful wildness to perplex the scene.

('No' + adjective + noun + verb / 'No' + adjective + noun + verb . . .). Such an effect, in both garden and poem, will eventually become soporific, as Pope realises. He criticises the garden for excluding anything that might suggest disorder; consequently, the trees themselves are 'nodding', or falling asleep, from boredom.

Buildings and gardens have rhythm, though it is a rhythm that strikes the eye, not the ear. Pope is suggesting that this garden's rhythm is too unvaried. The eye soon wearies from contemplating perfection and needs the added distraction of some 'pleasing intricacies' to enliven its interest. Similarly, as Pope is well aware, the ear soon tires of uniformity of rhythm in poetry. Constant variations of pace and metre are called for, in order to keep the mind alert, and Pope manages to create such 'intricacies' despite the confines of the heroic couplet. Even in the above passage, where the regularity of metre is meant to mirror, in a mocking manner, the unimaginative mathematical perfection of the garden, Pope does not allow the metre itself to become too somnambulistic. Just when the reader might be in danger of drifting off, Pope inserts a spondee into the stream of iambs ('Gróve nods ăt gróve') and prevents the attention from wandering. For a monotonous rhythm defuses all possible tension in a poem and with a decrease in tension comes a growth in indifference. A poet will pay constant heed to the effects that his sound patterns are having on the reader's ear to ensure that he is stimulating interest rather than stifling it.

Structure

Structure is the way a poem is put together: how it is built. Structure has a sort of rhythm of its own. This is not a metrical rhythm, based on the sound pattern of the poem, but a larger rhythm running through the entire poem and one that is based on the flow of ideas rather than on the flow of sounds. In fact, structure could be said to be the 'rhythm of ideas' in a poem. This operates most palpably in sonnets but there is also a rhythm of ideas involved in longer poems. A reperusal of Owen's 'Anthem for Doomed Youth' will reveal the rhythm of ideas in operation in a shorter poem – within the 14-line structure of the sonnet form.

A quick glance at the way that Owen's poem is set out on the page typographically shows that it is split into two sections: one of eight lines and the other of six. This is a pattern discernible in even the earliest sonnets. Since the sonnet originated in Italy, in the 14th century, the names given to these two parts are of Italian derivation: *octave* (the first eight lines) and *sestet* (the remaining six). Not all sonnets split so neatly into eight and six-line 'halves' and some sonnets have no discernible split at all. But, in general, such a division is the rule rather than the exception among sonnets. It is a division that is both structural and thematic: there is a syntactic pause at this point, at the same time as the words of the poem indicate an interlude, or breathing-space, in the exposition of the content. Such a pause is often accompanied by a change of attitude in the speaker of the poem. In other words, a change of perspective usually occurs between the octave and the sestet: this change is referred to as the *volta* (or 'turning-point'). And such a shift from one mood to another, while not essential to a sonnet, lends, when it arises, an air of greater comprehensiveness. Here is a poet who is not simply bombarding his audience with an emotional outburst: his poem is the product of thought as well as passion.

As for the structure of Owen's sonnet, it is evident that the opening line of the octave comprises a question and that the rest of the octave sets out to answer it. The question suggests that there ought to be some kind of religious ceremony for those slaughtered on the field of battle; the answer provided demonstrates that there can be none, that these young victims of war die in the midst of a holocaust from which God is conspicuously absent. This same question-and-answer structure is repeated in the sestet, where a similar question is initially asked: the question of who will light candles for the dead soldiers to expedite them on their way through purgatory toward heaven. Again the answer is the same: any kind of religious ritual would be a 'mockery', an insult to these victims who have been sent so senselessly to their deaths. Both questions are answered with a resounding negative ('Ónlў . . .', 'Nót . . .').

There is no difficulty in discerning where the volta occurs structurally in Owen's poem. But what effect does it have thematically? Closer inspection of the poem reveals a clear difference in tone between the two parts. Both questions raise the same issue: what consolation can religion bring to men who have been slain in such a bestial manner? But the tone of the two answers, although saying the same thing – that religion has no power to compensate for such annihilation – is quite dissimilar. The answer in the octave reproduces aurally the sounds of the battlefield, through the staccato rhythm of the onomatopoeic third line ('Only the stuttering rifles' rapid rattle'), its hard 'ă' sounds and alliterated 'r's suggesting the noise of the 'stuttering' guns. The tone here is predominantly that of anger. The poet's attitude, apparent in his diction, is that all religious trappings are 'mockeries'. A priest, even if he were present, would only 'patter out' words in which he had long since lost all conviction. The engines of war themselves provide, in a savage manner, the accompaniment of prayers and choral singing that the church has failed to supply. On the battlefield the celestial sound of the choir has been transformed into the demonic 'wailing' of the shells. The battlefield noises of the octave suggest a cacophonous black mass. This is the only tribute the dead will get: the madness that has destroyed them lives on to destroy others.

Then in the last line of the octave a transformation of tone is prepared for. After all the noise of the previous lines, the sounds of war are suddenly hushed and only the plaintive notes of the 'bugles calling for them from sad shires' can be heard. The scene shifts from the battlefield to the home front, where the last post is being sounded in their home counties for the dead soldiers. This is a preparation for the tone of the sestet, where the focus is no longer on the scene of slaughter but on the effect of this butchery on those that the victims have left behind. The sestet is much quieter in tone. The clamour of the octave is stilled and the poet's mood moves towards resignation. Whereas the emphasis in the octave is on sounds ('passing bells', 'prayers', 'choirs'), the focus in the sestet is on soundless tributes to the dead ('candles', 'flowers', 'pall', 'blinds'). The battle is over. Religion can aid neither the deceased nor the bereaved. Emotion is more sincerely expressed by comrades than by choirboys and it is the tears in the eyes of the former that show greater respect than the candles held ritualistically in the hands of the latter. The paleness of complexion of their sweethearts and wives is a more sincere tribute to the worth of the dead ones than any religious funeral ceremony could express. The final couplet emphasises that all is now still, for ever; and nature itself ('each slow dusk') adds its note of unutterable sadness.

The structure of the sonnet is based on two 'movements'. The first provides the clash of cymbals, the blaring of the brass, the loud discords of the battle arena; while the second introduces a slower pace, an *andante*, an acceptance of inevitability. So the poem is an anthem, after all. It moves from tension and discord towards a kind of resolution and harmony. The intervention of the bugles at the end of the octave is the key for this transition in music, theme and tone.

Rhymes and Sound Effects

Rhyme, alliteration and assonance are the means by which the poem makes its appeal to the ear. Together with rhythm – which is the 'percussion section' of the poem – they constitute the 'music' that distinguishes the poem from prose and lifts it into the realm of song. Whereas the imagery offers visual pictures, the rhymes and sound effects add the soundtrack. A reader not only sees the poem but hears it too, as, for example, in these lines from Tennyson:

> The bare black cliff clanged round him, as he based
> His feet on juts of slippery crag that rang
> Sharp-smitten with the dint of armed heels.
>
> ('Morte d'Arthur', 188–90)

This description of a climber contains two devices for suggesting a difficult and perilous exercise. The opening line consists of ten monosyllables, with more than iambic stress, suggesting the jerky and hazardous nature of the man's progress; and the second line contains a three-syllabled word, 'slippery', compressed into two syllables by the demands of the metre, reproducing the insecurity of the climber's position. To keep his equilibrium he has to keep jumping, pragmatically, from crag to crag, just as the poem leaps irregularly from stress to stress.

In addition to these devices Tennyson uses *assonance* (repetition of the same vowel sound) and *alliteration* (repetition of the same consonant sound). There is a recurrence of the open vowel sound 'ă' in the first two lines ('black', 'clanged', 'crag', 'rang'), suggestive of the hollow resonance made by the man's steel-shod feet on the rocks, the clamour produced rebounding back from the neighbouring valley walls. An echo effect is created; as it is in the last line with the repetition of the 'ĭ' sound in 'smitten' and 'dint' although, as this is a closed vowel (pronounced with the mouth in a relatively shut position, the lips close together rather than far apart as for 'ă'), the sound produced is more subdued. Adding to the echo effect is the use of alliteration in the first line, where the reiterated plosives in '*b*are' and '*b*lack' and in '*c*liff' and '*c*lang' give extra stress to these four adjacent words, retarding the rhythm to emphasise the troublesomeness of the natural obstacle course. Alliteration is often referred to as 'internal rhyme'. In fact, it is the earliest sort of rhyme in English; Old English poetry was written according to a pattern of alliterative 'rhymes' before the idea of rhyming by similar vowel and final consonant sounds at the ends of adjacent or nearly-adjacent lines was developed. The point of either system of rhyming is to impose a pattern of linkage on the poem, to suggest that the individual words – quite apart from their interconnection to form a meaning – are linked with one another in sound. Words, that is, are interrelated *sonically* as well as *semantically*. Rhyme is like the melody line in a piece of music: it pleases the ear. It suggests an underlying order both in the poem itself and in the world in which the poem has been made.

The effect that rhyme has of imposing order and control over the subject-matter of a poem is particularly noticeable in the couplet. The couplet seems to 'round off' an idea, or tie it up neatly into a parcel. This is why a couplet often appears at the end of a poem: it provides a synopsis or summary of what has gone before. This technique is used in 'Anthem for Doomed Youth', where, although the first twelve lines are rhymed in four-line units (called *quatrains*), the last two form a rhyming couplet of their own and are thus set apart from what has preceded them:

Their flowers the tenderness of patient minds,
And each slow dusk a drawing-down of blinds.

Owen uses the couplet to give the sense of a finale: he is drawing down the blinds on his poem. This quality in the couplet of tying up what has gone before was understood by Shakespeare, who often concludes one of his blank-verse soliloquies with a couplet, whereby the speaker indicates that his previous verbal eruption is now ended and that a cooler conclusion has been distilled from it. In *Hamlet* the Prince of Denmark, after complaining passionately and at length about the universal corruption of the world, ultimately acknowledges ruefully that the reason he is so upset is because he himself is required to tackle the evils that encompass him. After a long blank-verse rumination he thus concludes with a couplet:

> The time is out of joint. O cursed spite,
> That ever I was born to set it right!

In this way Shakespeare permits his characters to come back down to earth after an extensive emotional flight, at the same time crystallising for the audience the exact state of mind that each character finds himself in at a particular crisis in the drama.

Rhyme, then, as well as adding to the music of the verse, serves the function of binding the structure and reinforcing certain aspects of the theme. The first five lines of Coleridge's 'Kubla Khan' demonstrate this:

In Xanadu did Kubla Khan	*a*
A stately pleasure dome decree:	*b*
Where Alph, the sacred river, ran	*a*
Through caverns measureless to man	*a*
Down to a sunless sea.	*b*

One of the commonest rhyming patterns, aside from the couplet, is the quatrain, in which a four-lined unit of verse has its lines interlocked by rhymes, in the pattern *abab, abcb* or *abba* (where *a, b* and *c* represent the different rhymes occurring at the end of the lines). Coleridge's poem begins with what looks as though it will be a quatrain. The first three lines rhyme *aba*, and one would expect the fourth line to rhyme with the second *b*, to complete the pattern. But instead the fourth line rhymes with its predecessor, and it is not until the fifth line that the expected *b* rhyme comes, concluding the initial 'unit'. The quatrain has been stretched into a 'quintrain'. Why has this been done? These opening lines are describing the legendary kingdom of Kubla Khan and are specifically setting the scene of the poem by picturing the progress, through this land, of the sacred river.

The suspension of the expected rhyme until the fifth line suggests the tortuous course of the river: both river and rhyme attain their deferred goal simultaneously in the 'sunless sea'. The meandering advance of the river has been subtly and successfully indicated by the rhyme scheme, which, like the river, reaches its end obliquely rather than directly.

Since 20th-century Western man often finds himself in the predicament of having lost sight of his God, his poetry tends to reflect his lack of faith in a greater order by being unrhymed and written in what is called *free verse*. Unlike blank verse, which, though unrhymed, does have a basic metrical pattern in every line, free verse is both unrhymed and metrically unpredictable: its lines, though they possess rhythm, have no common metre binding them together. Each line is 'individualistic', often existing in metric isolation from its closest neighbours. This is evident in Cummings's 'Portrait', where a long line suggestive of the sound of shots fired rapidly from a revolver ('and break onetwothreefourfive pigeonsjustlikethat') is followed by a short line expressing the speaker's breathless, and blasphemous, appreciation of such feats ('Jesus'). The music of the heavenly spheres, which at the height of Christianity was heard by all English poets enabling and encouraging them to write in regular rhythm and melodic rhyme-schemes, has become inaudible to modern ears. Hence the salient features of 20th-century poetry – unless it be written by a poet who has managed to retain, or rediscover, a Christian philosophy – are irregularity of rhythm and dissonance, if not complete absence, of rhyme.

The Great War of 1914–18 saw some of the first poetry to be written in the direction of dissonance and dismay. An example is 'Strange Meeting', by Wilfred Owen:

It seemed that out of battle I escaped
Down some profound dull tunnel, long since scooped
Through granites which titanic wars had groined.
Yet also there encumbered sleepers groaned,
Too fast in thought or death to be bestirred.
Then, as I probed them, one sprang up, and stared
With piteous recognition in fixed eyes,
Lifting distressful hands as if to bless.
And by his smile, I knew that sullen hall,
By his dead smile I knew we stood in Hell.

There is still a strong sense of 'order' in this poem, because of the strict adherence to iambic pentameter line-lengths. But in the 'half-rhymes' at the ends of the lines a discordant feeling creeps in. For Owen's poem does not 'rhyme' in its final vowel sounds but in the consonants that encompass them. The difference between a vowel and a consonant is that the former is a sound made by an unimpeded flow of air passing through the vibrating vocal cords and modified by the shape of the mouth; whereas the latter is a sound made when the flow of air is halted or hampered or in some way prevented from leaving the mouth freely. A vowel is musical: singers linger on the vowels of their songs and rush over, or omit, the consonants. For consonants are unmusical: they consist largely of hisses and growls (*fricatives* such as 's' and 'r') and clicks and bangs (*plosives* such as 't', 'k' and 'p'). So, for a poem to draw attention to the relationship between its consonant sounds and yet deny any accordance between the relative vowel sounds is to stress dissonance at the expense of harmony. The reader's 'ear' expects to hear the music of harmonious vowel sounds in such a poem. His consequent disappointment impresses him with a sense of there being something out of kilter in the poem. In 'Strange Meeting' further contradictions within the theme itself become apparent, showing that the lack of agreement between the final vowel sounds is neither whimsical nor accidental. The speaker in the poem meets a man who greets him as if with the sign of benediction, even though the location of the meeting turns out to be 'Hell'. Moreover, the man whom the speaker encounters has a 'dead smile': he is a phantom, not a man at all. And, as the poem continues, it emerges that this ghost who greets the speaker with such kindness in his eyes is the wraith of a soldier whom the speaker has slain and despatched to this underworld. By the consonance of the consonant clusters one's attention is drawn to the end of each line, where the disagreement in the vowel sounds disturbs the ear. The time is not only out of joint but out of tune as well.

After the trauma of the war it was difficult for poets to re-establish the vision of a divine order underlying all creation. From the earliest English epic *Beowulf*, written in the 8th century AD, to the more recent English poetry such as Tennyson's *In Memoriam*, written in the 19th, a confidence in the presence of a divine Being behind the mists of mundane existence had inspired writers to imitate their Maker and make music, harmony and order out of the raw materials of their trade. The First World War shattered this confidence. The poem with regularly rhymed units – of couplets, quatrains or stanzas – has come to seem a somewhat coy reaction to a world in which, in Othello's words, 'Chaos is come again'. Such a world view was, in fact, already in formulation before the outbreak of hostilities in 1914. The dissipation of the old vision probably began with the publication of Charles Darwin's *Origin of Species* in 1859, with its scientific attempt to demonstrate a spontaneous creation and accidental evolution in which no identifiable divinity had a hand. Then the work of undermining Victorian Christian confidence was carried further by the publication, eight years later, of Karl Marx's *Das Kapital*, with its exposé of the exploitative class-system. The shock waves from such iconoclasts as Darwin and Marx were penetrating the consciousness of the literary élite for the remainder of the century. The First World War simply accelerated the process.

Poets, together with painters and composers, had been attempting to cope with the problem of adapting their work to the character of their environment even before the war pummelled them into a sense of urgency. Rhyme was beginning to seem more and more irrelevant in an industrial society in which, according to Marx, alienation rather than communion was the *modus vivendi* of the masses. So rhyme, with its implications of relationship between differing elements, was coming to be regarded as obsolete. This is a process that has continued throughout the 20th century. Rhyme, when it is used, is employed for a special effect and not to imply belief in a metaphysical plane of being where all is harmony. The 20th-century poet tends to be sceptical of the existence of any 'world' other than this imperfect one which we inhabit. George Orwell summed up the mood of many contemporary writers when he wrote, in 1942, 'hardly anyone nowadays *feels* himself to be immortal'.

Rhyme, when it does occur in a 20th-century poem, often does so at isolated moments scattered throughout the body of the poem, suggestive of the random nature of our world and of man's apparently 'accidental' and unplanned evolution into a thinking being. At other times rhyme is hauled into a poem for a particular ironic or incongruous effect. In T. S. Eliot's 'Love Song of J. Alfred Prufrock', for example, written in 1911, some lines rhyme and other lines do not. This inconsistency, together with the uneven line-lengths, gives the poem a rather haphazard effect which reflects the uncertainty of its speaker Prufrock, a poet *manqué*:

In the room the women come and go
Talking of Michelangelo.

The desultory activity of the room where the bourgeois matrons 'come and go' is contrasted with the intense creative energies of Michelangelo, a name synonymous with all that was magnificent about Renaissance art. The pairing of his name, through the rhyme, with the comings and goings of guests at a cocktail party suggests how everything these days has become debased. Michelangelo's art no longer moves people profoundly: he has become merely a name to be tossed around in social chitchat.

As for the other 'sound' devices of poetry, the prevalence of alliteration should by now be apparent. It occurs, for instance, in Coleridge's 'Christabel':

Her gentle limbs did she undress,
And lay down in her loveliness.

Here the repeated 'l' sounds convey an impression of softness and tenderness – a 'lulling' effect – appropriate to the gently erotic image. Examples of assonance have also already occurred in the preceding pages and one more illustration of this device should suffice:

Thou watchest the last oozings hours by hours.

This line ends one of the stanzas of Keats's 'To Autumn'. The poet is trying to convey an impression of one of the characteristics of autumn: rest after the labour of the year is done. The duration of the leisurely occupation of supervising a cider-press is stressed by the long vowel sounds towards the end of the line: 'last oozings hours by hours'. 'Oozings' is an onomatopoeic word suggestive, in its long 'ū', of the slowness with which the liquid emerges from the machinery; while the repeated diphthongs in 'hours', together with the extra elongation produced by the plural form ('hours by hours' taking longer to say than 'hour by hour'), assist in creating the impression of an employment which is pleasantly relaxed and undemanding. Often alliteration and assonance work in combination with each other to produce the desired impact, as in this line from Keats's 'Ode to a Nightingale':

Through verdurous glooms and winding mossy ways.

The repeated long 'ū' sound in 'through' and 'glooms' together with the slowly-articulated semi-vowel 'w' in 'winding' and 'ways', plus the sibilance of the several 's' sounds, combine to slow down the rhythm and suggest the sinuous nature of the forest paths the poet is traversing. There is a caesura after 'glooms', emphasising the long vowel and applying a further brake to the rhythmic flow.

Thus the poet uses the tools of his trade – the words of his language – to fashion effects that call forth responses on intellectual, emotional and instinctual levels. The heart of a poem is its theme, and poetic devices only have a *raison d'être* insofar as they support it. The alliteration and assonance of Owen's 'stuttering rifles' rapid rattle' are there to provide a reflection in sound of the monstrous music of the battlefield that is the poem's main topic. A poem's apparatus must bear the burden of its theme to all the layers of understanding.

2 The Elizabethan Sonnet: Sidney and Shakespeare

Sir Philip Sidney (1554–86)

By the latter part of the 16th century the vocabulary and pronunciation of the English language had become more or less stabilised into something resembling English spoken today. This stabilisation coincides with what is more generally known as the *Renaissance*: the 'rebirth' of European man's awareness of his classical heritage from Greece and Rome and the resurgence of his questing spirit towards exploration and the acquisition of further knowledge in all fields. With the Renaissance came a new consciousness of the English language and a new confidence in its use as a medium for poetic expression, which found its richest and most sublime realisation in the works of Shakespeare. One of the new forms in which English poetry – including Shakespeare's – blossomed was the sonnet.

Both the structure and the subject-matter of the English sonnet came from the Italian founder of the sonnet form, Francesco Petrarca, known as Petrarch (1304–74). The standard Petrarchan sonnet has a break between the octave and the sestet – the volta – indicating that, as the poem progresses, the poet shifts from the plane of mere passive reporting to the higher one of active rationalisation or speculation about what he has reported. The first English sonneteers, Sir Thomas Wyatt, Henry Howard Earl of Surrey and Sir Philip Sidney, tended to imitate the Petrarchan form fairly faithfully, but even someone as early as Shakespeare, a near-contemporary of Sidney, was experimenting and developing a form of his own: the so-called

'Shakespearean' sonnet. Sonnet writers of later centuries have also adapted the form to suit their needs; but the basic blueprint of a 14-line iambic pentameter poem, generally rhymed, and usually including a volta at some point in its evolution, underlies all sonnets. The advantage of such a 'tight' organisation is that it brings the assertion of some kind of order over the emotional chaos that is so often the sonnet's subject-matter. The regularity suggested by the form brings often a serenity and sense of calm to the poet's bemused or distraught mental state. The messiness of individual human experience is offered some consolation by the order of the sonnet form and its suggestiveness of an ultimate, divine pattern underpinning the man-made representation.

This is the idea behind Petrarch's sonnets. Petrarch was in love with the married daughter, Laura, of the burgher of Avignon, in the Provençal region of southern France. Through his sonnets Petrarch managed to sublimate his earthly love for her and transmute it into a love of the divine, of God. Laura thus was 'idealised' by him into a type of heavenly virtue, losing all her earthly dross and becoming, in his vision, a pure heavenly body: the 'Sun'. Thus the subject-matter of the Provençal troubadour love songs – the beloved's cruel chastity, the lover's feeling of aloneness in the midst of others' gaiety – become, in Petrarch, elevated into an apprehension and adoration of the Godhead, of which the beauty of his forever-distant mistress is both emblem and testimony. It is a movement from concrete to abstract speculation. Petrarch's sonnets revolve around the earthly pains of the unrequited lover and their sedation through a contemplation of the divine order which informs all life. This is the subject-matter and the form that Sidney inherited and used, for his own ends, in his sonnet-sequence narrative *Astrophel and Stella*. Here is the thirty-first sonnet of the sequence.

With how sad steps, O Moon, thou climb'st the skies!
How silently, and with how wan a face!
What, may it be that even in heavenly place
That busy archer his sharp arrows tries?
Sure, if that long-with-love-acquainted eyes
Can judge of love, thou feel'st a lover's case,
I read it in thy looks; thy languished grace,
To me, that feel the like, they state descries.
Then, even of fellowship, O Moon, tell me,

Is constant love deemed there but want of wit?
Are beauties there as proud as here they be?
Do they above love to be loved, and yet
Those lovers scorn whom that love doth possess?
Do they call virtue there ungratefulness?

The poet is trying to express a personal or 'subjective' emotion through a conventional form – the sonnet. The several references to 'I' and 'me' stress the personal content of the poem, while the conventional images of Cupid ('that busy archer') and the 'Moon' emphasise that the poet is writing in a long-established tradition of poems about unhappy love and beautiful uncaring women.

The poet begins by associating himself with the moon and drawing a parallel between his own and the moon's 'case'. He fancies that the moon, with its 'wan face', has been denied the light and warmth of the sun, just as he is in the shadow of his own lady's displeasure. The moon is seen to be, like him, speechless ('silent') with grief and sadly climbs into the skies as if it, too, were ascending reluctantly to a lonely bedchamber. 'Even in heavenly place' the god of love is at work.

The link that the poet makes between himself and the moon is at first rather tenuous. He expresses it in the form of tentative questions: 'What, may it be . . .?' In the second quatrain he becomes more certain of the parallel he has drawn and moves from the interrogative to the declarative mood: 'Sure . . .'. He recognises in the moon a fellow sufferer: everything about the moon's appearance 'descries', or describes, the moon's lovelorn state. The poet's growing confidence throughout the octave in his at first timorous suggestion that he and the moon share the same unhappy love story prepares for the boldness of tone in the sestet. For by that time the poet has contrived to raise himself to the same sphere as the moon and he now claims an equality, or 'fellowship', with it. From the moon's point of view the 'values' of earth seem ridiculous. In heaven, the moon's 'sphere', constancy in love would be regarded as a prime virtue and not as the stupidity, or 'want of wit', it is deemed to be on earth. From heaven's more serene viewpoint the 'pride' of earthly 'beauties' appears as cruelty. Virtue there would not be termed ingratitude, nor would the person who bestowed love be scoffed at and scorned by the one who basked in the warmth of such love.

What Sidney has done in the sestet is bring all the canons of divine justice to bear on the unreasonable behaviour of his light-headed mistress. He has attempted, by linking himself with the moon, to enlist the forces of supreme disapproval on his side and to add supernatural weight to his own protestations. The questions in the sestet are all 'rhetorical': they all expect a resounding 'No!' as answer.

From this analysis the close identification between form and content in the sonnet should become clear. The poem begins with an image and with an application of that image to the poet's own subjective state. Then from the strength of this 'forced alliance' between poet and heavenly body the speaker moves back to what has caused his complaint in the first place: the cruelty of his mistress. The octave establishes the ground for the attacks that are to be made in the sestet. The latter begins with the word 'Then . . .', signalling that the speaker is going to draw conclusions from his foregoing remarks or is now switching to the offensive.

Sidney's sonnet has been approached here mainly through an appreciation of its structure, charting the progress of its syllogistic argument through the assumed naivety of tone and hesitancy of delivery in the octave to the straightforward belligerence of the sestet, culminating in the acerbity of the last line – a line given extra strength in its bitterness by its rhyme-linkage with the preceding line (it ends emphatically, in other words, with a couplet). Other analytical approaches could just as appropriately be adopted: for instance, the initial similarities, and later disparities, between the image of the moon and the 'lover's case' of the speaker could attract the main focus. However, having dealt – from whatever angle – with the 'body proper', the main theme or argument of the poem, we must conclude with some words on the 'incidental aspects', showing how all elements work together to form a coherent whole.

Firstly, the question of tone merits some consideration. The poem begins on a note of sadness or melancholy, quietly spoken. This quickly turns to smothered outrage in the sestet, where the poet's previous 'softness' is revealed as a mask behind which dwells an unquenchable resentment. The questions addressed, ostensibly to the moon, have a cumulatively ironic tone, calling for the reader's condemnation of the practices among beautiful women that could provoke such hurt.

Secondly, more might be said about the poem's one image: the moon. The moon, according to the Ptolemaic astronomical beliefs that were still current in Sidney's day, was the lowest of the spheres containing the planets which revolved around the earth (conceived as being the centre of the universe). Therefore the moon is the heavenly body which is the closest to the earth and thus the least perfect. Yet even so, it is obviously not 'sublunary' but 'extraterrestrial', relatively 'sublime', and in the poem it is identified even with the highest of the spheres, the 'heavenly place'. The moon combines both heavenly and earthly qualities. Through its proximity to earth, the poet is able to suggest that it too can feel earthly emotions; while, because of its kinship to the heavenly sphere, he is able to introduce divine justice into the dark hollows of his love affair. The choice of the moon-image suggests not only a unity between man and the natural world but an affinity between man and the supernatural world as well. There is an implication of cosmic harmony in the picture, against which the benighted cruelty of the earthly 'beauties' clashes in a discordant and therefore to be condemned fashion.

Thirdly, the diction of the poem might be mentioned. There is a contrast between personal and traditional 'voices' in the poem: much of this contrast comes through the diction, which juxtaposes the poet's uniqueness of feeling ('Then even of fellowship, O Moon, tell *me*') with the conventional phrases about 'proud beauties', 'long-with-love-acquainted eyes' and the 'busy archer' with his 'sharp arrows'. The poem's power and intensity derive from the tension between these two styles of diction: the personal and the predictable. The poet's experience, though individually new to him, is as ancient and oft repeated as human life itself. Sometimes diction combines with rhythm to produce a particular effect, as the penultimate line of Sidney's poem demonstrates. Here the regular iambic metre places a stress on 'that':

Thŏse lóveřs scórn whŏm thát lŏve dóth pŏsséss.

This helps to clarify the meaning of the line: *that* sort of love which torments the unrequited lover is an illness or infirmity – or even a sort of devil – which takes possession of the lover and which the beloved refuses to cure, or exorcise.

Finally, one point should be made clear. This analysis has referred to the 'subjective' voice of the poet; but it must be borne in mind that this 'subjectivity' may itself be a guise. In other words, the Astrophel of the whole sequence may be not simply a mask or persona for Sidney himself but a fictionally-created character in its own right. No matter how autobiographical a poem might purport to be, there will always be some amount of self-dramatisation in it. At the same time, though, there is a difference between the sort of persona created by Sidney – which seems more or less a dramatised representation of himself, or of how he would like to appear in the eyes of others – and the sort of persona created in later centuries by Robert Browning or T. S. Eliot, where the personality and point of view of the writer differ widely from those of his 'mouthpiece'.

William Shakespeare (1564–1616)

The 154 sonnets of Shakespeare were most probably written between 1595 and 1600, when the poet/playwright was in his early 30s. Many of the early ones are addressed to a young man, for whom the poet expresses altruistic sentiments of Platonic love; while the later ones introduce a third party, the so-called 'dark lady'. The two examples below are from the earlier phase. As with Sidney, a knowledge of the biographical background – which is anyway largely a matter of conjecture – is not necessary for an understanding of the poems. Each sonnet stands complete in itself and whether it is addressed to, or concerned with, people who are 'real' or merely fictitious matters little.

12

When I do count the clock that tells the time,
And see the brave day sunk in hideous night;
When I behold the violet past prime,
And sable curls all silvered o'er with white;
When lofty trees I see barren of leaves,
Which erst from heat did canopy the herd,
And summer's green all girded up in sheaves
Borne on the bier with white and bristly beard;
Then of thy beauty do I question make
That thou among the wastes of time must go,
Since sweets and beauties do themselves forsake,
And die as fast as they see others grow;
    And nothing 'gainst Time's scythe can make defence
    Save breed, to brave him when he takes thee hence.

In this his twelfth sonnet Shakespeare reflects on the disintegration wrought by the passage of time upon all natural objects. The poem is comprised of one long sentence, of which the first eight lines are composed of two subordinate clauses of four lines each: in these lines Shakespeare is cataloguing several individual instances of the effects of time on nature. The main clause is introduced in the third quatrain (lines 9–12), in which Shakespeare narrows his focus from the general overall view of the ravages of time to the particular prospect of the inevitable decay of beauty in the person to whom the poem is addressed. It is a process of deductive logic. From the preceding eight lines, in which the poet records his observations about universal decay in nature, the conclusion is reached – in the main clause of lines 9 and 10 – that the fading of beauty and vigour in the addressee of the poem is inescapable. To this pessimistic outlook the final couplet offers a ray of consolation, albeit a tenuous one: all that man can bring into the lists against time is his procreative faculty, which will at least ensure that the individual transmits something of himself through his children before death claims him.

The theme of the opening eight lines is that all things brilliant and vigorous in nature must fade and die. The alliterations of the first line suggest the unstoppable ticking of the clock, measuring out man's life span with an impersonal but inexorable regularity. The poet presents various images to illustrate his theme of the devastating effects of time. Daylight, which puts up a courageous struggle against the forces of darkness and disorder, must inevitably fade and fail each evening with the sinking of the sun. The brilliantly-coloured violet will lose its lustre once it has passed the peak of its growth cycle, the 'prime' of its existence. Similarly, the youthful head of black ('sable') curls will certainly in time lose its colour and vitality, turning first to 'silver', then to a lifeless 'white'. The colour progression of these images suggests the deterioration in quality and the loss of energy that affects all living organisms as time passes. In this opening quatrain Shakespeare moves from a plant image (the violet) to a human one (the head of hair). This is a method that he follows in the second quatrain also, and in the poem as a whole, since his main purpose is to point out analogies in nature that reflect on, and illuminate, the transitoriness of the human condition.

The second quatrain begins with a further image from the 'vegetable' world. Trees that are 'lofty' – aloof and proud – are eventually brought low and stripped of their finery ('barren of

The Elizabethan Sonnet: Sidney and Shakespeare

leaves'). The trees, which in the height of summer were able to provide protection from the sun to herds of cattle, are now not even able to clothe themselves against the coldness of winter. The point the poet is making is that even the most majestic natural creation (a 'lofty' tree) will ultimately prove helpless against the erosion wrought by time. This quatrain is based on the idea of the seasons, and depends particularly on the contrast between the health and vitality of created life in summertime and its miserable demise in winter. So the corn that flourished during the summer months quickly withers and is buried ('borne on the bier') when the season changes. This image is of the harvest: when the corn is cut and carried to the barn it is no longer 'green' with the sap and strength of youth but 'white' like the corpse of an old, bearded man.

In the third quatrain he draws the inference more particularly, applying it to one person: the addressee of the sonnet. The focus, thus, continues to be narrowed: from general observations to particular instances, from the impersonal to the personal. This person's beauty, like all else in the material world, has a vitality that is transient and the person himself (or herself) is foredoomed (he '*must*' decline) to an end of loneliness and aridity in the desert of his old age. The reference to the 'wastes of time' is the second image of sterility in the poem. This adumbration of the sense of desolation in one's old age prompts the one extenuation that Shakespeare, somewhat belatedly, offers in this poem as an antidote to the corrosive effects of time: the ability of natural species to reproduce their kind and the particular necessity that the addressee of this poem should do so. In the couplet time is seen as the reaper: the same force that, in the previous lines, put an end to 'summer's greenness', just as, with his scythe, he will eventually mow down each human life like so many stalks of wheat.

Since time's harvest of each individual life is irrefutable, the best that a human being can do is accept the inevitable and offer the only 'defiance' to time that he can: the perpetuation of his kind through the procreation of offspring. The application here to human endeavour of the same epithet, 'brave', as was used at the beginning of the poem to depict the efforts of daylight to withstand the encroaching darkness associates man's struggle against death with all the life-giving and life-rejoicing aspects of nature (sunlight, the vigour of fresh corn, the hues of flowers) in their perpetual fight against the threats of disorder and oblivion immanent in 'hideous night' and all the powers of evil abounding in the world. It is a 'brave' struggle, a noble conflict in

which man achieves dignity and the only victory that he is permitted
to enjoy: the satisfaction of leaving another generation behind him to
continue the battle when he himself finally succumbs.

The theme of time versus the individual also provides the starting
point for Shakespeare's 73rd sonnet but a rather different argument
emerges from it.

73

That time of year thou mayst in me behold
When yellow leaves, or none, or few, do hang
Upon those boughs which shake against the cold,
Bare ruined choirs where late the sweet birds sang.
In me thou see'st the twilight of such day
As after sunset fadeth in the west,
Which by and by black night doth take away,
Death's second self, that seals up all in rest.
In me thou see'st the glowing of such fire
That on the ashes of his youth doth lie,
As the deathbed whereon it must expire,
Consumed with that which it was nourished by.
This thou perceiv'st, which makes thy love more strong,
To love that well which thou must leave ere long.

Structurally this poem, like Sonnet 12, splits into three quatrains and
a couplet; but here the volta does not come at the end of the octave but
before the final couplet. This gives the effect of prolonging the
negative or 'fearful' aspects that the poet is presenting, before the
positive implications of the couplet are swung into the scale to
counterbalance the pessimism of the preceding twelve lines.
Diagrammatically the sonnet's structure could be presented thus:

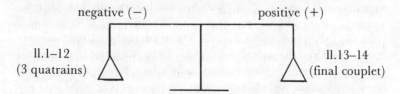

negative (−)   positive (+)

ll.1–12   ll.13–14
(3 quatrains)   (final couplet)

Each quatrain is composed of one sentence and contains one image.
All the images present aspects of life in its last stages. The focus of the

imagery gets narrower as the poem advances, at first 'catching' the attention by a general, panoramic sweep showing a wood in the season of late autumn, finally showing an old man nodding off before the embers of his untended fire. The purpose of this progression is to relate man's life cycle to mortality patterns in nature, showing how, as Hamlet's mother Gertrude expressed it, 'All that lives must die, / Passing through nature to eternity' – only in this poem there is none of the afterlife compensation implicit in Gertrude's short homily. Here there is a finality about death: at the end of life everything is 'sealed up', not to be broken. The compensation – if there is one – is not spiritual but earthly: it rests in the manifestation of the addressee's love for the poet in spite of the latter's visible decay and evidently imminent decease.

The three quatrains bludgeon the reader with images of gloom. Since these pessimistic premonitions are so persistent and over-whelming, the couplet strikes a note of courageous defiance. The love shown to the doomed poet is judged to be even 'more strong' because it is a love that is maintained in the face of death.

The first image depicts the season just prior to winter, when the sun is already low in the northern European sky and the trees have no longer enough vitality to sustain their foliage. This image is clearly visualised, with the self-correction in the poet's description ('yellow leaves, or none, or few') recapturing the actual process of cognition. The trees are personified as inadequately clad persons beating their arms together to try to keep warm, suggesting the bond between man and the natural world. The quatrain ends with a vivid 'close-up' of the boughs of the trees compared to stalls in a church choir, now empty both of leaves and of music. The comparison of bird-song to choral singing and the indication that such holy sounds are now a thing of the past ('late') perhaps imply that any possibility of religious consolation has been withdrawn from the poet, to whom death appears starkly as a void, characterised by the absence of light, warmth, music and, ultimately, of love as well.

In the first quatrain the approach of death in the natural world is emphasised and the poet is present only by implication. In the second quatrain he begins to assume more prominence, as is evident from the opening focus on 'me' rather than on 'that time of year'. The poet has first of all compared himself to a season of the year; now he compares himself to a certain time in the evening, when the sun has withdrawn its light and heat and only the 'afterglow' of twilight remains. Thus not only the focus but the time span of the images is retracting – and darkening. 'Black night' is imminent in this image and is seen as some hostile force lurking in the shadows before its appointed time comes. 'Night' here has the same role as 'winter' in the first quatrain: it is an emblem of approaching death, this time made more specific by its identification as death's henchman or *alter ego* ('death's second self'). Now even the energy of the bird-song has been forgotten. It is as if the speaker were ageing even as the poem advances.

In the third quatrain the focus has narrowed even further. From the initial 'outdoor' view of trees on an autumn day the poet brings us indoors, to his own fireside. Our purview, like his, is now limited to the coals crumbling into ashes in his hearth. It is no longer the sun that is the source of heat but only an old man's fire. With this diminution in the grandeur of the imagery comes a sense of growing depression. All the energy and beauty of the individual's life have been reduced to the 'ashes' that the spent man now gazes on. What previously sustained the speaker – his lust for life – now turns against him, making him cynical and listless and indifferent towards death. All his previous activity is seen as so much futile expenditure, since it all leads to this state of senile lethargy.

The images give a progressive picture of the physical decay and moral decline of the speaker. Thus the couplet, with its affirmation that the human being's capacity to love prevails in spite of all discouragement, gives an unexpected spurt of optimism. There is some hope for human nature after all. The opening 'this' of line 13 refers to all the accumulated impressions of physical and moral degeneration that the previous 12 lines have been piling up. And it is the addressee's capacity to maintain his or her love for the speaker who is so unflatteringly self-presented that constitutes the poem's final, if ephemeral, note of triumph. Even though he knows he must be deserted soon, when life finally leaves his body, the poet is, at any rate for the time being, not simply loved but loved 'well'. The nobility of man's nature is thereby signalled, even if the purpose of his existence remains dark.

3 The Early 17th Century: Donne and Herbert

John Donne (1572–1631)

The sonnets of Sidney and Shakespeare have suggested some of the ways in which the English sonneteers modified the form that they inherited – Sidney by introducing a tone of acidic complaint against women and Shakespeare by doing away with the octave/sestet division and replacing it by a structure of three quatrains and a couplet, thereby concentrating the conclusion of the sonnet into an effectively terse and pithy epigram. Donne confers an even more distinctive 'English' voice upon the Italian form.

Donne's poetry reflects the shifting sensibility of his age. The global explorations that had gone on in the 16th century were part of a questing spirit noticeable in all walks of life. Until this time the Ptolemaic model of the universe – propounded by the Alexandrian astronomer Ptolemy back in the second century AD – had held sway, offering as it did the comforting notion that the earth and its denizen, man, were firmly placed at the centre, as the focal point of God's regard. But in Donne's day Ptolemy's construct was being jostled aside by the theory of the Pole, Copernicus (1473–1543), who held that the earth went round the sun rather than vice versa. This idea had traumatic repercussions, since it showed the earth as being merely peripheral, rather than central, to the scheme of Creation. As Donne says, 'The new philosophy calls all in doubt'. The mood, then, at the start of the 17th century was one of scepticism: nothing could be believed unless it could be scientifically proved. Donne's poems are full of a new, 'unpoetic' sort of imagery: that of the telescope, of geometrical instruments, of minting machines and all the paraphernalia of the Renaissance laboratory. And if a woman declares her love, it must be taken with a pinch of salt, since such an emotion has no empirical basis and the chances are that the woman 'will be / False . . . to two, or three' before the day is out.

The sonnet has often been recommended as a good discipline for the apprentice poet because the tightness of its 14-line structure forces the writer to concentrate his thought, distilling it down to its essence. Shakespeare's sonnet sequence is said to have taught him the value of conciseness of expression. But Donne is a poet so filled with emotion that the 14 lines of iambic pentameter can scarcely contain it. There is tension between the 'medium' and the 'message': it seems as though the poet is in revolt against the disciplines – artistic and social – that restrain him.

Donne was born into a Catholic family in 1572, a time when many Catholics were persecuted for their beliefs and when all professional advancement was limited to Protestants. As an ambitious young man Donne studied law and converted to the Protestant religion possibly because, if he were to advance in the world, it was essential that he renounce his Catholicism. In the end it was not Donne's ambivalent religious status that stymied him but his injudicious elopement in 1602 with Ann More, the niece and ward of Sir Thomas Egerton, for whom Donne worked as private secretary. Egerton arranged for Donne to be imprisoned for a spell, having dismissed him from his service. His career in ruins, Donne spent several years in poverty, until he decided to try to repair his fortunes by answering the call of the church. He became an Anglican minister in 1615 and soon rose to become dean of St Paul's Cathedral in London.

There are, then, two distinct 'hemispheres' in Donne's life, and these are reflected in the two kinds of poetry that he wrote. In his youth he hoped for secular advancement, by way of a diplomatic career in government service. This was the period when he wrote his love poetry, most of which was produced before he was 25. After the scandal caused by his elopement Donne spent some years in the doldrums, writing an occasional poem for a patron. With his espousal of the church as his new destiny there was a renewed burst of poetic activity, this time of a religious bent. The energy and passion that had hitherto been directed towards women was now pointed at God. The quality that Donne's religious poetry has in common with his love poetry is its spontaneity of diction. The words strike a note which is colloquial and 'modern'. For example, one of his love lyrics begins,

For God's sake, hold your tongue, and let me love.

('The Canonization')

Donne displays a distaste and impatience towards the artifices of Petrarchan convention. He writes poetry of the city rather than of an idealised Arcadian countryside. Sidney's moon is looked at through an astronomer's, not a lover's, eye and Donne has no interest at all in the boughs, the birds and the beauties of nature that proved such an endless source of inspiration to Shakespeare. Donne's poetry is often called 'metaphysical', partly because of its scientific imagery (science was often referred to as 'metaphysics' in his day) and partly because of his unusual linking of physical objects to abstract metaphysical concepts (such as the comparison of a set of compasses to the love between a man and his wife in 'A Valediction Forbidding Mourning') with which they have apparently very little in common. The 'unromantic' qualities of Donne's imagery and tone have fallen on sympathetic ears in recent times: he was largely ignored in the 18th and 19th centuries and was 'rediscovered' at the beginning of the 20th by, among others, T. S. Eliot.

Here is one of the 'holy sonnets' produced by Donne in his later years, when he had relinquished his attempts to find completeness in a relationship with a human being and set about trying to establish a relationship with God.

X

Batter my heart, three-personed God; for you
As yet but knock, breathe, shine, and seek to mend;
That I may rise, and stand, o'erthrow me, and bend
Your force, to break, blow, burn, and make me new.
I, like an usurped town, to another due,
Labour to admit you, but oh, to no end.
Reason your viceroy in me, me should defend,
But is captived, and proves weak or untrue,
Yet dearly I love you, and would be loved fain,
But am betrothed unto your enemy.
Divorce me, untie, or break that knot again,
Take me to you, imprison me, for I,
Except you enthral me, never shall be free,
Nor ever chaste, except you ravish me.

The speaker is calling urgently for God to make His existence manifest and assuage the poet's fears of damnation. He seems to be bellowing out for God's attention and has worked himself into a state of frenzy which suggests his near despair at the unwillingness that God has so far shown to enter and alter his life. The poet has renounced his past profligate life and wishes to be born anew but he cannot believe in the efficacy of a forgiveness that does not involve painful punishment for sins confessed. He therefore calls out to God to use him violently; only through violence will he be able to feel that his reformation, his 're-formation' into a new man, has been effectively accomplished. To emphasise the force that he feels is necessary for his 'reshaping', he uses verbs of violent action, and at the same time he does violence to the iambic pentameter of the verse.

The first word of the poem indicates these two aspects. 'Batter' is an imperative, demanding that God should show Himself rather as the battering-Ram, the irascible Jehovah of the Old Testament, than as the kind and patient Lamb of the New. The stress falls on the first syllable, thus startling the hearer with a trochaic opening, emphasising that the poet is seeking every means of alerting the attention of a God who has hitherto seemed indifferent to his plight. He asks God to pound upon, and remould, his inner self, his 'heart'. God is addressed in all His three 'persons': as Father, Son and Holy Ghost. The poet demands *all* of God's attention. The verbs often come in groups of three, to reflect the tripartite nature of the Christian Godhead. The milder aspects of this God are revealed in line 2. So far God the Father merely 'knocks' on the poet's heart, in the meek manner of a suppliant. The Holy Spirit as yet only 'breathes' on the poet's soul, with insufficient strength to effect any change in it. And God the Son (with an implied pun on 'sun') merely 'shines' or radiates benevolence. But the poet is so hardened in his sinful ways that the 'diplomatic' approach of this liberal Deity is inadequate. The poet demands a much harsher and more vigorous attitude from God. He asks God to wrestle with him ('o'erthrow me'), in the way that the angel in the Old Testament had wrestled with Jacob.

Donne desires a complete psychological transformation; only a more energetic attack from divine forces can oust the wickedness planted so deeply within him. He therefore asks God to show more gusto ('bend / Your force') and to increase the intensity of His efforts, so that instead of merely knocking He will 'break'; He will 'blow' instead of simply 'breathe' and 'burn' rather than just 'shine'. What he longs for is to behold God as a blacksmith, rather than a simple carpenter; for on the vulcanic anvil he can be forged anew. To this end the verbs 'break, blow, burn' indicate the activity of the smithy not only in the images they give but in the sounds they convey. The heavily stressed plosives with which each of the verbs begins, linking them alliteratively to the initial 'batter' in sound as well as meaning, convey strongly the rhythm and the compressed and concentrated energy of the blacksmith's hammer as it pounds old metal into new material. Donne's various syncopations within the iambic pentameter line strain the fundamental rhythm almost to breaking point and demonstrate thereby the distractedness of his own mental condition. For instance, line 3 may be scanned

Thăt Í măy ríse, ănd stánd, ó'erthrów mĕ, ănd bénd,

which not only provides both an extra stress (six rather than five) and an additional unstressed syllable but leaves the line suspended in meaning, so that the reader has to rush on to the following line in order to find the object of the verb 'bend' and complete the sense. There is a similar disarrangement at the end of line 1. The unsettling changes of rhythm mirror disconcertingly the poet's own lack of equilibrium and give a discomfitting idea of the distance to be traversed between God and this beseecher if he is ever to find that peace which passeth understanding.

Having established that he needs to feel God working within him with all the power and purpose of a blacksmith, the poet goes on in the second quatrain to vary the image, while at the same time sustaining the same unsettling metrical effects. All four lines begin with reversed, trochaic feet. Not only is the rhythm disturbed but the syntax is tortuous. 'Reason, your viceroy in me, should defend me', would be a more orthodox expression. But an orderly rhythm and sentence structure would suggest calm and tranquillity of mind, which are the last things that the poet wishes to concede. This quatrain is built around the image of the sinful poet as a 'usurped town': he sees himself as territory which ought to show loyalty to God ('to another due') but which has been taken over ('usurped') and is being controlled by another (Satan). It is an image of possession – possession by the Devil. He is struggling to allow God into his life – the heavy trochaic stress on 'lábŏur' suggests the strenuous amount of effort he is putting in – but has so far failed. He needs God's help to expel the 'usurper'. He goes on to explain that even his reason – traditionally acknowledged to be the divine or God-given faculty or representative ('your viceroy') in man, separating him from the beasts – has betrayed its Creator and gone over to Satan's camp. If man's rational faculty 'proves weak and untrue', how much more powerless is his insensible body to resist whatever lusts of the flesh fall in its way?

The image of man as a town suggests his passivity and helplessness. The poet sees himself not only as a town held captive by an enemy and longing for relief but as a woman 'labouring to admit', in a sexual sense, her lover. The subsequent exclamation, 'oh', is thus not simply an expression of disappointment that the siege has not yet been lifted but the cry of a frustrated woman whose yearned-for lord continually refuses to satisfy her longings.

These sexual implications are further developed and embellished in the sestet of the sonnet. Donne pictures himself more and more in the guise of a hapless female, engaged ('betrothed') against her will to the Devil, yet capable of a much purer and more valuable ('dear') love for God. Like the captive-maiden of mediaeval romance, Donne is asking his Lord to ride in and rescue him from the clutches of the fiendish abductor. He is too weak to effect his own escape. He earnestly requests God to reciprocate his love ('would be loved fain') and demands that God give him evidence of His concern. If the speaker is to be severed from his sinful ways, it will have to be by a violent wrench which, on his own, he seems incapable of making. He therefore asks God, again in a three-verb cluster in which the verbs get progressively more violent, to assert Himself and come actively between himself and his seducer ('divorce me, untie, or break that knot'). Donne is here talking about spiritual love, the purer bond which grows between man and his God as opposed to the grosser tie which binds man to his world and which, all too often, strangles and chokes the development of the finer variety. Yet Donne is describing this spiritual love in terms of the love between men and women, showing that he desires to experience the love of God as something just as passionate as the sexual love he has enjoyed in his days of youth and carefreeness. Perhaps Protestantism, with its ruthless extirpation of the warm and comforting 'trappings' of Catholic religious practice, has made God seem too cold and forbidding a figure to the poet. Donne's imploring his Lord's return in the language of a languishing, sorrowful woman is a plea to God to make Himself more comprehensible on the human level, to reduce the distance that has grown up between Himself and His creatures.

The poem ends with two paradoxes. Firstly, the poet asks God to imprison or enslave him so that he may be free. Behind this is the idea that only by devoting himself to his spiritual well-being will the Christian be released from all the myriad sins that flesh is heir to. The 'livery' he wears as God's servant constitutes his 'delivery'. And the imperative 'enthral' indicates the speaker's desire that God should assume absolute ownership of him, as the master would take charge of a slave; moreover, this verb carries, through its other meaning ('bewitch', 'charm', 'bind with spells'), an expression of the poet's need for God somehow to enchant him so that his attention might nevermore wander to less worthy objects. The second paradox is a repetition of this idea in terms of the mistress/lover image that has developed out of the occupied town/rescuer image. Donne, depicting himself still as the unfulfilled female, declares that he will never be a virgin ('chaste') until he is raped ('ravished'). On a literal level this is obviously contradictory: the wisdom of it resides in its metaphorical level, as with all paradoxes. Donne recognises that he will only be purified if God possesses him utterly and by force. This would establish a dominion so complete and absorbing that all other temptations would be extinguished. As well as meaning, on the literal level, 'sexually violated', the word 'ravished' also carries implications of the rapturous delight that will flood into the soul of the sinner once the Holy Ghost enters his life.

The images, the diction, the syntax and the metre all combine to insist on this demand for what amounts to a physical intervention by God in the life of this habitual sinner. The emphasis on the sexual metaphor suggests that the speaker cannot relate to an abstract or intellectual idea of Godhead but seeks to secure the expression of God's love for him in the passionate, sensual way that he can more easily understand. Beneath the spiritual concerns of this holy sonnet the carnal consciousness of the younger Donne is still at work; he remains unable to grasp a reality that does not manifest itself in flesh, bone and blood.

George Herbert (1593–1633)

George Herbert's temperament was altogether different from Donne's. After graduating from Cambridge he had tried unsuccessfully to get a place at Court. He remained more or less unemployed and consciously useless for 11 years (from 1619 to 1630) and became tortured by a sense of the lack of purpose and meaning in his life. During this period he began – like Donne before him – to consider ordination as a priest but he constantly tormented himself by questioning his motives for such a step: was he thinking of becoming a priest solely in order to serve God or was he undertaking it as a means of solving his unemployment problem? Herbert's poems reflect this perpetual self-interrogation and the emotional seesaw it induced, varying from a soaring confidence in the love and approbation of God to a plunging, despairing fear that God has disowned His suitor.

In 1630, three years before his death, Herbert became priest of the parish of Bemerton, in Oxfordshire; and he finally found contentment in service to God. Both the poetry and the life of Herbert reflect his belief that the solution to the problem of self-centredness – from which all sin ultimately stems – lay in a total submission of the ego to God's will. Many of his poems end with the tension resolved by a trusting surrender of the self into the hands of the Lord. No doubt Herbert had taken to heart Christ's words, 'Except ye be converted, and become as little children, ye shall not enter into the kingdom of heaven' (Mark, xviii. 3).

Herbert's poetry reveals his awareness of the infinite possibilities for self-deception in man. Hence any poem that does not have as its sole aim the glorification of God is regarded as artificial. Herbert is constantly questioning the use of his own metaphysical imagery, as in 'Jordan (I)'. Any image that distracts the reader's attention, by its ingenuity, from the end it is supposed to be serving – the illustration of divine qualities – substitutes the shadow for the substance and is therefore inappropriate and sinful. Like the Protestant religion that he served, Herbert's poetry attempted to strip the potentially distracting ornaments and leave the simple naked truth, the picture of the ungarnished Godhead: to 'plainly say, "My God, my King"'. So his poetry tends to be simpler, more direct, barer of adornment than that of the ex-Catholic Donne.

Herbert's poems are a consecration of the whole man to heavenly love, as the prototype for all love. He complains that ordinary human love – which is merely a gross imitation of the ultimate love of the divine – has achieved a dominant position in the human psyche, so that people take it for the real thing, mistaking the copy for the genuine article. Sexual love is an erroneous obsession with the reflection rather than the reality, with the creature instead of the Creator. Through his poetry Herbert continually strives to lose his identity, to drown his egoistic desires in the ocean of God's love. He is always directing his attention away from himself towards God, unlike Donne, who is forever turning his regard back from the God he addresses and towards his own person. Herbert constantly strives to make God, not Herbert, the subject of his poetry. His motto was 'Not mine neither', meaning that he saw himself as not possessed of any peculiar poetic gift but as simply returning his God-given talent to the Maker who had originally lent it.

The emphasis throughout Herbert's poetry is on rebirth. Life itself is a continual battle between the ego struggling to assert itself and the soul, the inner voice, the unconscious perhaps, which quietly but persistently tells the ego to calm down and submit itself to God. This inner voice is often characterised in Herbert as 'a friend'. The typical internal dialogue of Herbert's verse, the altercation between ego and soul – or flesh and spirit – and its customary resolution, can be clearly witnessed at the end of 'The Collar':

> But as I raved and grew more fierce and wild
>   At every word,
> Me thoughts I heard one calling, 'Child!'
>   And I replied, 'My Lord.'

Once this harmony between ego and inner voice is achieved man is reborn but by the very nature of his being his rebirth is only temporary. The ego will continue to reassert itself and the process of rebirth will have to begin all over again: a viciously circular pattern that is acknowledged in 'Sin's Round':

> Sorry I am, my God, sorry I am,
> That my offences course it in a ring.

'Sin's Round' is an unusual poem for Herbert, in that there is no admission for the 'friend' Christ to come and assuage the poet's excruciating self-contempt. Nevertheless, the note of personal contact between Herbert and God can still be detected in his addressing the latter as '*my* God' (in contrast to Donne's more generalised vocative, 'three-personed God'). In the following poem the more usual note of intimacy between Herbert and his Master is evident.

Love (III)

Love bade me welcome: yet my soul drew back,
    Guilty of dust and sin.
But quick-eyed Love, observing me grow slack
    From my first entrance in,
Drew nearer to me, sweetly questioning,
    If I lacked any thing.

'A guest,' I answered, 'worthy to be here':
    Love said, 'You shall be he.'
'I the unkind, ungrateful? Ah my dear,
    I cannot look on thee.'
Love took my hand, and smiling did reply,
    'Who made the eyes but I?'

'Truth Lord, but I have marred them: let my shame
    Go where it doth deserve.'
'And know you not,' says Love, 'who bore the blame?'
    'My dear, then I will serve.'
'You must sit down,' says Love, 'and taste my meat':
    So I did sit and eat.

The tone makes this one of the most perfect expressions of the relationship between man and his Maker in the English language. It is a relationship based on charity or 'Love', a word which occurs six times in the poem's eighteen lines and gives the poem its title. Love is the cornerstone around which is built the new understanding between man and God, as covenanted in the New Testament ('For this is the message that ye heard from the beginning, that we should love one another': I John, iii. 11). The poet does not grovel before a God of wrath. He meekly asks for God's forgiveness, which is at once accorded with a compassion almost feminine in its gracefulness. Love, Herbert's interlocutor in this poem, is God in the person of His Son, the Creator wearing His most humane face, no longer the fearfully complex abstraction of Donne's distraught vision. Herbert has followed the Gospel precept of becoming again a child and has consequently experienced the Christian revelation that the essence of the man/God relationship resides in its simplicity.

Thus there are none of the contortions of syntax, the wrestling of the mind with the abstruse concepts of the Trinity or the scrabbling after the arcane metaphor, which are evident in Donne's sonnet. The language of Herbert's poem is mostly monosyllabic, the vocabulary plain, the sole image being that of the feast (representing the Communion service) to which the poet is so cordially invited. The rhythm is untortured, untormented, proceeding at a measured pace till it reaches its calm conclusion in

So I did sit and eat.

All is tranquillity; the soul of the poet has been succoured. He is asked to receive love and hereafter to pass it on to others, perhaps through his function as God's minister. The whole transaction is visualised as an invitation to a recalcitrant offender, 'guilty of dust and sin', to sit down and eat with a glamorous courtesan, 'quick-eyed Love'. But the image of this vivacious 'Love' is soon disarmed of any sexual potency in the dialogue that follows. The 'sweet' questioning and the 'smiling' catechism proffered by the hostess clearly show that carnal 'love' does not cross this Love's threshold – although it may underlie the poet's obvious 'shame' and feelings of unworthiness upon being called to Love's domain.

The Love who bids him welcome, though she does so with the gestures of a seductress ('drew nearer to me', 'took my hand'), evidently represents a passion that is not of the body. That is clear as much from the poet's reaction to her as from what she says herself. Having addressed her initially as 'my dear', he shifts to the invocation 'Lord'. The androgynous aspects of his host's character remove the scene of the poem's events to a more transcendental plane than was at first apparent; the 'quick eyes' of Love, in retrospect, become transmuted from the flirtatious glances of a *demi-mondaine* into the windows of the spiritual world with its promise of eternal life through Christ's sacrifice:

'And know you not,' says Love, 'who bore the blame?'

Herbert has used the invitation and the attraction of earthly love to lead us straight into the arms of *agape*, or Christian love. And at this culminating point of the poem the tense shifts from the past ('Love said') to the present ('says Love'), as if the poet's life of sin and of laying waste God's gifts in him ('I have marred them') was a temporary aberration merely, whereas the redemption promised him for dedicating his future to God ('My dear, then I *will* serve') is an eternally present blessing. Having accepted Christ into him through the Eucharist (' "You must sit down," says Love, "and taste my meat" ') the poet may rest assured of his salvation.

The whole poem is imbued with a soft effulgence, a quiet ecstasy, betokening perfectly the confidence and joy of the Christian who has accepted God into his heart. It is as if Herbert, in writing the poem, were obeying the injunction of Christ to 'Let your light so shine before men, that they may see your good works, and glorify your Father which is in heaven' (Matthew, v. 16). The poem records a state of internal harmony which is all too rarely arrived at among mortals and which even Herbert could not consistently attain. With its alternately long and short lines of regular iambic verse allowing plenty of pause for reflection, its simplicity of diction reflecting the speaker's success in rediscovering his lost childhood innocence and its portrait of Love demonstrating how all-embracing and merciful is the compassion of God, the poem remains a monument to the grace which can flow into the sinner who is not afraid to abase himself and confess himself – as Herbert elsewhere does – a 'worm'.

4 The Later 17th Century: Andrew Marvell

Andrew Marvell (1621–78)

There was great social upheaval in Britain in Marvell's lifetime. He grew up amid mounting tension between the rapidly rising bourgeoisie class, made rich from the trade and investments that had been increasing apace since the middle of the previous century, and the old-established landed-aristocrat class, defenders of the king's divine right to absolute rule and of their own privileged position as feudal landlords. The former, who became known as 'Roundheads' from the shape of the helmets they wore when civil war finally broke out in 1642, tried to assert themselves through the one channel that was open to them – parliament. Their attempt to use their access – through their elected members in the House of Commons – to parliament as a means of curbing the powers of the king and the aristocracy led to their being dubbed with the additional epithet of 'Parliamentarians'. The king's party were known as 'Cavaliers' or 'Royalists'.

Matters finally came to a head in 1642, when parliament refused to vote King Charles I the money he had requested; he dissolved parliament and war broke out. The king himself was captured and eventually beheaded in 1649, as a sign that not even kings, anointed with sacred oil as God's approved surrogates, were above the people whom they should both govern and serve. Oliver Cromwell was established as Protector of the Commonwealth and Britain remained for 18 years – from 1642 until 1660 – a republic, without a monarch, for the only time since the Norman Conquest of 1066. In 1660, however, the monarchy was restored with the recall of Charles I's son – Charles II – from France.

Marvell's life spans the pre-Civil War Stuart monarchy, the Civil War itself and the period of Commonwealth government that ensued and the Restoration of the Stuarts together with the uneasy peace between Roundhead and Cavalier that was thereby inaugurated. In times of such civil turmoil the judicious man keeps his thoughts to himself if he wishes to keep the head that houses them. Marvell being such a man, it is often difficult to fathom exactly what his political opinions were. His early sympathies seem to have been Royalist, inasmuch as many of his friends favoured the king's cause. Marvell was abroad during the early years of the Civil War but not long after his return in 1650 he published a poem, 'Tom May's Death', condemning the Parliamentarian cause and expressing Royalist sympathy. Yet five months earlier he had written 'An Horatian Ode upon Cromwell's Return from Ireland', in which, while his profoundest sympathy goes toward the hapless king, he seems to accept Cromwell's ascendancy as a historical necessity and even to admire the qualities of ruthlessness and austere militant Puritanism that had enabled Cromwell to gather in his hands the reins of state. This 'bi-focal' vision does not necessarily suggest that Marvell was two-faced or changed his opinions to suit his company; but rather that he shared the complex feelings of many of his contemporaries, who were nostalgic for the old feudal order and sorry to see it go at the same time that they acknowledged that that order was corrupt and that a new system, both more democratic and more efficient, must be instituted if the nation were to march, rather than limp, into the future.

However strong Marvell's Royalist leanings might have been until this time, from 1650 onwards he seems to have committed himself irrevocably to the Parliamentarian side. In 1659 he became Member of Parliament for his home town of Hull and retained this seat until his death 19 years later. In the unsettled times that followed the Restoration, when the power struggle between the upper and middle classes, between old and new influence, went on intermittently and underground, Marvell remained loyal to the Parliamentarian cause and to one of its staunchest defenders and servants, his friend John Milton – who referred to this hazardous period, when the knives of revenge twitched restively in their sheathes, as 'these dark days'.

The social flux going on around him no doubt encouraged Marvell to reserve his personal opinions to himself. In consequence, his poetry is devoid of the subjective outpourings that stream forth from Donne and Herbert. Marvell adopts a stance of cool, sometimes ironic, detachment from what he writes. Some critics interpret 'An Horatian Ode' as a poem which, in its comparison of Cromwell to a bird of prey, is maligning the Protector of the Commonwealth as an inhuman being, while others are of the opinion that Marvell's portrayal of Cromwell as a rigorous imposer of some abstract principle of justice is meant to elevate him to the level of a demigod. One thing is certain: when Marvell wrote poetry he reached for one of his various masks as unfailingly as he reached for his pen. Sometimes the persona is explicit, as when he speaks in the voice of a young maiden who has just discovered the presence of evil in the world, in 'The Nymph Complaining for the Death of Her Fawn'. More often, though, it is an implicitly-donned disguise, as in 'To His Coy Mistress'. The 'I' of Marvell's poems stands most probably for a general or archetypal human being summoned forth specially by Marvell for the occasion of the poem. So the speaker in 'To His Coy Mistress' advances the sort of argument used in any age by a man wishing to sidestep the barricades of conventional morality and persuade a young virgin to sleep with him. Marvell's own attitude towards the speaker of this dramatic monologue and his approval or disapproval of the arguments adduced by the seducer can only be surmised, not ascertained.

To His Coy Mistress

Had we but world enough, and time,
This coyness, Lady, were no crime.
We would sit down, and think which way
To walk, and pass our long love's day.
Thou by the Indian Ganges' side
Shouldst rubies find; I by the tide
Of Humber would complain. I would
Love you ten years before the Flood,
And you should, if you please, refuse
10   Till the Conversion of the Jews.
My vegetable love should grow
Vaster than empires and more slow;
An hundred years should go to praise
Thine eyes, and on thy forehead gaze;

Two hundred to adore each breast,
But thirty thousand to the rest;
An age at least to every part,
And the last age should show your heart.
For, Lady, you deserve this state,
20   Nor would I love at lower rate.
    But at my back I always hear
Time's winged chariot hurrying near;
And yonder all before us lie
Deserts of vast eternity.
Thy beauty shall no more be found,
Nor, in thy marble vault, shall sound
My echoing song; then worms shall try
That long-preserved virginity,
And your quaint honour turn to dust,
30   And into ashes all my lust:
The grave's a fine and private place,
But none, I think, do there embrace.
    Now therefore, while the youthful hue
Sits on thy skin like morning dew,
And while thy willing soul transpires
At every pore with instant fires,
Now let us sport us while we may,
And now, like amorous birds of prey,
Rather at once our time devour
40   Than languish in his slow-chapt power.
Let us roll all our strength and all
Our sweetness up into one ball,
And tear our pleasures with rough strife
Thorough the iron gates of life;
Thus, though we cannot make our sun
Stand still, yet we will make him run.

From its title this is evidently an address to a maiden who is 'coy', or bashful. The poem, predictably, contains an argument that will persuade her to be otherwise. From the way the poem is set down typographically this argument is clearly established as a three-part progression. The first part (lines 1–20) suggests what might have been if the conditions of life were dispensed differently. All the verbs are in the conditional tense ('We would sit down', 'I . . . would complain', 'love should grow'). So the first stage of the argument consists of an elaborate fantasy about the virtually endless endurance of the poet's courtship of his mistress and the imperceptibly slow advancement towards consummation in the marriage bed that he would be willing to suffer *if* there were no spatial or temporal boundaries ('Had we but world enough and time'). The whole structure of this first segment is built on the initial, conditional 'Had'.

'But', the next section begins, the world is not constructed thus; therefore we must forego such decorous behaviour, in order to recognise the reality of our condition and introduce some urgency into our love affair. Otherwise we will find that time has overtaken us and we fall, not into the marriage bed, but into the mausoleum. The third part of the argument is its conclusion – as indicated by 'therefore'. The poet would have been willing to go on paying court indefinitely to his mistress, were it not that time, being such an enemy to life, might intervene and cut them both off from the conjugational goal of such courtship. From this he draws the conclusion that it were best for them to make love at once ('*Now* therefore') rather than run the risk of being so cheated of their just deserts.

This is certainly a syllogistic, or false, argument. Having presented, in the first section, a languorous impression of an impossible timeless state, the speaker exaggerates, in the second, the proximity of death and thence proceeds, in the third section, to urge the lady to yield to his desires immediately, as if death were that moment knocking on the door. The whole of the first section is based on a suppositious situation: what would happen if the barriers of space and time were removed from human existence? If that should occur, the lady's coyness, or unwillingness to entertain the poet's suggestion that they make love, would be 'no crime'. The verbs in this section indicate the state of passivity that the poet says he would be willing to accept in such a timeless existence: he would 'sit down' and 'think', allowing her to go off to the Indian River Ganges and search for stones with which to adorn herself, while he would patiently await her return, merely 'complaining' about her absence, beside the humbler shores of the Humber River that passes through his native Hull. The poet here sees himself and his mistress in the traditional Petrarchan roles of tormented lover, obsessed by his passion, and cruel woman, giving her mind to other objects besides love.

The next sentence elaborates the idea of the eternal devotion of the man, coupled with the nonchalant attitude of his mistress. If human life were eternal, the speaker says, he would have begun loving the woman at some antediluvian date in the inconceivably remote past (ten years before Noah's flood), while she, since time is no object, could go on toying with him until some equally remote epoch in the future (until the Jews are converted to Christianity, an event which is not expected – by Christians – until just before the final apocalypse). His 'vegetable' love would grow infinitely slowly: 'vegetable' carrying the idea of the imperceptibly slow growth of some member of the plant kingdom, such as an oak tree. He indicates that, despite the lady's prolonged indifference, his love for her in such circumstances would continue to augment. The line

Vástĕr thăn émpĭres ănd móre slów,

with its initial trochaic foot and final spondee, proceeds at a leisurely pace, suggestive of the false sense of security into which such a complacent illusion lulls one.

The next six lines (13–18) are based on the conventional Petrarchan catalogue of the beloved's charms, adapted by Marvell into an arithmetical evaluation of her sundry physical properties. Starting at the top, the purest part (the 'forehead') of her body, he passes his assessor's gaze downwards and slyly places greater value on the erotic areas. The hundred years that the poet declares himself prepared to devote to the admiration of his mistress's eyes and forehead might seem excessive until one comes to the *two* hundred years that he is willing to devote to '*each* breast', followed finally by the totally disproportionate 'thirty thousand to the rest'. 'The rest' is probably a euphemism for the 'unmentionable' parts of his partner: sex, he is saying, is far and away the most important part of the love relationship. He is working round deviously to the end he has in view: an attempt to persuade the lady to dispense with all forms and preliminaries and succumb at once to his sexual advances. Finally, after all these aeons of quiescent adoration the lady's concealed love for the poet and her intention to submit to his desires will, he declares, be revealed ('the last age should show your heart'). He concludes this part of his argument by attempting to appease her vanity and her desire to be treated with respect and adulation ('Lady, you deserve this state').

Having tried to flatter the lady with blandishments, Marvell plants the next shaft in the armour of her virginity with his ensuing and emphatic 'But'. He introduces the idea of time as a threat sneaking up behind the unwary lover ('at my back'). It is a persistent threat, too, that he '*always* hears'. Time is 'hurrying near'. A sudden sense of urgency and haste is felt when the word 'hurrying', a trisyllabic participle, is forced by the exigencies of the metre into the confines of a two-syllabled pronunciation. Gone is the languid ease, the false security of the first section. The pace has quickened, giving support to the feeling of the fleetness of time. Time's chariot is 'winged' or expeditious – a reference also to the chariot of fire in which the prophet Elijah ascended 'by a whirlwind into heaven' (II Kings, ii. 11). Death may descend and whisk one away when least expected. The poet's theme has now become *carpe diem*, or 'seize the day': he suggests to his mistress that she should make the most of life now by warning her of the 'deserts of vast eternity' that await everyone. Life after death will be sexually arid, the once-vital body mouldering and merging with the desert sands.

He moves on to the familiar reminder of the transient nature of physical beauty ('Beauty that must die', in Keats's words); and adds that the cold marble tomb will be devoid of even the merest echo of his voice. Having made his lady familiar with the concept of the common grave that all humanity inherits, the poet goes on to associate her 'long-preserved virginity' with the tomb, implying that virginity itself is a death-force if maintained beyond the natural limit of puberty. He is warning her against keeping her maidenhead beyond the natural term of her maidenhood. Again, he is using arguments of some sophism to sway her to his will. In the grave, he warns, worms will 'try' to make sexual attempts on that place which she has kept so closely guarded from him. Whether or not it has been safeguarded from violation during life, it must succumb to assault after death – and the Elizabethan use of 'worm' as a slang word for the penis emphasises the sexual inference behind this image of his mistress's post-mortal humiliation.

In the last four lines of the second section these sexual hints are made plainer yet. The woman's 'honour', which restrains her from giving in to the poet's demands, is characterised by him as 'quaint' or old-fashioned. 'Queynte' is also a mediaeval word for the pudendum and is thus a pun – the poet is explicitly referring to the 'honour' which she places on her sexual impregnability. This concept of 'honour', together with the physical part it is used to protect, will inevitably disintegrate, just like the organ of the poet's passionate 'lust', and revert to insentient dust. In the last two lines of this section the poet draws a parallel between the grave and the 'fine and private place' of his mistress that he longs to inhabit. If she continues to deny him access, he warns, his passion will die and her own sterility will ensue. It is in order to drive home this threat of impending infertility that Marvell uses so many images of death, dust and decay.

Having apparently 'proved' that he would spend all the time that his lady's vanity requires in adoration and pleading and having then attempted to frighten her with a gruesome vision of a frigid old age, the poet proceeds to draw his conclusion. The lady is at the peak of her loveliness, at the height of her sexual vitality ('the youthful hue / Sits on thy skin like morning dew'). 'Morning dew' is suggestive of something moist, youthful and ephemeral – like the lady's beauty. He goes on to assert that the lady is bursting with suppressed sexual passion, 'instant fires' which only need a touch to be activated. She is psychologically and physiologically more than ready for sexual communion ('thy willing soul transpires'). He is deliberately misinterpreting the blushes which his outrageous suggestions have induced in her as indications of sexual desire, rather than as signs of 'coyness' or offended modesty.

The remainder of this 'pseudo-logical' conclusion consists of various images by which the poet is making his claim that he and his woman can defeat time by an act of copulation which will be such an intensely enjoyed moment that it will seem to stretch into eternity. They should turn the tables on time, he argues, and become the hunters instead of the hunted: 'like amorous birds of prey' they should devour time, or use it as profitably and energetically as possible, instead of tamely waiting for time to consume them, robbing them of their vitality by infinitesimal degrees ('Rather . . . than languish in his slow-chapt power'). In sexual communion, he says, they could roll themselves into a ball and thus make their own globe, their own world. Masculine 'strength' will be united with feminine 'sweetness' to form a totality. By 'tearing our pleasures with rough strife' they could break out of the prison which life becomes if they too passively accept the restrictions imposed on them by traditional taboos (such as virginity). It is better, he claims, to burn oneself out in a blaze of passion than to linger on indefinitely into a protracted but unfruitful and arid old age.

With this final salvo of defiance Marvell's – or Marvell's persona's – argumentative barrage has exhausted itself. Whether the lady will find enough ammunition to defend the bulwarks of her own position and probe the fissures and weak spots in her assailant's rhetoric rests outside the frame of the poem.

5 The Dawn of the Augustan Age: John Dryden

Marvell's poem shows a concern for the orderly presentation of an argument, albeit a falsely-reasoned one. This concern for order and ratiocination was, perhaps, symptomatic of a yearning for the restoration of peace and health to the body politic of Britain, which had been stretched and exhausted by the outbreaks and internal conflicts of the Civil War period. With the restoration of the monarchy in 1660 the nation hoped that the era of self-destructive squabbling was at an end. A desire for stability had been generated by the upheavals of almost twenty years of republican government.

The struggle between the monarch's wish for autonomy and the people's desire to tie him down with gravitational checks and balances ensured that the Restoration was not quite the return to an ordered calm that had been longed for, particularly when the tug of war was further complicated by Charles II's barely concealed Catholicism and by the overt espousal of the Catholic faith by his successor, James II, in 1685. Nevertheless, with the peaceful removal of the latter in the 1688 Revolution and with the establishment of the Protestant House of Orange on the throne in the persons of William and Mary, the way was prepared for a period of freedom from internal strife and external conflict which was to last for over a hundred years. With the advent in 1688 of a monarchy which was willing to pay more than lip service to the people and the parliament that had placed it there and which was perhaps prepared to acknowledge that its role in the British imagination was more symbolical than actual, the ghosts of civil war were at last laid to rest.

The long period of peace which was ushered in by the 1688

Revolution became known as the 'Augustan' age: this was because it was seen to resemble a period of serenity in the classical world – the reign of Augustus Caesar in Rome. The poetry of this era, stretching roughly from the 1680s until the French Revolution of 1789, is notable for its attempt to mirror the tranquillity so eagerly sought as the goal of life by the members of upper-class, educated society. The religious and civil struggles of the mid-17th century had exhausted their conscripts. Now these battle-torn men demanded a respite: a period in which they could relax and cultivate their gardens and their minds and take delight in realising the amount of order that could be imposed upon both. It was as if Milton had prophesied the coming of the Augustan age in *Samson Agonistes* (1671), when at the end of the militant Christian-hero's struggles against unbelievers, betrayers and Philistines, there remains nothing but 'calm of mind, all passion spent'. With the Augustans passion was banished to the backstage area of the theatre, where it would remain until the Romantics brought it once more beneath the spotlight.

Augustan literature delights above all in the display of reason. At last, it was felt, man had arrived at a point where he could control both his destiny and his environment. Augustan man saw a Great Chain of Being, a hierarchy in nature and supernature, leading up from the lowest forms of animal and vegetable life to God Himself, the ultimate Link in the Chain. Man was at an intermediate point: above the beasts but below the angels. All levels of life, whether high or low, natural or supernatural, were linked by the spirit of the Creator that informed them all. This cosmic hierarchy was reflected in the social hierarchy which had made some men masters and other men servants: the frequent exhortations to the less fortunate to accept their situations as divinely appointed demonstrates the conservative tendencies of Augustan philosophy. The Augustan universe was in perfect mechanical order and ticked away methodically under the benevolent eye of its Creator and Instigator. There was a rational plan to the universe and all arts in the Augustan age – whether manifested in the control of nature's wildness through the artfulness of landscape gardening, in the binding of poetry's wanton tendencies within the straitjacket of the heroic couplet or in the emergence in architectural design of façades of mathematical precision and symmetry – gave enthusiastic expression to the newly-won belief in the supremacy of reason.

John Dryden (1631–1700)

The first major poet to give expression to the longing for order in every area of life was John Dryden. He voiced the suspicion towards the imaginative and the emotional that had become so prevalent in his day. 'A Man is to be cheated into Passion, but to be reasoned into Truth', he wrote in 1682; and his poetry, with its predilection for a logical line of argument in which all human fancies and feelings are subjected to the rule of reason, set the tone and established the style of poetry for generations to come.

By 1660 Dryden had developed a scepticism about the integrity or worth of any human effort. He nursed the fundamentally conservative attitude that it was better not to tamper with the state of the world one had inherited:

> all the happiness mankind can gain
> Is not in pleasure, but in rest from pain.
>
> (*The Indian Emperor*, IV. i)

Like his fellow poets Milton and Marvell, Dryden had been employed by Cromwell's Commonwealth régime. He was disappointed by the backstage wranglings among the chief members of the republican administration, while the Restoration, with its resumption of court intrigue and power politics, disgusted him further and deepened his doubts about man's capacity to govern himself. 'Common quiet is mankind's concern', is how Dryden formulated one of his basic beliefs. Man, he held, should not in either politics or religion concern himself over much with the finer points of doctrine or dogma but should rest satisfied with the broader principles that his ancestors had bequeathed to him. Thus Dryden, in obedience to his own precepts, became a Tory in politics and a Catholic in religion, submitting himself to the party and the church that were the most authoritarian, in the belief that they would also supply the strongest guarantees of social order.

This penchant towards order influenced Dryden's poetic technique. He was constantly trying to 'reform' the rhythm of English poetry, to instil a regularity into its metric pattern; and it is largely thanks to him that the heroic couplet became the established norm for several decades after his death. He did not invent the heroic-couplet form – it had already been exploited by earlier poets such as Sir John

Denham and Edmund Waller – but he tightened its structure so that each couplet tended to be a self-contained unit or symmetrical step in the logical development. His poetry is primarily the poetry of ratiocination: each couplet is like a brick laid sequentially in the erection of his argument.

Dryden was not only a poet but a linguist, highly conscious of the richness which the English vocabulary could display through a judicious word choice and a rigorous paring by the poet of the unfunctional and the ugly. He tried to express, through his poetry, an underlying sense of grace, proportion and unostentatious splendour. In this way his approach to poetry writing was 'sensible' rather than 'sensational': the feelings might provide the source of a poetic or dramatic theme, but it would be the head that would take charge of this theme and direct it into channels where it would ripple harmoniously and soothingly to the ear. For Dryden, the need for control – over both experience and the poetry employed to record it – was paramount. From Dryden's poetry one gains a vision of the poet as architect. He 'found the language brick and left it marble', in the assessment of Samuel Johnson. Rhyme was regarded by Dryden as a necessary rein to check the imagination from running away into regions of complexity and obfuscation: it kept the creative faculty firmly under the management of the rational. 'For imagination in a poet is a faculty so wild and lawless, that, like an high-ranking spaniel, it must have clogs tied to it, lest it outrun the judgement', he explained.

His doubts about any theories of human progress find their expression in the satires for which Dryden is most famous. However, the example from Dryden given below is from another mode – that of elegy. Both satire and elegy have classical origins (originally Greek, both genres were further refined by the Latin poets Juvenal and Ovid, among others) and both tend to be resurrected and achieve great prominence during a period of retrenchment and cautious conservatism such as that which followed the Restoration. Satire emphasises man's imperfections and suggests that, since he is naturally corrupt, he should give up trying to perfect his society and cling instead to the imperfect one that he has inherited; while elegy suggests that the only time a man can be regarded as potentially noble and perfectible is after he is dead and can no longer disappoint us.

An elegy is a poem expressing sorrow or lament, originally for ill-success in love. By the 17th century, however, the intentions of the early Greek elegists had been overlooked or forgotten and the elegiac mode was used almost exclusively for meditative verse, usually on the occasion of someone's death. The 'voice' one expects to hear from an elegiac poet is one of restraint, compassion and appreciation towards the departed soul. The age of Dryden could still accept the death of the individual as the outcome of God's inscrutable will: an occurrence provoking sadness but not madness. Man's life could be seen to be, in Dryden's words, 'all of a piece throughout', for it began and ended with its Maker. Thus the elegy in English poetry becomes part of the Christian funeral ritual. *Ave atque vale*, or 'hail and farewell', is the elegiac theme: a last appraisal of the deceased's virtues before his body is committed to the clay.

The heroic couplet, with its rigorous sorting and ordering of the manifold fragments of human experience into two-line units of rhyming verse, was an assertive declaration of faith in a Creator who was similarly tidy in His habits and who perpetually strove, like the Augustan poet, to make harmony out of dissonance, order out of chaos, pattern out of random happenings. By 'boxing in' his representations of life in heroic couplets and turning the key of rhyme upon them, the Augustan poet believed himself to be acting in the image of his Maker.

To the Memory of Mr Oldham

Farewell, too little and too lately known,
Whom I began to think and call my own:
For sure our souls were near allied, and thine
Cast in the same poetic mould with mine.
One common note on either lyre did strike,
And knaves and fools we both abhorred alike.
To the same goals did both our studies drive;
The last set out the soonest did arrive.
Thus Nisus fell upon the slippery place,
10 While his young friend performed and won the race.
O early ripe! to thy abundant store
What could advancing age have added more?
It might (what nature never gives the young)
Have taught the numbers of thy native tongue.
But satire needs not those, and wit will shine
Through the harsh cadence of a rugged line:
A noble error, and but seldom made,

When poets are by too much force betrayed.
Thy generous fruits, though gathered ere their prime,
20 Still showed a quickness; and maturing time
But mellows what we write to the dull sweets of rhyme.
Once more, hail and farewell; farewell, thou young,
But ah too short, Marcellus of our tongue;
Thy brows with ivy, and with laurels bound;
But fate and gloomy night encompass thee around.

To the couplet's inbuilt quality of balance Dryden brings reinforcement by grouping words in pairs instead of deploying them singly. There are two examples of this technique in the opening couplet: the poet John Oldham is mourned for having been 'too little and too lately known' (the repeated 'too's and alliterated 'l's emphasising the linkage between this pair of epithets) and is described as someone whom the poet Dryden had only just begun to 'think and call' his own. This presentation of ideas in 'pair bondings' rather than just as single concepts gives an added feeling of consonance, or unity, to the elegy. The second word in each pair tends to develop from the idea expressed in the first word: not only was Oldham's work recognised by too few people, such recognition as he did secure was only accorded him tardily. To the equipoise of the couplet form is added the poise of Dryden's judicious coupling of epithets that support and enhance each other.

The poem conveys the response of the urbane, well-balanced late 17th-century gentleman to the demise of one of his contemporaries. It suggests sophisticated sadness: a grief firmly under the grip of reason. So sober an approach might prepare us to expect a poem which is elegiac in manner only: a work of merely formal rhetoric in which all expression of personal sorrow has been repressed, if it had ever existed. Such a work would be either dull or hypocritical and Dryden promptly precludes such ominous expectations by introducing a personal note in the second line of his tribute. Not only was the late Oldham 'too little and too lately known' by the world at large but his acquaintance was made only belatedly by Dryden himself: he was just beginning to 'think and call' him his own – both as a friend and as a member of the poetic fraternity – when death unkindly intervened. The sense of personal bereavement is introduced and continues to reverberate beneath the more formal cadences of rhetoric, tone and rhythm in the poem.

The second couplet (lines 3–4) enhances this idea of a personal bond between the dead poet and the living one. The sense of poetry as a universal brotherhood of the spirit is suggested ('sure our souls were near allied'). Poets, it is inferred, are more aware of the inward life than their non-poetic fellows: there is a special 'mould' for forming their souls. And the particular sympathy between Dryden and Oldham is specifically forged by the linking of their two souls in the end-rhymes 'thine' and 'mine'.

Dryden now goes on to distinguish further links between himself and his dead soul-mate (lines 5–6). He uses the image of the lyre – a stringed instrument used by Greek poets in classical times – to establish more firmly the spiritual 'oneness' of all poets. Neither time nor space can cleave the poetic fraternity: Oldham is associated with the same instrument that Homer had used in the 8th century BC. Both Dryden and Oldham struck 'one common note' when writing their poetry. This was the 'note' of satire, as line 6 makes clear: 'knaves and fools we both abhorred alike'. Again, in the last word of the couplet, the kinship between the two poets is stressed. This kinship is developed once more in the next couplet (lines 7–8), though the image is changed slightly to suggest this time that the poets coexisted in a state of rivalry. But if there has been a contest between them, it was a friendly one. The metaphor that expresses this rivalry is that of the Olympic games, which again argues that there is no fundamental difference between classical and modern times: the same spirit of self-improvement and striving after individual excellence illuminates the best of modern men just as it had inspired the heroes of ancient Greece.

The 'studies' of the rival poets 'drove' them on 'to the same goal', the winner being he who would first publish his verses and receive the public applause accorded to the winner in the Olympic stadium. On this occasion 'the last set out the soonest did arrive': that is to say that Oldham, 22 years younger than Dryden, found public favour and recognition sooner. Dryden might be expected to experience some rancour, or to make some comment on the arbitrariness of public taste, as a result of his long neglect in comparison with his precocious rival; but he does not do so. He is a generous loser. In lines 9–10 he even alters an anecdote from Virgil's *Aeneid* to reinforce the sense of inherent nobility and unselfishness among poets. Casting himself as the runner Nisus, he explains that his tardiness at the winning post of public honours is owing to his having slipped and fallen, thus permitting his younger competitor to overtake him and reap the prize. In the original legend Nisus allows his friend Euryalus to win the race but does so by grabbing the ankle of the runner-up, Salius. Such ungentlemanly conduct would be inappropriate to the spirit of friendly rivalry and generous fair play that Dryden wishes to demonstrate and he alters the classical source accordingly. Besides, 'winning the race' is not necessarily so desirable as it might seem. The line 'The last set out the soonest did arrive' takes on another significance in the context of the whole poem. Oldham gained not only the acknowledgement of the public but the attention of death by his youthful exploits: both claimed him sooner than they were to embrace the more circumspect Dryden.

Since Dryden's rival has arrived precipitately at the twin goals of fame and death, any jealousy that Dryden might have felt is tempered by compassion and commiseration that one so young (Oldham was 30 when he died) and full of promise should have been snuffed out. And it is Dryden's magnanimity that gives the poem its overall air of serene and studied calm, of nobly expressed sentiments in which nothing acrimonious or censorious is allowed to intrude. Dryden goes on (lines 11–12) to praise his younger rival by suggesting that, although young, he had already reached perfection. 'O early ripe!' is an exclamation which, at the midway point of the poem, suggests that the barely-restrained emotion of grief is about to burst forth. The measured 'reasonableness' with which the verse progresses on its regular iambic feet is counterpointed by intimations of emotions that the poet is with difficulty controlling. Thus passion and reason are kept in perfect counterpoise throughout the poem.

The metaphor of 'early ripeness' suggests several things. For one, Oldham has 'ripened' sooner than expected: his verse has revealed a maturity unlooked for in one so young. Then, like fruit which has acquired fullness, Oldham has been plucked by death – prematurely, since his is an 'early' ripeness. Furthermore, the characteristic of fruit which becomes ripe early is often a certain bitterness which might have been sweetened had the fruit remained longer on the tree. This last implication is the only criticism – and that a fairly mild one – which Dryden permits himself in the poem. The late Oldham's verse was characteristically bitter: he wrote only satire, a mode with a tendency towards harshness and acerbity. Whereas if he had stayed longer on the tree of life, Oldham's verse might have mellowed a little and generated some of the sweetness of which Dryden's tribute to him is a prime example. More years 'might' have allowed Oldham to diversify a little, even to the extent of producing the sort of patriotic poetry ('the numbers of thy native tongue') in which Dryden on occasion indulged and which needed something other than an unvaried satirical exhibition of mordant wit. Still, the implications of Oldham's limitations as a poet are kept to a minimum, and having sown this little seed of doubt about Oldham's claim to poetic greatness, Dryden proceeds to stifle it in the next couplet (lines 15–16) by suggesting that satire is a genre sufficient unto itself. Satire does not need mellifluous 'numbers' (verses): its intellectual sharpness, or 'wit', alone is of enough significance to override all other considerations. Dryden gives an indication of the sort of rough music in Oldham's verse to which he is referring, in

Thrŏugh thĕ hársh cádĕnce ŏf ă rúggĕd líne,

where the hitherto smoothly-flowing iambic pentameters are interrupted by an agglomeration of syllables with no ear-pleasing rhythm or melody: the line itself illustrates its own 'harsh cadence'.

Dryden goes on to suggest that the spontaneous vigour of Oldham's rough verse is preferable to the monotonous correctness of the sort of poetry which he is currently writing himself. 'Advancing age', although it matures what is bitter and sweetens it, takes some of the edge off one's youthful passion and may replace a vigorous harshness by a melodious dullness. Lines 19–21 constitute a triplet, a three-lined unit which in itself exemplifies the comparison which Dryden is making. The verse moves quickly, with adolescent sprightliness, up to its half-way point at 'quickness'; after the caesura at this point the long 'ū' in 'maturing' slows the pace of the verse, and the concluding Alexandrine (a line containing one extra foot) further retards the progress and suggests the soporific quality that may creep into poetry when its creator grows older and leaves his early passionate and venomous diatribes for the predictable anodyne and 'dull sweets of rhyme'. Dryden, in his role of the older poet, is effacing himself in order all the more to enhance the rather limited achievements and abilities of his late rival.

The poem, in other words, is a fine example of Dryden's sense of balance: of the 'decorum' which was such an essential ingredient in the character of the 'gentleman'. The equilibrium held in his poem is that between myth and reality: the myth that Oldham was a great poet worthy of comparison with classical predecessors and the reality that he was, in fact, a poet of only mediocre merit. This balance is maintained right to the end where, as is fitting in a funeral poem, the similarity between the dead person and a classical forbear is left as the final image. Oldham does not appear in his own name but is designated as 'Marcellus': elements of truth and fiction are again interwoven, so as to convey the impression that the dead Oldham is being mythologised into someone greater than he actually was. Marcellus was the heir of the Emperor Augustus and died at the age of 20, so by implication Oldham is mantled in associations of nobility, classical greatness and youthful promise tragically cut short. Yet, on Dryden's own admission, Oldham's achievements in this world indicate that he was in fact a very ordinary mortal.

This is not simply, however, a final, fallacious parting compliment. The last two lines of the poem suggest that the late Oldham does have more in common with classical antecedents than might meet the eye. Death unites all, and Oldham has now gone beyond the grasp of Dryden. He has been translated into the sphere of great classical poets and is crowned with the traditional coronet of laurel. Yet this is an ambiguous triumph, a Pyrrhic victory; for he is also crowned with ivy, the wreath for the dead. Oldham, in other words, has only found greatness and recognition in death: at the same time that he is encircled with laurels he is encompassed by 'gloomy night'. The extra foot of the final Alexandrine (line 25) emphasises the sombre finality of Oldham's departure from the human scene: he has gone where no man may follow, with nothing but the dubious rewards of a posthumous poetic fame to light him on his journey to the underworld. Dryden's careful balancing of classical allusion with colloquial sentiment succeeds in bringing closer together the worlds of 'then' and 'now' and showing that they have one overriding concern in common: a fearful ignorance before the frontier of death.

6 The Early 18th Century: Pope and Swift

The 17th century had witnessed a long and exhausting struggle for supremacy. The fluctuations between royalist fervour and republican yearnings and between Catholic 'legitimacy' and Puritan iconoclasm, to all of which much of Dryden's verse bears witness, finally levelled off, in the last decade of the century, into a general feeling of religious and political tolerance. The 18th century, the era of the 'Great Peace', has its roots in the Restoration and really begins with the accession of William and Mary to the throne in 1688.

Britain, from force of habit, found herself embroiled with France a couple of times during the 18th century, but these were wars that occurred on the distant soils of India and America and in no way affected the feeling at home that a modicum, if not a millenium, of tranquillity had at last arrived. There was still a good deal of anti-Catholic sentiment, particularly when two Jacobite rebellions, brewed in Scotland, tried to re-establish the Stuarts on the throne, in 1715 and 1745; but otherwise, religious toleration was the order of the day. It was an age of profound conservatism: the Revolution Settlement of 1688 took on some of the aura of a totem or a shibboleth, particularly in the speeches of Edmund Burke, and to attempt any interference with it to accommodate a more democratic parliamentary system was regarded as sacrilege. Only at the end of the century, when ripples from the French Revolution spread across the Channel and began to rock Britain's firmly anchored ship of State, did the question of change in the constitution of British society begin to circulate more urgently.

Alexander Pope (1688–1744)

Alexander Pope is in many ways a typical voice from the first decades after the English Revolution: a voice of common sense, of distrust towards passion and empassioned men, of faith in the supremacy of the rational faculty above men's other qualities and of belief in a logical God. According to this philosophy the social system should be left undisturbed because it has been ordained by a God whose purposes, while they might appear to be mystifying or even cruelly unjust, are beyond man's capacity to question ('Presume not God to scan', warns Pope). No one has a licence to agitate or attempt to alter the universe which God, in His ultimate wisdom, has engineered. 'Whatever is, is right', Pope affirms in his *Essay on Man*. At its least inspired, this kind of conservatism can degenerate into complacency on the one hand and, on the other, into a terror of change which is every bit as irrational as the clamours of the radical 'hot-heads' whom it accuses in the name of reason. Conservatism finally finds itself holding an untenable position and has to give way before the new forces for change which are generated in the march of time. Thus the defenders of tradition in Britain found themselves ultimately forced to bow before the progressive forces and permit the reform of parliament, as their precursors had permitted the 1688 Revolution Settlement, though they managed to balk the inevitable advance until 1832.

It would be incorrect to see Pope merely as a reactionary with his gaze turned nostalgically towards the past while he nurses a facilely optimistic vision of the present state of his society. In fact, Pope's view of Britain in the first decades of the 18th century is far from complacent and hints that beneath the powder and the wig the 18th-century 'gentleman' is no less atavistic in his desires than the animals whom he so much despises as his inferiors in the Great Chain of Being. The 18th century may have brought manners to perfection, just as it has smoothed and polished the 'rough diamond' of the heroic couplet bequeathed to it by Dryden. But behind this smoothness and suavity of exterior man is as corrupt and depraved as he ever was.

In Pope's satires, which express this pessimistic side of the poet's outlook, the elegant poise of the carefully sculptured rhymes and rhythms contrasts with the far-from-elegant behaviour of the characters so elegantly framed. How far short the activities of such characters fall below the standards of excellence implied by the rhythmic and semantic 'completeness' of the heroic couplet is made more emphatic by the immaculate perfection to which Pope had brought the art of couplet composition. If, as Dr Johnson claimed, Dryden had transmuted the 'brick' of English poetry into 'marble', it was left to Pope to apply the polish to the stone. 'Dryden's page', says Johnson, 'is a natural field . . . diversified by the varied exuberance of abundant vegetation; Pope's is a velvet lawn, shaven by the scythe, and levelled by the roller'. The 'velvet' form of Pope's satiric verse serves as an added indictment of the behaviour that it encases.

Satire attempts to draw attention to certain discrepancies between a society's ideals and its practices. The satirist's aim is to demonstrate how far short of ideal patterns of noble behaviour human conduct actually falls; and he usually sets out to emphasise this disparity by consciously exaggerating the baseness, the pettiness and the selfishness at the root of human action. The personages of a satire – be they real or only representative figures – have very often the features of cartoon characters, or 'caricatures', because only their quirks, idiosyncracies, foibles and personal defects are singled out for attention – to the exclusion of any redeeming qualities. The satirist's purpose is not to comfort his audience but to discompose it: to jolt it from its complacency by holding before it a distorted mirror in which only its worst features receive prominence. Like the cartoonist, the satirist aims to amuse his audience by demonstrating the ridiculous pomp and pretentiousness that clothe so much of human behaviour. Yet it is not simply a question of raising a laugh, for behind the flying ink of the cartoonists and satirists there rests a serious intent: to reform an imperfect world and make it a better place to live in. The satirist serves a social function. One could visualise the body politic, or indeed any human society, as a living organism constantly tending to develop inner corruption, on which satire acts as a purgative and a restorative, cleansing it and making it whole again. Like many a purgative, the taste of satire is often bitter and painful to swallow.

Satire has its range of 'tastes' or flavours. There is, for instance, in the early 19th century the 'gentle' satire of Jane Austen's novels, which, while poking fun at upper-class behaviour, never suggests that any radical alterations – either in the composition of society or in the psychological structure of the people who incorporate it – are necessary. Such satire provokes amusement and a feeling of kindness and sympathy towards beings who are obviously selfish and imperfect, but not maliciously so.

Some satire, on the other hand, seems to have been engendered in fury against the writer's fellow creatures and comes spitting off his pen with the accumulated venom of a snake pit. Examples of such satire can be found in the 18th century in plenty: in, for instance, the works of Jonathan Swift, whose King of Brobdingnag in *Gulliver's Travels* classifies mankind as 'the most pernicious race of little odious vermin that nature ever suffered to crawl upon the surface of the earth', and in Pope's *Dunciad*, where mankind is destined for the reign of dunces, an era of ubiquitous stupidity when 'universal darkness buries all'. When this darker satire is ingested, the laughs come less readily and one is made to reflect more seriously on whether mankind is, after all, redeemable. The only saving graces in a satiric vision of such density are the writer's own self-evident brilliance and powers of wit and imagination. As long as man can express himself so eloquently, all hope is not lost for humanity. The satirist is, in the last analysis, the conscience of the human race: he is a social reformer and a preacher who uses the tricks of distorting mirrors and funny stories to exhort, cajole, encourage and bully his fellow men into purifying and re-educating their souls.

Some of the techniques of satire may be seen in action in Pope's *Rape of the Lock*, first published in 1714. This section – from the poem's first canto – describes the dressing table (or 'toilet') of the heroine, Belinda.

> And now, unveiled, the toilet stands displayed,
> Each silver vase in mystic order laid.
> First, robed in white, the nymph intent adores,
> With head uncovered, the cosmetic powers.
> A heavenly image in the glass appears,
> To that she bends, to that her eyes she rears;
> The inferior priestess, at her altar's side,
> Trembling, begins the sacred rites of pride.
> Unnumbered treasures ope at once, and here
> 130   The various offerings of the world appear;
> From each she nicely culls with curious toil,
> And decks the goddess with the glittering spoil.
> This casket India's glowing gems unlocks,
> And all Arabia breathes from yonder box.
> The tortoise here and elephant unite,
> Transformed to combs, the speckled and the white.

Here files of pins extend their shining rows,
Puffs, powders, patches, bibles, billet-doux.
Now awful beauty puts on all its arms;
140   The fair each moment rises in her charms,
Repairs her smiles, awakens every grace,
And calls forth all the wonders of her face;
Sees by degrees a purer blush arise,
And keener lightnings quicken in her eyes.

Perhaps the most remarkable thing about this passage is its tone. A panoply of sacred imagery ('robed in white', 'priestess', 'altar', 'offerings') is applied to the description of something inconsequential: the preparations of a young girl prior to meeting her 'beau'. There is, thus, a disparity between the gravity of the diction and the levity of the action. Belinda's absorption in her physical charms is treated by the poet with a solemnity and reverence usually reserved for loftier themes. From this disequilibrium between language and topic springs the satiric tone: evidently Pope is mocking his heroine, insinuating that she is regarding her own person with the awe and devotion that properly belong to God.

The first two lines of the extract establish the poet's 'mock-heroic' approach. Belinda's dressing table (something 'ordinary') is treated as though it were an altar (something sacred or 'extraordinary'). It is normally 'veiled', as if too holy to be profaned by the gaze of ordinary mortals; and each jar of cosmetics (the 'cosmetic powers' Pope calls them, implying an ironic, mock-heroic analogy between the 'cosmic powers' and these trinkets) has the appearance of the Communion cup ('silver vase'). All is arranged 'in mystic order', suggesting that the sequence in which each item of make-up must be applied is a divine secret known only to the initiated. Belinda is the high priestess of this 'mystic order'; her serving-maid, it emerges later, is merely the 'inferior priestess'.

It is at once apparent, therefore, that to Pope's heroine beautification is the same thing as beatification. To be beautiful is to be blessed. She has confused salvation in the next world with salvation in this and is cultivating her body with the intention of catching a husband, displaying to this end all the intensity and high seriousness which she ought rather to direct towards the nurturing of her soul. She is dedicating herself to an earthly lord, instead of to the heavenly Lord, and for this misapplication of her energies Pope satirises her and all young ladies like her. Yet it is evident that Pope is amused rather than enraged by Belinda's folly; his tone is humorous rather than bitter, indulgent rather than bilious. If Belinda is a sinner, she is a sinner on a small scale.

The picture of Belinda's sacrilegious self-devotion is built up couplet by couplet. Each ensuing couplet adds to the 'sacred' atmosphere of the first couplet, so that by the end of the description Belinda's bedroom has acquired the ambience and all the accoutrements of a chapel. The 'nymph' (Belinda at the early-adolescent time of life when she is light of body and of mind) 'adores' her bottles of cosmetics: she pays them the respect of religious devotion because they do have the 'power' to transmute her – though bodily, rather than spiritually. Pope describes a quite natural situation as though it were a sacred occasion, alluding to Belinda's long undergarment in terms of sacerdotal vestments ('robed in white') and suggesting that her head is 'uncovered' for religious rather than practical purposes. The 'heavenly image' that appears in the 'glass', or mirror, is of course Belinda's own. When Belinda bends forward to apply her eye make-up – a task calling for concentration and close inspection of her mirror-image – Pope chooses to interpret it as a movement of abject obeisance. Like Narcissus, Belinda is lost in adoration of her own person.

The religious references continue. Belinda's cosmetic routines are called 'sacred rites' and the maid, who is no doubt nervous lest she make a mistake in the painting of the mistress's countenance and call forth her anger, is described as 'trembling', as if awestruck by the proximity of the divine. By maintaining the analogy between sacred and profane rituals, Pope encourages his reader to recognise how far short men and women generally fall of the perfection they might achieve.

In the ensuing couplets the adorning of Belinda's person continues. The various contents of her jewel and make-up boxes ('unnumbered treasures') are referred to as if she were a 'goddess' (line 132) to whom these gifts have been rendered in homage by her devoted subjects or worshippers around the globe ('the various offerings of the world appear'). These 'treasures' have, of course, come from distant lands, but under compulsion rather than voluntarily, culled from several outposts of expanding British mercantilism. Belinda, in other words, is the recipient of the produce of other lands grasped by Britain's colonial adventurers and bought for or bequeathed to Belinda by virtue of her privileged class position. What she is wearing is the booty of 18th-century imperialism, as Pope intends us to understand from his use of the phrase 'glittering spoil' (the 'spoil' or plunder of war) to describe the jewellery with which Belinda's maid 'decks' her. Thus India has been deprived of precious stones and the Middle East of perfumes (lines 133–34) for the furtherance of Belinda's sex appeal. The extent of this theft of the treasures of foreign nations is indicated by Pope's claim that '*all* Arabia breathes from yonder box': the wealth and vitality of the Orient have been captured for Belinda's frivolous self-indulgence, while Arabia itself is left destitute and, perhaps, lifeless (since its 'breath' is now contained within Belinda's perfume box).

The natural world has been despoiled by the spirit of commerce (lines 135–36). Long-lived and majestic animals are summarily killed and 'transformed' into trivial objects for a lady's boudoir, to satisfy the trader's instinct for a quick profit. Belinda, one assumes, is ignorant of the origins of her tortoiseshell and ivory combs: she takes them for granted as part of the heritage due to a young lady of the leisured class. Yet Pope's satire seems to be ranging beyond the 'type' of thoughtless and privileged female adolescent and striking at the roaming activity of Britain's merchant adventurers. The metamorphosis of the mighty elephant into a tiny ivory comb, an object beneath one's regard, suggests a society which translates the noble into the ignoble: a community in which spiritual, moral and aesthetic values have disappeared in the rush to satisfy grosser appetites. *The Rape of the Lock* is probing beyond Belinda's personal and venial shortcomings to focus intermittently on another and more serious 'rape' than that indicated by its title.

Pope is more indulgent to Belinda herself than he is to her society at large. In lines 137–38 he pokes further fun at his heroine by cataloguing the other items of her dressing table. Firstly, her innumerable hairpins are described as if they were an army of anonymous foot soldiers, ranked in lines for their commander-in-chief's (Belinda's) inspection. These objects are at least kept by Belinda in an orderly fashion. The next line, however, suggests that this young lady is not always quite so meticulous. The other items at her fingertips are strewn about her table-top in a manner devoid of all discipline. Cosmetic aids ('puffs, powders, patches') are intermingled with love-letters ('billet-doux') and in the midst of all this disarray are found 'bibles'. Pope implies, by juxtaposing the eternal book of divine

Love and the ephemeral letter of secular love, that to Belinda the Word of God has no more significance than the word of her beau and that both may be equally neglected in her preparations for further sexual conquests. The use of the plural form of the word ('bibles' rather than 'Bible') enhances the feeling that for Belinda the Bible is not a book apart. She has several copies instead of the single one which is all that is necessary. Belinda, it seems, is not much interested in nurturing her soul and it may be that her 'bibles', lumped together as they are with her other trinkets and 'glittering' paraphernalia, are collected more for the delight she takes in the surface beauty of their gilt-embossed covers than for any more spiritual joy she might reap from a perusal of what is clasped between those covers.

The passage ends with the application of Belinda's cosmetics to her face, a procedure which is described in terms of a hero arming himself for a battle. To Belinda, the task of conquering and subduing a man to the point where he will beg her hand in marriage is a serious undertaking, calling for all the painstaking preparation of a military campaign. As the magic of the make-up begins to work Belinda's stature grows ('The fair each moment rises in her charms'); she is undergoing a veritable metamorphosis. The satire, however, is magnanimous. Pope does not suggest that the cosmetic chemistry transforms something commonplace or ugly into something rich and strange; he merely implies that the process elicits 'wonders' which until now have only lain dormant in Belinda's physiognomy, waiting to be brought out. Her smiles have simply to be 'repaired' a bit, her various 'graces' awakened and the salient features of her facial structure made more apparent through the beautician's art. As Pope goes on to demonstrate later in the poem, in the male-orientated 18th-century society in which Belinda is trying to make room for herself such arts as she uses in her battle with the opposite and more privileged sex are altogether excusable.

In the last couplet Pope's tone of light banter against his heroine becomes more explicit. The 'purer blush' that the make-up paints on Belinda's face is a comment made by the poet with his tongue in his cheek. Belinda's use of rouge to implant an artificial blush on the cheek must create, contrary to what Pope says, blushes which are *less* pure than those which arise of their own accord. Similarly, the 'lightnings' which dart from Belinda's eyes – perhaps a mock-heroic allusion to the thunderbolts used by the Greek god Zeus to impale his enemies – are made sharper and more alive ('quickened') by virtue of her dexterity with the cosmetic materials. Pope is using language ironically; he obviously intends the opposite. The eyes in poetry are conventionally the 'windows' of the soul; Petrarch and the courtly-love poets looked upon the eyes of their mistress as the most divine feature of her, and it is through their eyes that lovers such as Chaucer's Troilus and Criseyde first communicate and fall in love with each other. In Shakespeare's *Romeo and Juliet* Romeo refers to Juliet's eyes as 'Two of the fairest stars in all the heaven'. Thus one feels that when Belinda coats her eyes with cosmetics, she is transgressing against her truer self; and the whole make-up ritual emerges as a desecration rather than a consecration of her latent qualities. She is cultivating the body at the expense of the soul. It is this to which Pope wishes to draw his reader's attention through his mock-heroic analogies; and it is this for which Belinda, along with her whole circumambient social milieu, is being satirised, in the hope that the reader may learn from Belinda's myopia to reject the ephemeral and artificial values of personal adornment for those which are real and lasting.

Jonathan Swift (1667–1745)

The early decades of the 18th century are remarkable for the spirit of pessimism which dwelt in the hearts of the most gifted writers. Pope, in *The Dunciad*, prophesied that the proliferation of third-rate literature by the hacks of Fleet Street would culminate in a lowering of intellectual and, in consequence, of ethical standards, to the point where 'Morality expires' and no 'human spark is left, nor glimpse divine'. In prose, Pope's friend Jonathan Swift was even less optimistic about mankind's ability to subdue his baser instincts and rise above mediocrity, sloth and selfishness. At the end of *Gulliver's Travels* Gulliver finds himself so thoroughly disgusted by the antics of his fellow creatures that he takes himself off to live in the stables, preferring the wholesome odour of simple horses to the moral offensiveness of devious humans.

In the first half of the 18th century, and beyond, writers in Britain perceived themselves as the torch-bearers of the rational light of God in a world into which darkness and disintegration were always threatening to make inroads. Hence the prevalence of the satiric form during this epoch. Writers such as Pope, Swift and Johnson made constant reference to their classical forbears in ancient Rome, who had held similar beliefs in the serious and sacred purpose of their writings. Satire must teach as well as entertain, alerting its audience to the catastrophic dangers that attend a relaxation in moral standards. The Roman poet Horace shared the low opinion of mankind which the satirists of 18th-century Britain were later to hold, and he knew, as they did, that men turn to books for pleasure not instruction, so they must be enlightened surreptitiously, beneath the guise of entertainment: 'the man who has managed to blend profit with delight wins everyone's approbation, for he gives his reader pleasure at the same time as he instructs him' *(Ars Poetica)*. Thus Pope's *Rape of the Lock* makes its reader smile magnanimously at the moral blindness of its heroine; but it also informs him, through her ultimate downfall, of the perils of narcissism and spiritual ignorance.

In general, the 18th-century poet takes for subject-matter his social environment and the nature of human beings ('The proper study of mankind is man', according to Pope's dictum). The poet employs his argumentative faculties in an effort to guide mankind by the light of reason towards an apprehension of the errors of his ways. For this end the heroic couplet is eminently suitable: the poem can progress step by step, in a logical way. When he uses the heroic couplet the poet is 'bound' to plod systematically through his argument, pausing for breath and reflection at the end of every alternate line. Thus the format of heroic-couplet verse automatically imposes a more or less 'reasonable' tone on the poem's content. At that time, if a writer wanted to give vent to an emotional outburst, he would have to resort to the medium of prose, as Swift did in *Gulliver's Travels*. However, in the poem that follows (published in 1708) Swift appears in a more genial mood, willing to marshal his sentiments within the regimentation of the couplet.

A Description of the Morning

Now hardly here and there a hackney-coach
Appearing, showed the ruddy morn's approach.
Now Betty from her master's bed had flown,
And softly stole to discompose her own;
The slip-shod 'prentice from his master's door
Had pared the dirt and sprinkled round the floor.
Now Moll had whirled her mop with dext'rous airs,
Prepared to scrub the entry and the stairs.

The youth with broomy stumps began to trace
10 The kennel-edge, where wheels had worn the place.
The small-coal man was heard with cadence deep,
Till drowned in shriller notes of chimney-sweep:
Duns at his lordship's gate began to meet;
And brickdust Moll had screamed through half the street.
The turnkey now his flock returning sees,
Duly let out a-nights to steal for fees:
The watchful bailiffs take their silent stands,
And schoolboys lag with satchels in their hands.

The couplet is used here to delineate a picture of London at dawn.
Swift accumulates a sense of the ethos of the city by enumerating the
sundry activities of its inhabitants at this early hour. Each couplet
registers a new impression, animating the canvas with sight and
sound, until by the end of the poem the picture is complete. No single
object or person attracts the main focus, as Belinda does in *The Rape of
the Lock*. Swift's perspective is instead panoramic: he presents a broad
sweep of the human industry being conducted both in the light and in
the shadow of the London streets. For a visual equivalent one could
turn to the satirical drawings of William Hogarth. To both artists, the
essence of urban society was the manifold, though hardly noble,
activities of swarming humankind.

Within the boundary of each couplet Swift works hard to create an
effect which is simultaneously suggestive and precise. Like his
contemporaries through the major part of the 18th century, he
explores not himself but his world in his verse. His is not, however, the
strictly objective eye of the camera: Swift is giving a satirical slant to
what he sees. The satirical angle is effected by the selection of
incidents and the choice of vocabulary, which ensures that the
presentation of the facts is not a 'neutral' one. Thus all the schoolboys
displayed are laggards, unwilling to work, with not a 'swot' among
them. The vocabulary throughout the poem has been chosen by Swift
with the intention of conveying the low moral tone of city life. Even
the dawn itself has a 'ruddy' complexion, as if it had spent the night
with a port bottle. And this fits in precisely with the apparently
mystifying understatement with which the poem begins. Why should
the relative infrequency of hackney-coaches give sign of the new day
approaching? Because up to this moment these vehicles have been
busy conveying their gentlemen-hirers to and from all-night

carousals and debaucheries or secret assignations with their mistresses. Only with the end of night does such unwholesome activity become more sporadic; but so contagious and widespread is this metropolitan degeneracy that, in the poet's fancy, nature itself is getting up with a hangover.

The implication that the city's inhabitants do things under cover of night that they dare not do by day is developed in lines 3–4. Betty, the servant, having passed the night in her master's bed, hastens to 'discompose' her own, to give the false impression that she has spent an innocent night alone. Night in this city is the time for disorder: neither the moral order that places sexual restraints upon unmarried people nor the social order which places hierarchical barriers between upper and lower classes is respected. Day, on the other hand, is the time for 'discomposing', for deception, for lying and covering up one's traces until the evening returns to permit a resumption of former unprincipled practices. Clandestinity is the watchword by night and by day.

The animation of the city at this early hour arises from the activities of the labouring classes. Betty leaves her master sleeping in his bed, while the apprentice (lines 5–6) is engaged in cleaning the workshop where he is learning his trade in preparation for the later arrival of his master. The next couplet shows 'Moll' (like 'Betty', another generic name for a servant) vigorously whirling and scrubbing at the filth deposited by her betters. The contrast between the industriousness of the lower classes and the idleness of their social superiors is made more striking by the fact that the tasks of the former have already been accomplished by the time the poet begins his record: Betty *'had* flown', the apprentice *'had* pared the dirt' and Moll *'had* whirled her mop'. The servants, in other words, have been busy not only at the crack of dawn but before it.

The poem is based, like most English poetry, on a Greek model – in this instance, the pastoral idyll. The idyll is a short descriptive piece, and the pastoral idyll usually depicts – for example, in the work of Theocritus (3rd century BC) – the shepherd or shepherds going forth at dawn, when all nature is glistening with freshness, to tend their flocks. The only flocks in Swift's poem are, of course, the gaoler's. Swift's poem is a satiric version of the idyll – a 'mock-idyll' – with the innocence of the rural scene replaced by the corruption of the urban setting and the simplicity of the rustic peasants substituted by the wily dishonesty of their urban counterparts. Swift would expect his readers to be familiar with the idyllic mode of poetry, and indeed the satiric effect of his poem depends very much on his audience keeping constantly in mind the implied comparison between the two worlds of the idyllic and the actual. In both settings – ideal rural and real urban – it is the working classes who are up and about to greet the new day, while their masters lie abed until later. The speaker of Swift's poem, by his tacit admission that he was not around to record what happened earlier, seems to place himself in the category of the leisured classes.

In lines 11–12 Swift adds a soundtrack to his picture. The itinerant merchant of household coal advertises his wares in a deep voice appropriate to the profundity of the earth from which his product is mined; while a more piercing cry issues from the lips of the chimney sweep, probably a small boy whose voice has not yet broken ('shrill'), walking the streets in search of someone to hire his lithe and nimble frame. The phrases 'cadence deep' and 'shriller notes' suggest music, perhaps the music of bird-song which greets the shepherd of the pastoral idyll. But in the city the birds are silent, their melodic warblings replaced by harsher, human tones. With the voices of the sweep and the coalman the dawn chorus of the city streets commences and is soon joined (lines 13–34) by the 'screams' of a local lunatic, 'brickdust Moll', so called perhaps because her clothes are dusty from the derelict buildings where she sleeps by night. Beneath her high-pitched cries another sound is overheard: the steady, continuous mutterings of the creditors ('duns') who are gathering at the gate of an overspending aristocrat to reclaim from him their financial dues. This is the one specific reference in the portrait to the upper classes and it is not a flattering one: 'his lordship' is apparently a man who is financially bankrupt and, by implication, morally so as well.

The poem drops innuendoes about a spiritually destitute ruling class and suggests some of the repercussions on social order that will ensue. Thus, immediately after the reference to 'his lordship's' predicament the demented madwoman is heard wailing 'through half the street' like a banshee predicting the chaos that is to come. A corruption at the top will run through and infect the whole social fabric and a sign of the spreading decay comes to light in the penultimate couplet. The gaoler, whose job is to keep the criminal element under lock and key so that it is prevented from harming the social organism, is in fact releasing the prisoners each night so that they will give him a portion of their new-stolen loot. The final couplet continues to suggest a demoralised community. The bailiffs, waiting to issue their writs on the debt-ridden upper classes, are lurking like vultures, anticipating the demise of a moribund society. And the closing image of the 'lagging' schoolboys going unwillingly to their studies suggests that there will be no salvation, through greater self-awareness, from the coming generation.

Even though Swift is aware of man's inclination for self-indulgence, the tone of his poem is one of tolerant acceptance rather than wrathful indignation. This is apparent from the humour of his presentation: in the 'soft' deception practised by Betty to preserve the appearance of innocent nights, or in the affectionate relationship established between the turnkey and 'his flock', living in symbiotic harmony based on a 'duly' regulated rapport. In Swift's vision man is no more than an animal, no matter what finer pretensions he may give himself, and it is man's animal vitality which this poem celebrates while implicitly mocking his fatuous endeavours to refine his ineluctable nature into something purer.

7 A Tilt towards Romanticism: Thomas Gray

The dominant spirit of the 18th century was a controlled and rational scepticism. Poets did not expect great or noble deeds from their fellows nor even from themselves. Fears about man's inherent incapacity for self-improvement and doubts about his ability to alter his environment for the better led to a *laissez-faire* attitude towards politics. Man, in Pope's words, was a 'chaos of thought and passion, all confused' and any alteration in the structure of his government must, given mankind's centrifugal tendency towards anarchy, be an innovation for the worse. Hence the conservatism for which the 18th century is renowned. As such attitudes became more entrenched the longer the century advanced, it was not surprising that they invited reactions. The most notable of these was the French Revolution of 1789, which wiped out the French monarchy and aristocracy and challenged all the previously held assumptions about the sacred and inviolable structure of society. This event had repercussions throughout Europe, causing many a monarch to tremble on his throne; and it was probably the French Revolution that encouraged the nascent Romantic movement in Britain to burst forth into full flower at the end of the century.

Romanticism, however, did not arrive *tout d'un coup*, overnight on the wings of the French Revolution. There were many harbingers in the previous decades, ranging from the 'nature' poetry of James Thomson through the 'graveyard' poetry of Edward Young to the 'Gothic' novels of Horace Walpole and Clara Reeve. Romanticism came with éclat but its way had already been prepared.

Romanticism is a term which has been attached retrospectively to

94

categorise the new upsurge of self-confidence and the abounding energy which is evident in the works of the poets writing at the end of the 18th and the beginning of the 19th centuries. Broadly speaking, the 'Romantic' poet looked to himself, rather than to the world around him, for his subject-matter. Wordsworth's *Prelude* is subtitled *Growth of a Poet's Mind,* indicating that the poet now believed his own interior landscape to be as interesting a field study as was the human society to which he belonged. In consequence, the Romantic poet often preferred to withdraw altogether from society, the better to concentrate on mining the sources of his own hidden wealth. Such a denial of the poet's integral part in the social organism would have been unthinkable to Pope or Johnson, who considered man to be a social animal and strictly limited in respect of his own internal resources.

But where the 18th-century writer sought to impose limits upon human potential the Romantic writer strove to remove them. Where the 18th-century poem advocates passive acceptance of the human lot the Romantic poem discovers a surge of optimism, a faith in the limitless possibilities for the individual to rise above the corruptions and degradations of his worldly environment through the force of his imagination. And it is this belief in imagination which distinguishes Romantic poetry from that which immediately preceded it. The Romantics discovered the creative function of the imagination, possessed and realised to a large extent by Shakespeare and the Elizabethans but on the decline ever since until, in the Augustan era, reason had been proclaimed as man's most divine faculty to which all others must submit. For the Romantics, the rediscovery of what Coleridge called 'the shaping spirit of imagination' offered a whole new dynamic for the conception of poetry and the shackles inherited from the Augustans were joyfully thrown off. The heroic couplet was by and large discarded and blank verse, as a freer form of expression, came into a popularity it had not known since the 17th century.

What the spontaneous birth of the 'Romantic' movement involved was a fundamental shift in the role of the poet. Where he had hitherto been functioning as a mirror, passively reflecting the world around him while allowing himself the occasional sardonic remark or wry interjection, he now saw himself as a creative agent, endowed with a mind which could – through 'imagination' – arrange and reconstruct the materials that it received. The poet – and man himself – was no longer perceived as a puny being with strictly limited possibilities of more or less worthless achievement. Once more he was conceived of in Hamlet's terms, as a being 'infinite in faculties! ... in apprehension, how like a god!' The poet could now retire from the distraction of the city streets, the social gatherings, the pomp and circumstance of court and commercial life, to the sanctum of his own mind, where he could observe a new and more radiant cosmos. It was an exhilarating discovery.

Thomas Gray (1716–71)

Some poets in the middle years of the 18th century were already making tentative moves in the direction of Romanticism. One of them was Thomas Gray, whose 'Elegy Written in a Country Churchyard' – of which the first nine stanzas appear below – could be seen as an 'intermediary' stage, a bridge between the restrained 'classicism' of Pope and Johnson and the effusive 'Romanticism' of Wordsworth and his confrères.

The curfew tolls the knell of parting day,
    The lowing herd wind slowly o'er the lea,
The ploughman homeward plods his weary way,
    And leaves the world to darkness and to me.

Now fades the glimmering landscape on the sight,
    And all the air a solemn stillness holds,
Save where the beetle wheels his droning flight,
    And drowsy tinklings lull the distant folds;

Save that from yonder ivy-mantled tower
    The moping owl does to the moon complain
Of such, as wandering near her secret bower,
    Molest her ancient solitary reign.

Beneath those rugged elms, that yew-tree's shade,
    Where heaves the turf in many a mouldering heap,
Each in his narrow cell forever laid,
    The rude forefathers of the hamlet sleep.

The breezy call of incense-breathing morn,
    The swallow twittering from the straw-built shed,
The cock's shrill clarion or the echoing horn,
    No more shall rouse them from their lowly bed.

For them no more the blazing hearth shall burn,
  Or busy housewife ply her evening care;
No children run to lisp their sire's return,
  Or climb his knees the envied kiss to share.

Oft did the harvest to their sickle yield;
  Their furrow oft the stubborn glebe has broke;
How jocund did they drive their team afield!
  How bowed the woods beneath their sturdy stroke!

Let not Ambition mock their useful toil,
  Their homely joys and destiny obscure;
Nor Grandeur hear with a disdainful smile
  The short and simple annals of the poor.

The boast of heraldry, the pomp of power,
  And all that beauty, all that wealth e'er gave,
Awaits alike the inevitable hour:
  The paths of glory lead but to the grave.

The poem's rhythm is emphatically iambic. From the opening line,

Thĕ cúrfĕw tólls thĕ knéll ŏf pártĭng dáy,

the alternately stressed syllables ring out loud and clear in imitation of the steady intoning of the curfew bell, the image that ushers in the poem. This bell, with its note of sustained melancholy, establishes the tone of the poem. To the poet's mind it is a 'knell', or a parting tribute, tolling for the day that is dying. This reflection puts the poet into a meditative frame of mind and launches him on the course of rumination that he is to follow in the ensuing stanzas. Gray's elegy is 'written in a country churchyard'; and from the poem's title and the funereal note of the opening line it is clear that death will be the dominant theme of the poet's speculation.

For such a theme the structure that Gray has chosen is most apt. He does not write in couplets but in four-line stanzas, each stanza advancing at an unhurried, measured pace, unfolding each image of the departing day and the approaching night – and the thoughts they inspire in the poet – in a simple, uncomplicated way. The poet is in no rush; the whole night stretches before him and he luxuriates in the prospect of being free to allow his thoughts to range wherever they will, even if they gravitate towards the dark topography of death. For though the corpse in its clayey resting-place is the nucleus around which the poet's fancies soon come to revolve, such a topic does not lead him to despair but rather towards an acceptance of the evident truth that 'the paths of glory lead but to the grave'. The rhythm of the poem points to the universal but undemonstrative rhythm of life. The first stanza affirms this, with its gong-like bell, its herd of cattle taking its meandering course 'slowly' across the meadow and its farm labourer, homeward-bound, planting his tired feet with the same 'plodding' regularity, and at the same unhurried pace, as the poem itself.

These initial images create the appropriate atmosphere for the meditation that is to follow. Having observed his fellow men obeying the summons of the 'curfew' and retiring behind their doors and shutters for the night, the poet is left alone. In the first stanza the focus narrows down from the world around him to the final 'me', the 'ego-tistical sublime' that Keats would detect at the centre of Wordsworth's verse. Yet, since he is not a fully-fledged 'Romantic', Gray does not see his position of solitude at this point of gathering dusk as an opportunity to plunge within himself and drag forth some long-buried psychic treasure into the light of poetic consciousness. Instead, the poem continues as before, registering the impressions that come to the poet from both without and within, while he himself remains uninvolved. A Romantic poet, on the contrary, would have actively engaged his mind in the images that came to it, imaginatively fusing a unified vision, or 'higher reality', out of the disparate elements. Gray, by contrast, remains a somewhat dry observer, cataloguing what he sees around him without attempting to relate the phenomena of external nature too intimately to his own inner life.

Nature, which figures frequently in the poetry of the Romantics, serves them chiefly as a stimulus to wider-ranging inquiry, either inward through the chasms and caverns of the poet's own soul or outward towards an exploration of the heavens and a definition of man's part in the universal scheme of things. The 'pre-Romantic' poet, on the other hand, is much more restrained in his reflexes to the animal and vegetable kingdoms. It is the 'external' reality of nature that strikes him, rather than its 'internal' essence or hidden meaning; and he goes about the task of tabulating its phenomena dutifully, with a detached and dispassionate eye. Thus, while Gray differs from the bulk of his contemporaries in considering the natural scene at all, he undertakes his peregrination through the nocturnal world of bestial sights and sounds with the imperturbable aplomb and exactly-measured gait of a village policeman.

The second stanza clearly illustrates how Gray conceived his role as a passive receptacle of the impressions that came to his senses. The effects that the 'glimmering landscape' and the 'droning beetle' make on the sight and the hearing are duly registered but the poet himself remains disengaged, his passions undisturbed. The 'solemn stillness' that governs all around him reigns in his own soul, too. When his contemplation of nature does eventually stimulate a response in him it is not an intuitive emotional reaction but rather a carefully-weighed, deliberate and, above all, rational reflection. This is not to say that Gray's more 'reasonable' attitude to the natural world is necessarily inferior to the 'spontaneous overflow of powerful feelings' characteristic of the Romantics' more participatory response. But it does suggest that for Gray the instinctive reaction to life's phenomena is not to be trusted: it must be filtered still through the funnel of reason before finding expression in a diction and a metre intended to tranquillise rather than agitate. Gray, like his contemporaries, believed in keeping nature at arm's length; the day had not yet arrived when he might have said, as John Keats was to say more than half a century later, 'if a sparrow come before my window I take part in its existence and pick about the gravel'.

The 18th century, with its love of the landscaped garden and its preference for the 'picturesque' in art, desired nature to be 'tame': something that the mind could cope with. Gray's poem shows where his predilection lies: in the direction of a nature that is neither unruly nor unpredictable. Thus the images that come to him during his vigil are those he is predisposed to receive. The evening contains no surprises. So, in stanza 2, the beetle 'wheels' in 'droning flight', the monotonous 'droning' sound encouraging a relaxation towards sleep. The sheep in their folds are 'lulled' by the 'drowsy tinklings' of their bells: an example of pathetic fallacy, suggesting that Gray, intent on having all the natural phenomena in consonance with his soporific mood, is more interested in imposing an anthropomorphic interpretation on the sheep's behaviour than in any independent observation of the habits of such animals. Creation of the initial mood is Gray's first task: he must establish a relaxed, sleepy atmosphere so that he may proceed to meditate aloud. Thus he projects onto surrounding nature the 'drowsiness' that is an essential preliminary to his poem.

The third stanza shows more clearly how Gray credits nature with human feelings and intentions. The one creature that is stirring at this crepuscular hour is the owl, a bird traditionally identified as a harbinger of death and therefore appropriately discovered in an ancient 'ivy-mantled tower' overlooking the graveyard. Gray interprets the bird in a fanciful 'humanised' way, without doing violence to its actual behaviour: the owl's whooping call, he claims, is a sulky moan of protest levelled against the poet who dares to disturb, at this untoward hour of the night, 'her . . . solitary reign'. The bird's human dimension is suggested by the use of 'her' rather than 'its', just as when referring to the beetle the poet mentions 'his' droning flight. Gray is wrapping his night creatures up in human coats.

The poet's primary aim – the evocation of those moments before slumber when the mind, on the threshold of sleep, is relaxed and reflective – is attained. Gray selects those elements in animal life which assist this purpose, excluding those that might not. Nature is disciplined by the poet's rationalising sensibility. It is not allowed to behave too chaotically: there has to be a *reason* for the owl's weird, unearthly cry, and the poet duly supplies it. Nor is the darkness permitted to become too overwhelming: the landscape 'glimmers' in stanza 2, subsequently to be illuminated by the moon of stanza 3. It is a comfortable rather than a disquieting obscurity: a vapour rather than a void.

In stanza 4 Gray approaches the main preoccupation of his elegy: the passing from life of the former inhabitants of this small village (the 'forefathers of the hamlet'). His thoughts are guided in this direction by the encompassing darkness and by his awareness of the trees in the churchyard, shading the graves of the villagers. These 'rude' people, uneducated but honest, are now imprisoned 'forever' in a 'narrow cell'. Yet some of the claustrophobic horror of death is lessened by Gray's euphemistic assertion that the cemetery gives 'sleep' to these worn-out peasants and not utter annihilation; an impression which is furthered by his depiction of the trees standing guard over the beds of the 'sleepers' and the turf that covers them 'heaving' like blankets tossed about by a slumberer. It appears that the hamlet's forefathers might at some future time shake off their present hibernation. The tone of the poem, though solemn, is not morbid. The graves' tenants may have departed 'forever' from this world but they are at the same time resting prior to their journey to the next.

The freshness of the 'incense-breathing' morning and the sweet odours emanating from its opening flowers can make no impression on the olfactory organs of the grave-dwellers. Nor can the swallow's 'twittering' reach their ears. Their senses, along with their bodies, are stilled and 'mouldering' with the turf. They will be equally heedless of the cockerel's reveille and the hunter's horn. Only the Judgement-Day trumpet now has the power to reach them and 'rouse them from their lowly bed' ('lowly' signifying both their humble station during life and the subterranean nature of their present resting-place).

Gray has begun now to celebrate the life that the dead ones have left: the exhilarating scents of the fields, the chattering activity of the birds, the excitement of the fox hunt, the health and vigour of the countryside where nothing is ersatz (even the shed is 'straw-built' with materials provided by nature). He develops this in stanza 6 with an evocation of the domestic joys that are perforce a thing of the past for the churchyard's tenants. The welcoming warmth of the fire, the bustling ministrations of a matronly wife and the affectionate attentions of his offspring, all serving to compensate the workman at the end of a day's hard labour, are treasures all the more precious for their inevitable impermanence. Gray's tone here is one of nostalgia and regret, not of despair: the regular measure of the iambic feet, if nothing else, reassures us. With so much love evident in the earthly cottage, how impossible that such love should not be magnified a thousandfold in the heavenly mansion.

In stanza 7 Gray pays tribute to the physical energy of these late husbandmen, 'rugged' as the elms which now watch over their remains. The 'yielding' of the harvest crop suggests that the corn only surrendered after a tough struggle; and the peasant must have developed military virtues in himself to combat the 'stubborn glebe' and wrest a subsistence from it. He had to fight nature and to dominate it; and in the end even the trees of the forest 'bowed' down before him, acknowledging him as master. But for the labourers who now lie beneath Gray's feet, demobilised by death, the glory of such physical power is departed. The harvesters have themselves been harvested and the earth over which they had hitherto reigned supreme now rests on top of them. Yet there is something so 'natural' about this cycle of events that one's sorrow must be tempered by acceptance.

Gray goes on to justify his calling the attention of his literate middle and upper-class readers (personified, not too flatteringly, as 'Ambition' and 'Grandeur') to the humble lives and deaths ('destiny obscure') of the illiterate peasantry. Death, the great leveller, does not recognise social class, physical beauty or cultured accomplishment; all such superfluities must be deposited at the entrance to the 'narrow cell' that awaits poor and rich alike:

> The paths of glory lead but to the grave.

The poem has its roots evidently well-embedded in the 18th-century poetry of moral tutelage. Yet its tone is not as drily didactic as, for example, a poem on a similar theme by Johnson might have been. The graveyard atmosphere anticipates the terrors called forth later in the century by similar settings in the Gothic novels of Ann Radcliffe and M. G. 'Monk' Lewis. There is in Gray, however, a passive acceptance of the known facts of life and death which is notably absent from the more febrile writings of the Gothic novelists and Romantic poets who were to follow in his wake. He is, after all, a man of his time and the moral of his meditation is none other than the classically conventional *sic transit gloria mundi* ('thus pass all the glories of this world').

There are, however, two aspects at least in which Gray foreshadows those writers of a more turbulent epoch and for which he is sometimes dubbed 'pre-Romantic'. Firstly, he has forsaken the city streets to seek stimulus from the rural environment. He shows a sensitivity towards nature and an awareness of its power to trigger off human emotions and musings, even though neither nature nor the thoughts it inspires are allowed to trespass beyond the limits preimposed by the poet. Secondly, the poem seems to map out, at the end of its opening stanza ('leaves the world to darkness *and to me*'), a subjective terrain which, in the event, is left unexplored. Having indicated his own place in the panorama, Gray turns his gaze outward and keeps it there. The self-examination which the first stanza seems to promise is not forthcoming. Neither chaos from the inner world nor turmoil from without is allowed to intrude to the point of disturbing the even flow of perfectly-weighted aphorism.

Although Gray may have experienced the occasional atavistic twitch – the urge to let sentiment overrule sententiousness – he was, finally, too much a man of the 18th century to allow the last word to any other voice than that of reason.

8 Romanticism: Blake, Wordsworth, Keats, Byron and Shelley

Towards the end of the 18th century a growing disgust among writers with the rationalistic bias of their predecessors can be discerned. The wit that was once so fresh and vigorous in the writings of Pope and Swift had become dull and predictable. The edge had gone off it. For inspiration writers began to turn towards more mysterious or numinous aspects of experience and towards the world of their dreams, territories which had been out of bounds to the Augustans. The Gothic novelists gave a further impulse to the writer to follow the impromptu, 'irrational' leading of his imagination and to body forth in words the images of his deepest fantasy, however grotesque and horrible these might be.

To William Blake the world of matter was a false 'reality', concealing the true reality, which was spiritual, numinous and eternal. Blake, regarded as a lunatic by the society in which he lived, wrote in isolation, a prophet without an audience. Other poets of the time were possessed by the same intense desire to promote the spiritual and imaginative at the expense of the rational. The lid was lifted from Pandora's box: ghosts, goblins and 'frightful fiends' stalked across the poet's landscape. Gone was the world-weary urbanity of the Augustans. The poet was no longer ashamed of responding to life with the wonder and amazement of a child, of greeting each new day as a minor miracle in itself. Coleridge, in *Biographia Literaria*, expressed this notion of the importance of safeguarding the child's freshness of response within the poetic temperament, remarking that:

To carry on the feelings of childhood into the powers of manhood; to combine the child's sense of wonder and novelty with the appearances which every day for perhaps forty years had rendered familiar . . . this is the character and privilege of genius.

Or, as Wordsworth put it, 'The child is father of the man'. The child's imagination is unfettered and his response to life 'truer' than the conditioned reflexes of the adult; and the poet must continue to cultivate his spontaneous emotions and become again as a little child. The poet's concern, as expressed by Wordsworth, was with 'common life' and 'ordinary things', from which he must extract the inner significance, exposing for all to see the hidden beauty of the humble.

Blake had a similar reverence for the mind of the child, and throughout his life he condemned the social 'system' of Britain, which was then rapidly industrialising and 'rationalising' as it did so its exploitation of child labour and its warping of the infant intellect through mechanical and soulless methods of education. In Blake's view, the educational principle which insisted on clipping the wings of the child's free-flying imagination and ringing him with prohibitions and inflexible dogma was one of the most flagrantly criminal legacies from the Age of Reason; for

How can the bird that is born for joy
   Sit in a cage and sing?

('The School Boy')

The Romantic poets realised in common that the child, by virtue of his uncluttered imagination, is closer to spiritual truth than the adult can ever be. In the words of Wordsworth the child 'beholds the light, and whence it flows'; until, unfortunately growing older in an insanely rational world, 'Shades of the prison-house begin to close'. Understanding this as they did, the Romantic poets encouraged in themselves a childlike attitude towards experience, an openness towards life in all its aspects.

The most intense perod of Romantic creativity lay between 1789 – the year when Blake's *Songs of Innocence* was published – and 1824, the year when George Gordon, Lord Byron died. The Romantic urge certainly lived on after 1824, just as it had already been in evidence before 1789, but the Romantic surge was finished when Byron expired in a foreign land fighting for the cause of a people not his own. It should be remarked that even at the height of this Romantic flood tide undercurrents from the Age of Reason were still traceable. The novels of Ann Radcliffe, for example, for all their evocation of the supernatural and their hints of unspeakable human misconduct, provide 'rational' explanations for the horrors they have raised, while the villains stop short of committing the ultimate depravity; Jane Austen's fiction, written during this epoch, reflects an eminently 'sensible' attitude towards life and a particularly contemptuous dismissal of the supernatural in her mock-Gothic novel, *Northanger Abbey*; while Lord Byron himself, who in his poem *Childe Harold's Pilgrimage* delineates a particular sort of 'Romantic' hero-figure, a man self-dependent and isolated against a hostile world, elsewhere deplores some of the by-products and excesses of the Romantic attitude and longs for a return to Augustan level-headedness ('Oh! ye shades / Of Pope and Dryden, are we come to this?').

Reason, in other words, was not abandoned altogether, even at the height of the artistic revulsion against it. But it had ceased to be the arbiter supreme. Horizons which had threatened to remain closed for ever, while reason held sway, were once again thrown open, offering an incentive to a new generation of poets to launch themselves into hitherto uncharted waters.

Perhaps at no other time in the history of English literature had so many gifted poets been writing simultaneously. It was as if a forest fire had ignited spontaneously, spreading in several directions at once. With Byron's death in 1824 the last of the flames was effectively snuffed out; for although Wordsworth and Coleridge were to live on for many more years, the 'first fine careless rapture' and the concentrated energy and vision of their youthful verse was already, as Wordsworth had foretold in his 'Ode: Intimations of Immortality', gone beyond recall:

At length the Man perceives it die away,
And fade into the common light of day.

The poetry written in the last decade of the 18th century and the first two decades of the 19th exhibits an exultation of spirit, like a child capering in the fields after his release from a gloom-laden schoolroom. With the passage of time this initial euphoria naturally exhausted itself. It is perhaps no accident that three of the major Romantics (Keats, Byron and Shelley) died early, as if all that was most precious in their lives had been poured onto paper in their youths, leaving them to face a barren and 'posthumous existence' (in Keats's words), the kind of intellectual afterlife that Wordsworth endured.

But during those three decades the creative activity of these writers was at its highest pitch. Keats sensed that his era had been blessed with a higher than average quota of genius, as he remarked in one of his sonnets:

Great spirits now on earth are sojourning.

('Addressed to Haydon')

Yet these 'spirits', though at work contemporaneously, were labouring independently of one another. Wordsworth's and Coleridge's collaboration in the 1798 *Lyrical Ballads* was a rare example of cooperation, soon to be followed by a rupture and a pursuit of separate poetic paths. The integrity of the individual vision (the 'egotistical sublime') was of supreme importance and nothing must be permitted to impair it. The poet was no longer the gregarious being with a social consciousness that had been his Augustan counterpart. He now tended to withdraw from the social scene and to produce poems from his isolation, peopling them with beings of his fantasy in a landscape of his imagination. Even when a Romantic poet did feel impelled to write on a contemporary social theme, the product was often couched in such heady idealistic terms that the reader might find himself involved in the inner workings of the poet's brain rather than in any wider, more 'objective' context.

The poets were like lone navigators, each invisible to the others but all following the same guiding-star in the heavens. They all held more or less to the belief that the concrete world of material 'appearances' served only to divert man from the real, eternal truths about Creation. It was Blake who first formulated this thesis, telling his reader to penetrate the surface world of nature and grasp its spiritual sap, its heavenly essence: to see not merely with but '*through* the eye'. The Romantic eye is an organ not only of perception but of penetration. Thus, beause of a generally shared faith in a permanent world beyond this transitory one, a world 'closed', as Blake said, 'by your senses five', Romantic philosophy tends to be ultimately optimistic. Even death is a door opening, not inwards to the claustrophobic 'narrow cell' of Gray's inhumed peasantry but outwards, offering release from this world where, as Keats saw, 'youth grows pale and spectre-thin and dies', to the 'eternal Silence' envisioned by Wordsworth, where all of life's contradictions will be reconciled.

William Blake (1757–1827)

William Blake lived for 70 years, was a visionary from his childhood and never lost the capacity of seeing life around him glowing with inner glory where lesser or more prosaic men would have perceived nothing extraordinary. 'Everything that lives is Holy', asserted Blake, and he spent his life writing poems that attempted to overthrow the tyranny of Reason and reawaken man to the wonder of his own nature and of Creation itself. As a child he saw streets and fields filled with angels or sometimes devils. When he was four years old he saw God looking at him through a window. In later life he claimed that his poetry was 'dictated' to him by spirits.

The Britain in which Blake was living had recently discovered steam power and was just beginning to realise the enormous potential for accelerated mass-production that this discovery offered. It is often said that, whereas the French had a political Revolution at the end of the 18th century, the British had an economic one – the Industrial Revolution. The harnessing of steam power stimulated the creation of gigantic mills and factories; to the Romantic poets such acts were acts of anti-Creation, desecrating as they did both the face of the natural landscape and the souls of their human employees. The rural weaver, whose hand-loom had become unprofitable in competition with the new machine-looms, was recruited from his cottage home and made to work with many others in a huge factory. New towns were built around the new industries and 'England's green and pleasant land' changed overnight to grey streets from which the sun was banished by the belching smoke of factory chimneys. At the same time a parallel technological and scientific revolution was making it more profitable for landowners to farm large fields. The resultant enclosures, often absorbing both the peasant's own small allotment and the commons on which he relied as grazing land for his few units of livestock, forced many farm labourers to turn their backs on the soil of their 'rude forefathers' and feed themselves to the new towns where the machine was master. For the first time great masses of people, underfed and overexploited, were conglomerating in small areas and the slums mushroomed to accommodate and incarcerate them: the industrial proletariat was born.

A large and obvious gap was opening between the few at the top of society (the factory and landowners) and the many unprivileged people at the bottom. This social rift caused a future Prime Minister, Benjamin Disraeli, to describe Britain as a land split into 'two nations' (in his novel *Sybil*, published in 1845). Other 19th-century novelists, such as Charles Dickens, Elizabeth Gaskell and Charles Kingsley, made similar protests about the harm being done to the nation's soul by its reckless rush to industrialisation. But by the time they were writing the process was irreversible. All of this Blake foresaw and he foretold it in his longer 'prophetic' poems: by engrossing himself in the material world man risked paralysis in his spiritual life. A common emblem in Blake's early poetry is the free-ranging child caught, taken from the fields and turned into a chimney sweep.

An engraver by trade, Blake combined the two arts of poetry and painting, illustrating his poems with his own designs. He worked in complete isolation from his fellow poets, and, from some of the remarks made in the margins of his copies of Wordsworth's works, he seems to have felt little sympathy with at least one of them. Probably, in going his own individualistic way he was merely adhering to a dictum of his to which his fellow Romantics would also have subscribed: 'I must Create a System or be enslaved by another Man's'. The liberty of each person to 'create a System' was seen as vital to Blake: only thus could man hope to realise himself and discover wholeness of being, uniting reason with passion, conscious self (the Freudian *ego*) with unconscious (the *id*). The resulting state of psychological well-being would be worth sacrificing the world to gain; and for this reason Blake loathed the idea of making artistic compromise for commercial profit. His individual self was regarded as territory so sacrosanct that Blake even made strong attacks in his poetry against the intrusive and destructive force of his wife's devotion, characterising the latter as a jealously possessive female will.

Whereas the Industrial Revolution alarmed Blake into prognosticating visions of doom, the French Revolution inspired him with hope for mankind's future. Unlike fellow Romantics such as Wordsworth and Coleridge, who after initially supporting the French Revolution turned against it in consequence of the Jacobin excesses and the Reign of Terror (1793), Blake always remained sympathetic to the aims of the revolutionaries. To him, the French

Revolution was a sign that man was at last waking up to his full potential and would finally realise his proper nature, hitherto dormant. If imagination in each man were aroused, mankind would become as one Man, united by sympathy and shaken from apathy and ennui.

Blake's *Songs of Innocence*, from which the first poem below is taken, contains lyrics in which the spontaneous and imaginative response to life shown by children predominates. The oppressive adult world hovers in the background but the children have not yet begun to bend beneath its crushing weight: they remain, in both senses of the word, unaffected.

Holy Thursday

'Twas on a Holy Thursday, their innocent faces clean,
The children walking two & two, in red & blue & green,
Grey headed beadles walked before, with wands as white as snow,
Till into the high dome of Paul's they like Thames' waters flow.

O what a multitude they seemed, these flowers of London town!
Seated in companies they sit with radiance all their own.
The hum of multitudes was there, but multitudes of lambs,
Thousands of little boys & girls raising their innocent hands.

Now like a mighty wind they raise to heaven the voice of song,
Or like harmonious thunderings the seats of heaven among.
Beneath them sit the aged men, wise guardians of the poor;
Then cherish pity, lest you drive an angel from your door.

Holy Thursday, more commonly known nowadays as Ascension Day, celebrates Christ's rising into heaven, 40 days after His crucifixion, and the guarantee thereby given of salvation for the individual human soul. It should be an occasion for great rejoicing and the children in Blake's poem respond accordingly, without any prompting. There is a contrast throughout the poem between the natural hopefulness of the young and the spiritual blindness and implicit hopelessness of their elders.

An unusual feature of the poem is the inordinate length of its lines, most of which are composed of seven iambic feet, with a long pause at the end of each line and a shorter pause in the middle, after the fourth foot. Blake is describing children 'walking two & two', under the watchful eye of their guardians and the long lines of iambic verse suggest to the reader's ear the rhythm made by the long lines of marching children. Furthermore, the metre of these 'fourteeners' (or lines of 14 syllables) is one in which most ballads, or stories in verse, are written. Such ballads often have a 'romantic' or 'fairy tale' subject-matter; and there is an implicit irony in the contrast between the 'innocent' associations evoked by the ballad metre and the implications within the poem of a paradise lost to corrupt and cynical adults.

The word 'innocent' occurs in the poem's first line and reappears in the eighth. Blake apparently wants to stress this quality in his children, reinforced by the 'cleanliness' of their faces. The children have a natural purity, undefiled as yet by experience. Yet there may be another, more sinister reason for their 'clean' faces, suggesting how already the adult world is impinging on their spontaneous lives and threatening to warp their growth. The children, inmates of an orphanage, are resplendent in their 'red & blue & green' uniforms and may have had their countenances scrupulously scrubbed by their guardians before being regarded as presentable at church. In other words, the adults may be more concerned with external appearances (the children's neatness) than with internal preparedness for receiving the spiritual seed of the Christian gospel.

The children's guardians, the 'beadles', are characterised as 'grey headed': they are associated with dull, nondescript colour tones in contrast to the bright primary colours that imbue the children. Furthermore, these old people are identified with the 'wands as white as snow', the sticks which they carry to enforce discipline and order among their juvenile charges. The whiteness here is not that of purity but of 'snow', suggesting the emotional coldness of the church that the beadles serve. The colour contrasts between young and old reinforce the poem's opposition between the untutored gaiety, warmth and living spirituality of the children and the intellectual torpidity of their supposed superiors. The children seem immeasurably nearer to God than their elders; and when they arrive at St Paul's Cathedral they 'flow' into its high dome as if in defiance of the physical law of gravity which keeps the older generation so firmly anchored to the surface of the material earth. The comparison of the children to the 'waters' of the River Thames enhances this impression: Blake seems to be invoking the Thames as an earthly type of the River of Life of the Book of Revelation (a river of which Blake painted a celebrated watercolour), thereby suggesting that the children are moved by the force of an innate spirituality, which is still fresh within them when it has long since been stifled in the beadles.

There are so many of these unwanted urchins that they set up a 'hum', suggestive of a swarm of bees; '*but*', Blake assures us, though these orphans may constitute a pestiferous nuisance to the municipal authorities that are obliged to take charge over them, they in reality manifest a holy and religious presence of which their governors, in their purblindness, remain wilfully and unblissfully ignorant. These 'thousands of little boys & girls' are, in the poet's more penetrating vision, 'multitudes of lambs', each one of them a little living emblem of Christ, the Lamb of God, who brought a message of hope to a world that would not listen.

Biblical references continue in the final stanza. The sound of the children's singing voices is 'like a mighty wind', an allusion to the 'rushing mighty wind' that visited the Apostles at Pentecost, filling them all 'with the Holy Ghost' (Acts, ii. 2–4). This is an appropriate reminder of the victory that both young and old are supposed to be celebrating: the triumph of the spiritual over the material, the soul over the body, as it had been made manifest to the original Apostles through Christ's ascension into heaven ('while they beheld, he was taken up; and a cloud received him out of their sight': Acts, i. 9). The children open their hearts spontaneously to God, in the manner of the early disciples, and the Holy Spirit rushes in. The child is the man's superior and while the latter 'sits' rooted to the clay the former is carried, by the strength of his untrammelled imagination, to another world ('the seats of heaven among') where his artless hymn of praise is echoed and amplified to the proportions of 'harmonious thunderings'.

At the end of the poem the ironic note, which has been sounding softly in the background until now, becomes dominant. The older members of this congregation are labelled as 'wise guardians of the poor'. On the face of it this is a tribute to their age and suggests that their grey hairs have brought sagacity. But the last line of the poem suggests that the 'wisdom' of these wardens of the poor does not spring from any source more sublime than that of mere self-interest. It is not the transcendent wisdom of the ancients that has come to them with the passing years but the narrow wisdom of the self, bent on securing its own ends. For the final line, with its proverbial ring, intimates that charity should only be shown to the less fortunate ('cherish pity') as a kind of life-insurance policy. Only by condescending to bestow one's charity on life's underprivileged can one be certain of attracting the approval of the angels and thus of guaranteeing oneself a niche in the next world. This is the 'wisdom' of the 'aged', as seen by Blake: a wisdom generated by self-concern.

The aged men in the poem are imprisoned in an egoism which prevents them from participating in the spiritual life which is all around them, if they had eyes to see and ears to hear. They wrongly exercise a calculated 'pity', rather than responding to one that springs spontaneously from the heart. Such enslavement to the voice of reason has debased them to a level at which the voice of heaven can no longer reach them. Although there is evidently an enormous gap between what Blake called 'the two contrary states of the human soul' – the 'Innocence' of the recently-born and the 'Experience' of the adults – there is not much doubt in this poem that the victory belongs to the children. Their faces are transfigured with a 'radiance' which their warders cannot quench with their disciplinary switches. Touch them who dare; they are in the lap of the angels. Thus the poem – despite the bitter dregs left by its final ironies – remains predominantly wholesome and optimistic and so finds its place among the other *Songs of Innocence*.

As the child grows into adulthood he finds himself, in Blake's view, more and more enmeshed in the prohibitions of his social environment. Blake condemned state religions and the conventions of morality, holding them largely responsible for the repressed half-lives that adults were forced to endure. He was an early protester against the shackles of conformity, the 'mind-forged manacles' as he called them. 'Sooner murder an infant in its cradle than nurse unacted desires', counselled Blake in his belief that outward-reaching energy – sexual or other (what psychologists might nowadays term *libido*) – would, if thwarted or repressed, turn inward and destroy the individual. This is the situation charted in *Songs of Experience*. The example that follows reveals something of Blake's horror at the way in which the individual soul may be obstructed and disfigured by an authoritarian milieu.

The Garden of Love

I went to the Garden of Love,
And saw what I never had seen:
A Chapel was built in the midst,
Where I used to play on the green.

And the gates of this Chapel were shut,
And 'Thou shalt not' writ over the door;
So I turned to the Garden of Love,
That so many sweet flowers bore,

And I saw it was filled with graves,
And tomb-stones where flowers should be:
And Priests in black gowns were walking their rounds,
And binding with briars my joys & desires.

From the first stanza it is evident that the world of childhood innocence has been left behind. The speaker *'used* to play on the green'. He no longer does so, because a 'Chapel', the edifice of institutionalised religion, has been erected on the ground where he previously roamed at will. The 'Garden of Love' suggests the paradise of childhood, when the child gives his love unthinkingly to those around him; only as he grows into more awareness does he perceive that love unbidden is not always returned. Once this consciousness has dawned on him ('I . . . saw what I never had seen') his image of life as a garden of love collapses. The artificial construction of man's religion is seen to be squatting plumb in the centre ('built in the midst') of the erstwhile play area, like a bird of prey. The 'Chapel' is not new; it has always been there. But this is the first time that it has intruded on the growing child's consciousness. A shadow is consequently cast: life is no longer the endless plain of 'green' and lush fertility that it had hitherto seemed to be. The child is losing his 'greenness': it is a joyless maturity, bereft of promise.

The second stanza reveals more about the nature of man's religion. It is a faith which emphasises the negative rather than the positive aspects of spiritual life, for the chapel has as its motto, 'Thou shalt not'. This is a creed which prohibits rather than encourages; it seeks to curb the child's spirit and his natural inclinations rather than nourish them. Furthermore, the child is not even allowed access to his Father, for 'the gates of this Chapel were shut'. It is as though God had turned His back on the child, and the unnatural growth of the bleak chapel building pushes itself up as a stark symbol of His newly-disclosed indifference.

The adolescent 'speaker' of the poem recoils in horror from the institutionalised adult world that awaits him and turns instinctively back towards the world of sweet-flowered innocence which has hitherto succoured and sustained him. But, of course, innocence once lost can never be recovered. The growing child is increasing in consciousness and he cannot revert to a state of blissful ignorance. As T. S. Eliot says in 'Gerontion', 'After such knowledge, what forgiveness?' The speaker in Blake's poem cannot return to his childhood state because the adult world has impinged upon and impaired his vision, superimposing on his image of a God of love its own image of a God of hate. As the third stanza shows, the intuitive optimism of the child is replaced in adolescence by a mounting despair. Gone are the sweet flowers; tombstones and graves have taken their place. The circumambulating priests, in the name of a dour and distant Deity, occupy themselves in tying up ('binding') the child's natural inclinations ('joys & desires') so as to restrict their development. Moreover, they use the thorny stems ('briars') of rose bushes for this purpose, taking delight in punishing the child for the very nature which God had endowed him with.

The rhythm changes at the end of the poem. The first two and a half stanzas have bounced briskly along on lilting trimeters of fundamentally anapaestic (ˇˇ´) feet. But in the last two lines the rhythm gets bogged down. Blake adds an extra foot: the anapaestic trimeter turns into amphibraic (ˇ´ˇ) tetrameter and the jolly jogging canter of the earlier part of the poem changes to a weary footslog, as if the interfering priests become tangible in the poem itself. The reader is retarded and becomes entrammelled in their weed-infested plots. They bind both the feet of the running child and the feet of the loping poem. The joyous sprightliness of the first part is replaced by a final bemused aimlessness.

Blake's poem is intended as a warning rather than a prophecy; the wilderness need not be the final state. Once one has apprehended and acknowledged the divinity that underlies all of created life the brick chapel and similar ominous, but ultimately inconsequential, appurtenances will evaporate as though they never had been. And the garden of love may miraculously reappear: it is within the capacity of man's divinest attribute, his imagination, to recreate it. Once sprung (or resprung) into action, such vision would enable man to surpass the obstacles of his material environment, to leap into a world of his own creation or recreation, to enrich his own life immeasurably; or, as Blake put it,

To see a World in a Grain of Sand
And a Heaven in a Wild Flower
Hold Infinity in the palm of your hand
And Eternity in an hour.

('Auguries of Innocence')

William Wordsworth (1770–1850)

William Wordsworth elected, in his Preface to the 1802 edition of *Lyrical Ballads*, to 'choose incidents and situations from common life' as subject-matter for his poetry and to dispense with the Augustan style of poetic diction and replace it with 'a selection of language really used by men'. Blake had already shifted the focus of his poetry towards 'incidents and situations from common life' in writing about the generally neglected subject of orphaned wards of state; and in the unadorned simplicity of his diction and the straightforward 'reds & blues & greens' of his imagery he was already anticipating the preference for language pruned of all baroque embellishment that Wordsworth declared.

Wordsworth was aiming at a new sincerity in poetry. 'All good poetry', he said, 'is the spontaneous overflow of powerful feelings'. Thus he located many of his poems in 'common life' and featured peasants, unmarried mothers and village idiots, not from a burning social urge to expose the problems of the downtrodden but primarily because he could communicate 'powerful feelings' in a more authentic manner through the mouths of unrefined, illiterate cottagers than through the cluttered rhetoric of more educated actors. The unschooled agricultural worker spoke straight from his heart: he had not been taught to clothe his naked emotions for the sake of decency. The poet, Wordsworth felt, should cultivate in himself a similar raw simplicity. To this end, Wordsworth rejected the metropolitan 'ant-hill' (as he called London in *The Prelude*) at an early age and sequestered himself in the countryside, where he could study its inhabitants and its manifold natural phenomena.

As he discloses in *The Prelude*, Wordsworth enjoyed a deep-seated belief, impressed on him from his childhood experiences in the Lake District, that there was a 'Presence' underlying, informing and giving unity to all nature. Behind all the depictions of natural scenes in his poetry there rests an awareness of the indwelling Presence of the

Creator, lending meaning to the natural world and to man's experiences. Nature, to Wordsworth, was not mere matter, the logical outcome of scientific cause and effect. Nor was God the remote watchmaker of the Augustans. Wordsworth endeavoured to bring God closer to earth and to lift earth closer to God. He fetched the Creator down from the distant heavens to which the Augustans had consigned Him and installed Him in the natural environment.

To respond to natural scenes with the unalloyed emotion that Wordsworth advocated required a simplicity and lack of sophistication that only peasants or children owned. Thus both of these 'types' – 'stereotypes' even – appear frequently in Wordsworth's verse. Their close relationship with the natural world renders them apt to express sincere sentiments about it.

> Those weeds, and the high spear grass on that wall,
> By mist and silent raindrops silver'd o'er,
> As once I passed, did to my mind convey
> So still an image of tranquillity,

says the 'old man' in Wordsworth's poem, 'The Ruined Cottage'. And this instant rapport between unlettered man and his natural environment Wordsworth was able to cultivate in himself once he had retired to the countryside:

> My heart leaps up when I behold
>   A rainbow in the sky.
>
> ('My Heart Leaps Up')

Realising, like Blake, that the child had an immediate apprehension of his Creator that was denied to the adult, Wordsworth looked back to scenes from his own childhood as sources of inspiration for many of his poems. Certain impressions are engraved vividly on the *tabula rasa* – the receptive new-born mind, uncluttered and empty of innate ideas – which could never be etched with equal intensity on the adult brain. Wordsworth called such impressive moments in the experience of the child 'spots of time'. The task of the mature poet was to retrieve these 'spots' from his childhood memory bank and register them for ever in his poetry. Wordsworth referred to this process as 'emotion recollected in tranquillity'.

In other words, the older Wordsworth could, through the channel of memory, explore dispassionately what the younger Wordsworth had passionately undergone. What was originally a subjective response is 'recovered' for the sake of an objective analysis and synthesis, through the workings of memory and imagination. In this way there is a magical chemistry between the older and younger 'selves' of the poet: an alchemy which helps to distil Wordsworth's clearest insights and most lucid poetry. This distinction between the older and younger self can be demonstrated from some of Wordsworth's 'Lines Composed a Few Miles Above Tintern Abbey', where he refers to himself as he had been 'when first / I came among these hills':

> I cannot paint
> What then I was. The sounding cataract
> Haunted me like a passion; the tall rock,
> The mountain, and the deep and gloomy wood,
> Their colours and their forms, were then to me
> An appetite; a feeling and a love,
> That had no need of a remoter charm,
> By thought supplied.

His 'appetite' for feeding on the natural features of the landscape as a boy was basically sensual, animal, unthinking. But only by the mature man can the 'thought' be 'supplied'. Sifting in tranquillity through the raw material of his fledgeling emotions, the poet can extract what was golden and illuminate it through the conscientiously-acquired skills of his craft.

Yet, as Wordsworth discovered and indeed forecast, such a dependence on personal recollections entailed a serious drawback. For as the poet grew older his memories would fade and with the passing years the child's acuity of vision would be lost, along with the power to write poetry. Wordsworth's poetic career exemplifies his doubts about the diminishing source of poetic inspiration, just as Blake's long creative life illustrates his faith in the eternally active springs of imagination. For Blake it was the impersonal *state of mind* of childhood, not the personal memory of it, that counted, and he was still forging new visions into his old age. Wordsworth's best poems had all been written by the time he was 35, before half his life was done; after that the 'visionary gleam' illuminated him less and less often. The well of childhood memory had run dry.

One of Wordsworth's most vividly captured recollections was his description of daffodils at Ullswater.

I Wandered Lonely as a Cloud

I wandered lonely as a cloud
That floats on high o'er vales and hills,
When all at once I saw a crowd,
A host, of golden daffodils;
Beside the lake, beneath the trees,
Fluttering and dancing in the breeze.

Continuous as the stars that shine
And twinkle on the milky way,
They stretched in never-ending line
Along the margin of a bay:
Ten thousand saw I at a glance,
Tossing their heads in sprightly dance.

The waves beside them danced; but they
Outdid the sparkling waves in glee;
A poet could not but be gay,
In such a jocund company;
I gazed – and gazed – but little thought
What wealth the show to me had brought:

For oft, when on my couch I lie
In vacant or in pensive mood,
They flash upon that inward eye
Which is the bliss of solitude;
And then my heart with pleasure fills,
And dances with the daffodils.

The theme is the poet's isolation from his fellow men and the compensation for this 'loneliness' in a heightened sense of sympathy with nature. The speaker is identified as 'a poet' in stanza 3 and it seems that his status as such is what sets him apart from the 'host' of his fellows and causes the drifting 'loneliness' acknowledged in the first line. Yet his elevation above his fellows who *do* have a defined purpose to their existence is suggested by his comparison of himself to a 'cloud', which implies a certain serenity in his alienation. The poet 'floats on high' over the vales and hills of the world, superior to the ups and downs of life, the alternate fits of optimism and depression to which more ordinary mortals are subject. He has extirpated his earthly roots, has ceased to be moved by the thought of worldly gain and has yielded himself instead to the currents of nature: he is willing to follow wherever the voice of intuition should direct him.

The daffodils are encountered as if they were a 'crowd' of fellow beings. They 'dance' and 'toss their heads'; they constitute a 'jocund company', infecting the poet with their animated 'glee'. He seems to discover a sense of kinship with them that he has apparently failed to find with members of his own species. He enjoys at this moment a feeling of *participation mystique* with nature. It is a moment out of time, an experience that can be perpetually recalled: a 'flash' of insight into eternity. The poem begins in the past tense ('I wandered') but the vision of the daffodils transcends the limitations of time. The daffodils remain with the poet always ('They flash upon that inward eye'): they not only danced in the past but are dancing in the present and will dance in the future as well.

From the image of the daffodils, confined 'along the margin of a bay', the speaker's vision expands to include the whole universe. The 'golden' radiance of the daffodils is cosmically reflected by the 'twinkling' of the stars of outer space. The 'waves' also partake of this cosmic gaiety. The poet's participation in the 'dance' of the daffodils indicates his involvement in the whole dance of the cosmos: his sense of oneness with Creation. He is flooded with a sensation of well-being, which comes to him in a 'flash', a split second out of time that is nevertheless eternally present to him whenever on his couch he lies. Then, when the pressures of life in the workaday world cause the poet to retire 'in vacant or in pensive mood', the daffodils revive in his memory to display to him once more their song and dance of sheer *joie de vivre* and rekindle in him the urge to join in their celebration. Their image on his 'inward eye', the door of visionary perception into eternal truths, more than compensates for the lack of significance in his mundane life that strikes his outward eye, leaving it 'vacant', hollow and depressed. The daffodils have offered the poet the assurance that true wealth is intangible, invisible and, ultimately, inexpressible; and this recognition furnishes him with an inexhaustible store of positive inner energy with which to combat the baleful, negative presentiments of a world without purpose.

The experience recounted in this poem is one of those 'spots of time' which, Wordsworth elsewhere insisted, constitute the most significant moments in life. They are instants of epiphany, immediate inundations of spiritual illumination (Wordsworth's 'heart' even now 'fills with pleasure' at the recollection) and Wordsworth captures them in words which are similar to those used by a later, Jesuit poet, Gerard Manley Hopkins, when relating a similar mystic euphoria:

> In a flash, at a trumpet crash,
> I am all at once what Christ is.
> > ('That Nature Is a Heraclitean Fire and
> > of the Comfort of the Resurrection')

This same feeling of joyful entrance into a timeless world, beyond the margin of the bay, of a coalescence between sensual and extrasensual perceptions to produce a blinding awareness of 'God, who is our home' (Wordsworth's expression in his 'Immortality' ode), underlies all the 'bliss' which informs Wordsworth's vision of the daffodils. It is the bliss of religious certitude, a preview of the peace which passeth understanding.

In his Preface of 1802 Wordsworth vowed to employ only the 'language really used by men'. This pledge is perfectly fulfilled in the next poem.

She Dwelt Among the Untrodden Ways

> She dwelt among the untrodden ways
> > Beside the springs of Dove,
> A Maid whom there were none to praise
> > And very few to love:
>
> A violet by a mossy stone
> > Half hidden from the eye!
> – Fair as a star, when only one
> > Is shining in the sky.
>
> She lived unknown, and few could know
> > When Lucy ceased to be;
> But she is in her grave, and, oh,
> > The difference to me!

There is nothing arcane or archaic about the diction in this poem. Every phrase, with the possible exception of the rather poetical 'dwelt' for 'lived', might occur naturally in normal discourse today, nearly two centuries later, including the euphemistic 'ceased to be' for 'died'.

The opening stanza introduces the idea of the intrinsic loneliness of the human condition. 'Lucy' passed a life of modest seclusion, her charms and virtues not attracting any particular notice. Nobody praised her and few people loved her; only with her demise is her true worth felt for the first time when, ironically, it is too late to give her her just reward of attentive affection. Three allusions to a state of virginity are made in this first stanza. The country tracks that pass Lucy's dwelling-place are unused, 'untrodden'; the water that she lives beside is the pure source, the 'springs' of the River Dove; and she herself is a 'Maid'. The countryside, for all of its unpolluted advantages over the city, does not, it seems, provide fulfilment to its inhabitants. Both the pathways and the maiden are unfrequented.

This impression is deepened in the second stanza by the two sharp images between which it is divided. Firstly, the girl is pictured as a vividly beautiful but unassuming and retiring flower, the 'violet', which prefers to hide itself in the shade of a rock, rather than display its attractions in the full light of day. The image suggests a girl who is by nature unassertive: one who may well pass unremarked if there be a more forceful personality in close attendance to cast a shadow over her. The 'mossy stone', in other words, may refer to the dominant and self-assured 'leader' of the Romantic revolution, Wordsworth himself, the 'moss' indicating the experiences of life that have already accrued and adhered to him; and the 'half-hidden' violet may suggest his sister Dorothy, his constant companion in life, but in whom the overbearing quality of her brother's presence induced occasional nervous disorders. The image suggests a woman naturally self-effacing, whose gem-like qualities might pass unrecognised in a world predisposed to be attracted only by all that glistens.

In the second of this stanza's images the girl is envisioned as a solitary star shining in the heavens. The suggestion of the girl's physical beauties embedded in the previous 'violet' image is superseded now by the impression of a spiritual radiance that emanated from her. The poem's one variation of rhythm occurs here, at its half-way point: the initial iamb becomes a trochee. At the same time the stresses fall on two long vowels, so that, musically and thematically, the verse here soars to its sublimest point:

Fáir ăs ă stár.

Just as mariners navigate by a particular star, the speaker of the poem has guided himself by the 'shining' example of 'Lucy' (the name comes from the Latin word *lux*, meaning 'light').

Lucy was 'unknown' during life, and the nuance of 'know' in the sense of 'carnal knowledge' is possibly another discreet reference to Lucy's virginal state: she was 'unknown' to, and by, men. They are unaware of Lucy's demise not only because of the spiritual distance that has separated her from them ('few *could* know'): they are constitutionally incapable of esteeming Lucy, alive or dead, blind as they are to her hidden treasures. In other words, Lucy is, at the time of her death, not simply a physical but a *spiritual* virgin: the spring of her love, in all senses of the word, remains untapped. The world is too busy looking around itself to see the 'star' above: its eyes, too long accustomed to operating on a horizontal plane, cannot make the adjustment to the vertical plane of spiritual values and thus Lucy lives and dies anonymously. The observation is similar to that expressed in another of Wordsworth's poems:

> The world is too much with us; late and soon,
> Getting and spending, we lay waste our powers.
>
> ('The World Is Too Much With Us')

Such quiet beauty as Lucy has been endowed with is likely to be trampled under the world's foot before it can attract the eye of its appreciation.

Wordsworth expresses an intensely 'private' emotion in a way to arouse sympathy among the 'public' at large. Lucy, as he says in another poem, is now beyond the reach of anyone's pity or love:

> She neither hears nor sees;
> Rolled round in earth's diurnal course,
> With rocks, and stones, and trees.
>
> ('A Slumber Did My Spirit Seal')

Ultimately, in the 'Lucy' poems, he acquiesces in the fact of death as life's 'natural' termination: Lucy has become a part of the planetary pattern. The poet may grieve but he does not despair.

John Keats (1795–1821)

John Keats knew of the proximity of life and death and the neighbourhood of joy and pain: the transport of pleasure 'turning to poison while the bee-mouth sips'. Despite his epitaph to himself as 'one whose name was writ in water', Keats's popularity since his death at 25 has been more consistent and enduring than that of any of his fellow Romantics. Perhaps his premonition of an early end impelled him to value all the more feverishly the various physical sensations that are superabundantly present in his verse, packing each line with richness just as the 'Autumn' of his ode 'fills all fruit with ripeness to the core'.

The profusion of sensuous imagery in Keats's poetry is not merely a paean to the pleasures of the flesh: it is often the most effective means Keats has at his disposal for communicating a half-glimpsed eternal 'truth'. It is his way of trying to express the abstract by the concrete. The intangible reality can be represented by something of tangible beauty, since

> 'Beauty is truth, truth beauty', – that is all
> Ye know on earth, and all ye need to know.
>
> ('Ode on a Grecian Urn')

Keats is not a poet who is content to linger among sensual delights for their own sake. He is well aware that the physical appetite palls and that only spiritual food can supply perfect repletion. Bodily delights soon satiate; as he remarks in this 'Ode on a Grecian Urn', they leave

> a heart high-sorrowful and cloyed,
> A burning forehead and a parching tongue.

Earthly pleasures may be 'sweet' but unearthly ones are 'sweeter', since one can never have too much of them. In art, Keats suggests, are found prototypes of the perfect world where soul and body may discover utter contentment. Thus he claims that the 'unheard' melodies 'played' by the musician engraved on the side of the Grecian jar enrich the beholder more than if he could actually hear them. The physical ear tires quickly, the spiritual ear is tireless:

therefore, ye soft pipes, play on;
Not to the sensual ear, but, more endeared,
Pipe to the spirit ditties of no tone.

Art, in this perspective, is an anteroom to the next world, bodying
forth intimations of the immortality that awaits one there.

The poet–artist, though, is a hybrid being: he may have one foot in
the next world but the other foot remains firmly rooted in this. Thus
there are days, as Keats himself experienced, when the 'enchanted
portals open wide' and the poet's imagination can travel effortlessly to
'that far seat of bliss'. But there are other times when the strain of
wrestling with intellectual issues at the very edge of human sentience,
when the act of engaging in 'solitary thinkings, such as dodge /
Conception to the very bourne of heaven', is a far more exhausting
and unrewarding enterprise. To enter this ideational world the poet
must become dead to the earthly one. To 'pry 'mong the stars, to
strive to think divinely', he must endeavour to escape from his body
and 'feel uplifted from the world'. At times such as these it seems 'rich
to die'.

Periodically in his poetry Keats addresses death with apparent
yearning, asking it to 'take into the air my quiet breath'. This has led
some critics to accuse him of a death-wish, pointing to the rash
walking tour of Scotland in 1818 – a rain-sodden ramble that
provoked Keats's fatal tuberculosis – as further evidence of his
seeking a premature end. In his poetry however, Keats is not seeking
a termination to his existence but a furtherance of it when he calls upon
death to relieve him of all the incongruities, banalities and failures
that he must suffer in this earthly world in which pathetically
impotent human beings can do little more than acquiescently 'sit and
hear each other groan'. The desire for death usually implies the
aspiration, however unrealistic or unrealisable, of finding refuge in an
imagined and flawless world of sensual and spiritual joy without end.

The poem which follows is a sonnet which, produced early in his
career, first proclaimed Keats to be an authentic poetic voice, another
of the 'Great Spirits' which 'on earth [were] sojourning' at this critical
moment in literary history.

On First Looking into Chapman's Homer

Much have I travell'd in the realms of gold,
And many goodly states and kingdoms seen;

Round many western islands have I been
Which bards in fealty to Apollo hold.
Oft of one wide expanse had I been told
    That deep-brow'd Homer ruled as his demesne;
    Yet did I never breathe its pure serene
Till I heard Chapman speak out loud and bold;
Then felt I like some watcher of the skies
    When a new planet swims into his ken;
Or like stout Cortez when with eagle eyes
    He star'd at the Pacific – and all his men
Look'd at each other with a wild surmise –
    Silent, upon a peak in Darien.

The sonnet is woven on the orthodox frame of octave and sestet. The octave offers a description of the poet's extensive 'travels' and of his ultimate arrival at the fabled kingdom of Homer; while the sestet proceeds to a revelation of the emotional transformation that this last voyage wrought on him.

The poem launches on a trochaic foot before falling into a preponderantly iambic rhythm ('Múch hăve Ĭ trávĕll'd ín thĕ réalms ŏf góld'), thus stressing the quantity of voyages that the speaker has undertaken ('Múch'). Like the Spanish conquistador Cortez, whom he introduces towards the end of the poem, he is a well-seasoned traveller, not easily amazed by new discoveries. Like Cortez, too, he seems to have visited the 'realms of gold', the fabulously rich Aztec and Inca civilisations of Central and South America, ravaged by the Spaniards. But Keats's ravaging, if he is guilty of any, has occurred, like his travels, on the metaphorical plane: he has plundered not countries but books, filling his mental coffers with other men's immaterial treasures. The metaphorical intentions of his travels are evident from the poem's title: 'looking into' indicating a first sampling of a particular book, in this instance the epics of the classical Greek poet Homer in the English version of George Chapman, the Elizabethan poet-translator.

Good books are presented as 'realms of gold', lands loaded with precious minerals. Reading, in other words, is a richly rewarding experience: it emancipates the mind and introduces it to foreign 'states and kingdoms', to a variety of concepts that are strange to it. Reading is an exploration of the human topography rather than the physical landscape; and one is just as inexhaustible as the other. The poet refers initially to some of the literary works he has already navigated. He has sailed 'round many western islands', inhabited by poets who hold a tenancy from their lord, Apollo. This allusion to the Greek god of music and beauty, with its suggestion that all later 'western' European poets have been inferior by comparison with those of the classical age, prepares for the imminent panegyric to Homer.

The Greeks, Keats suggests, achieved a perfection in art that is unlikely ever to be surpassed. This is an unusual compliment to 'classical' times from a 'Romantic' poet, for the two concepts of classicism (a preference for order, symmetry and stasis) and Romanticism (an uninhibited, dynamic and often disorderly venturing into forbidden territories) are generally deemed to be diametrical opposites. Yet Keats manages to reconcile the spirit of classicism with that of Romanticism by infusing the former with the vitality of the latter; so that the rock-solid world of Greek statuary and the permanence of the Parthenon pulsates with new life and takes its place serenely and harmoniously in the ever-expanding universe of Romantic vision. Classical art is not cold, dead and irrelevant but has an essential, tutelary role to fulfil in the comprehensive Romantic conception of life. It is not a hermetic world, sealed off in the seclusion of the distant past but a 'wide expanse' without evident limits, an unconfined area which the poet talks of in the present tense, a region whose air is not musty and stale but ever 'pure' and 'serene'. Classical art, in its perfection, offers a perpetual refuge of calm and blissful repose for the spirit that finds itself ground down by the cares of this troublous world: a theme which Keats was to take up again in his 'Ode on a Grecian Urn'.

Once he has reached those purer heights, the reader finds himself revived by the balmy breezes that encompass him (the long vowels in 'breathe its pure serene' enhance the sensation of a hardly-won tranquillity). For Keats, the attainment of this summit is the high point in a long series of literary expeditions: the El Dorado towards which the traveller has long been obliquely sailing. Having, in the octave, described his introduction to Homer as the climax of his bookish meanderings, Keats proceeds in the sestet to elaborate the effects that the achievement of his goal have produced in him. It is, above all, his feelings ('Then *felt* I . . .') at this climactic moment in his life that he is at pains to analyse. But emotional states are by their very nature intangible and evanescent. To give a clearer idea of what his feelings were on the discovery of Homer, Keats develops two similes and these constitute the entirety of the sestet.

The first simile is short and relatively 'undeveloped'. The poet compares his activity as a bibliophile to that of an astronomer, a 'watcher of the skies'. Both occupations necessitate a withdrawal from the world of everyday affairs and a concentrated search for signficant signs in a more abstract world: stars, as well as books, may offer clues to the origin and purpose of man's existence. Keats wants to suggest the feeling of intense excitement that the astronomer, accustomed as he is to perusing the same old celestial system day after day, undergoes when an entirely new planet unexpectedly appears at the trim of his vision, his 'ken'. It is, quite literally, a whole new world which manifests itself. For both astronomer and poet the perspective of the universe shifts perceptibly as a result of their discoveries. The cosmos is not something static, immobile and defined once and for all in star charts: it is dynamic, animated and instinct with unpredictable possibility. The 'new planet' does not merely drift into the astronomer's lens: it actively 'swims' to get there. Similarly, the universe of books is not composed of so many volumes of dead leaves gathering dust on library shelves. Death and dust may, as the Elizabethan poet Thomas Nashe said, have 'closed Helen's eye' but they have not succeeded in stopping up the mouth of the poet who wrote about her in his *Iliad*: his voice rings out 'loud and bold' as ever. Just as mariners guide their course by looking heavenwards to the stars, so we ordinary mortals may navigate our passage amid the reefs and whirlpools of life by observing the lights left behind by 'great spirits' such as Homer.

The second simile brings us back to earth again but develops the implications of the limitlessness of the universe and the limitations of man's puny understanding of it. But it is optimism and not pessimism which is uppermost in the 'wild surmise' with which the explorer Cortez greets the vision of a new, unsuspected ocean that suddenly presents itself to his predatory gaze on a Central American mountain top. Keats no more than glances, in his mention of Cortez's 'eagle eyes', at the destructive aspects of the Spaniard's character, which introduced pillage and genocide to the civilisations of Central America. He is primarily concerned to illuminate the more 'Romantic' features of Cortez's profile: the restlessness which urges him ever onward and which shows up again in many of Lord Byron's heroes, the indomitable pride of the 'eagle' which recognises nothing

uperior to itself and the irrepressible energy which manifests itself
n at a moment of apparent quiescence. Cortez 'stares' rather than
zes at the new ocean, as if challenging its right to be there. The
alisation that the world contains another enormous and uncharted
sea, with the possibility that there are other continents and other seas
beyond that, is something for which reason has not prepared this
hard-bitten adventurer and 'all his men'. The band of explorer-
brigands, like the solitary reader, has been rewarded for its efforts
with a vision which takes away its breath and leaves it 'silent'. The
caesura which follows this initial trochee retards the progress of the
last line and reinforces the suggestion that, for Cortez's band as for
Keats, the moment of discovery is a moment out of time. Such a
moment often comes as a blinding light, temporarily depriving the
recipient of the use of his physical senses (as in St Paul's conversion on
the road to Damascus). Keats is trying to make the reader share a
sensation which, by its very nature, cannot be defined in words and he
does this by suggesting how men of other 'professions' would react,
gazing with vertiginous wonder and ecstasy from the 'peaks' of their
endeavours, towards the ever-opening vistas extending endlessly
before them.

It is in this vision of life as an ever-unfolding experience that the
poem is intrinsically Romantic. Pope had recounted a somewhat
similar experience to Cortez's when he referred to a mountaineer who
had climbed what he believed to be the highest Alpine peak only to
find that 'Alps on Alps arise', that he had conquered but a negligible
surface area on the infinite face of the globe. But Pope's rationally
enlightened vision communicates a sense of weariness rather than
elation at the prospect of a creation too deep and too broad to be
measured by the limited faculties of man. To Keats, however, such a
prospect is sublime rather than depressing. It fulfils his vision of life as
a continually expanding experience, charged with a promise which
not even death can disappoint. Reason once given the lie and put
firmly in its place, it is possible to 'surmise' wildly. There are no
limits, no horizons, no frontiers: the questing spirit, the imagination,
may, as the hero of Keats's *Endymion* demonstrates, journey ever
onwards, as high as the moon and as deep as the ocean bed, in
anticipation perhaps of the glorious freedom it will enjoy once death
has finally released it from the body's pentitentiary.

George Gordon, Lord Byron (1788–1824)

In many ways George Gordon, Lord Byron was not a Romantic at all. A radical in politics (he died defending the cause of Greek independence against the Turks at Missolonghi), he was nevertheless an archconservative in poetry who insisted that Pope and the Augustan versifiers had been wrongly maligned by Wordsworth and his fellow Romantics and that consequently 'we are upon a wrong revolutionary poetical system . . . not worth a damn in itself'.

A measure of Byron's admiration for Pope can be taken from his first major poem, *English Bards and Scotch Reviewers* (1809), written entirely in couplets and in the biting tone of Augustan satire. The satiric vein remained a recurrent feature of Byron's poetry, and was perhaps the result of his aristocratic approval of *sang-froid* and his upper-class impatience with some of the more exaggerated enthusiasms expressed by poets of more bourgeois extraction (for example, Robert Southey's deification of the pathetically insane monarch George III, which Byron ridiculed in *The Vision of Judgement*). In Byron's poetry reason has not been entirely thrown over in favour of passion and imagination.

Byron, however, has supplied the world stage, both by his life and in his poetry, with its major Romantic protagonist: the 'Byronic' hero. Developing hints from the beetle-browed villains of Ann Radcliffe's two most celebrated Gothic novels – *The Mysteries of Udolpho* (1794) and *The Italian* (1797) – Byron gave deeper shades of ambiguity to what society stigmatises as 'evil'. First appearing in *Childe Harold's Pilgrimage* (1812) and reincarnated in many subsequent poems, the Byronic hero is a man whose superior intellect and passionate devotion to a chosen way of life renders him aloof from his fellow men and condemns him to a life of loneliness. He is a being whom no social fabric could comfortably accommodate; and, like Byron himself once his love-affair with his half-sister Augusta Leigh had become known, he is ostracised from his native land and condemned to spend the rest of his days in exile, anticipating the fate of Dr Frankenstein's unwanted monster in Mary Shelley's novel. The Byronic hero is generally darkly handsome and may generate an unsolicited passion in women whom he encounters in his wanderings but for whom he, with his soulful eyes ever fixed on the one deep well of his primary sorrow, can kindle not a spark of answering affection. With only his anguish for company, despising all those who compromise, existing above and beyond the strictures of good and evil, the Byronic protagonist is the Romantic hero *par excellence.*

Of all the Romantic poets, it is Byron who exhibits the richest variety of 'voices': sometimes trenchant, sometimes tender, now beseechingly gentle, now bitterly reproachful. His diction ranges from the crudest vernacular to the most lyrically sublime. Here is one of his more encomiastic effusions.

She Walks in Beauty

She walks in beauty, like the night
   Of cloudless climes and starry skies;
And all that's best of dark and bright
   Meet in her aspect and her eyes:
Thus mellow'd to that tender light
   Which heaven to gaudy day denies.

One shade the more, one ray the less,
   Had half impair'd the nameless grace
Which waves in every raven tress,
   Or softly lightens o'er her face;
Where thoughts serenely sweet express
   How pure, how dear their dwelling-place.

And on that cheek, and o'er that brow,
   So soft, so calm, yet eloquent,
The smiles that win, the tints that glow,
   But tell of days in goodness spent,
A mind at peace with all below,
   A heart whose love is innocent!

One of the distinctions of Romanticism is its inclination to idealise. Only too conscious of the great disparity between the world's grotesque miscreations and the perfect compositions ideated by the intellect, the Romantic poet never ceases to hope that one day the earthly form will match the heavenly one, believing against all the evidence that total equilibrium, full harmony and perfect peace are not the prerogatives of heaven alone. In Byron's poem the idea of such perfection informs every line. The rhythm itself (iambic tetrameter) unfolds gently, serenely, while the diction employed ensures a constant flow of mellifluous vowel sounds: for instance, the three diphthongs and the one long vowel in the line 'Of countless climes and starry skies', guaranteeing that each stressed syllable is savoured to the full. The sound of the verse itself augments the impression of the beauty amid which the lady walks. It murmurs in soft seductive sibilance ('Which waves in every raven tress, / Or softly lightens o'er her face'), meandering through the consciousness like the wisps of hair traversing the lady's countenance. At last man's warring elements have found stasis and equilibrium in the presence of this anonymous 'she'.

The lady walks not on earth but in the domain of the stars, swathed in the cloak of an incandescent 'beauty'. She is at once identified with 'all that's best', her ideal beauty reconciling all the contrary dark and light aspects of human nature, her becalmed facial expression ('aspect') beaming forth goodwill and equanimity. In her person the human being is no longer split into two contentious factions: the 'dark' of the instinctual self (the *id*) and the 'bright' of the reasoning personality (the *ego*). She is an exemplar of psychological wholeness, shining forth to despondent mankind like a moral lighthouse. In her perfect equilibrium is seen the reconciliation between heaven and earth. The impeccable combination of her dark and light aspects (her 'shades' and 'rays') the poet sees as the gift of some heaven-borne 'nameless grace', inducing in him a feeling of religious awe. The woman has nothing unhallowed about her: even the physical shell of her bodily 'dwelling-place', the temporary abode of her 'sweet' unsullied thoughts, is 'pure' and 'dear', as if the very strength of her chastity has transmuted earthly flesh into a substance of essential and precious divinity. The speaker resembles the enraptured Orsino in Shakespeare's *Twelfth Night*, who expresses a similarly ebullient estimation of the virtues of his beloved:

Here comes the Countess; now heaven walks on earth.

The woman is purged of all sublunary elements: she is Eve before the Fall. She can nurture only 'innocent' passion, all her days in this world are endured with a 'goodness' that knows no evil, her glazed forehead is never ruffled or wrinkled by the emotions of anger, envy or discontent. The reader may justly wonder whether Byron is talking about a 'real' person at all. The 'she' in the poem, that is to say, may not represent any beauty of the poet's terrestrial acquaintance but may simply indicate a projection of his postulated soul-mate, the woman he spends his waking life in quest of, the one who will bring him peace. In Jungian terms, she may be the *anima*, the female opposite needed by each male to make him whole, the perfect partner for whom he never ceases to search. She is the subject of H. Rider Haggard's novel *She*, the woman who promises to make man psychically complete, the quarry who by her nature is unattainable in this flawed existence.

Byron does not always wax so lyrical about the fair sex. His satire *Don Juan* introduces a woman who is very much of the earth, earthy: the fiery Julia, 'married, charming, chaste, and twenty-three':

> Her glossy hair was cluster'd o'er a brow
> 　Bright with intelligence, and fair, and smooth;
> Her eyebrow's shape was like the aerial bow,
> 　Her cheek all purple with the beam of youth,
> Mounting, at times, to a transparent glow,
> 　As if her veins ran lightning; she, in sooth,
> Possess'd an air and grace by no means common:
> Her stature tall – I hate a dumpy woman.

Julia has a 'cheek all purple' and 'lightning' in her veins and her face and hair have been artfully arranged into a veritable mantrap. There is nothing unknown about Julia, no 'nameless grace'. She exudes the all too 'transparent glow' of sexual desire. The poet concludes his description of Julia with a reference to her physical height – 'her stature tall' – in spite of which the impression lingers that this is a woman whose aspirations and ambitions gravitate most definitely downwards. Despite her vertical elevation, she is impelled by horizontal inclinations. *Terra firma* is her natural habitat not 'cloudless climes'. She lives in a world of concrete realities; to more abstract concerns she remains indifferent. As an afterthought the speaker of the poem adds his *cachet* of approval to the woman he has just presented, declaring roundly in the emphatic couplet that he dislikes plump women. This reinforces – through the bizarre insertion of the colloquial word 'dumpy' – the premise which the speaker has been trying to establish throughout the stanza: that, no matter how glamorous the exterior, woman is after all no more than mere flesh and blood.

Of these two Byronic extracts, the first would probably be nominated as the more 'Romantic', while the second harks back to its antecedents among the 18th-century satirists. Byron's tone is more sublime, more 'emotional' in the first extract; while in the second it is drier, more detached, altogether more 'reasonable'. The first poem describes woman in all her transcendental potential; the second delineates her in all her human frailty. There is compassion in both portraits. A key word in the first poem is 'tender'. The poet's vision of the lady is bathed in soft light. It is an expression of enthusiasm but kept within the bounds of reason; it is no eulogistic frenzy written under the influence of an intoxicating idealism, when, as Swift remarked, 'a man's fancy gets astride on his reason . . . and common understanding as well as common sense is kicked out of doors'. Byron's tone of appreciation is as restrainedly 'soft' and 'calm' as the lady herself, his poem as undemonstratively effulgent as the nimbus that envelops the object of his praise. It is well-tempered acclamation throughout.

The second piece, while focusing on a woman of a very different stamp from the first 'beauty', is, in its way, no less complimentary. Byron's view of woman is comprehensive: having illustrated her capacity to function as man's spiritual beacon, he now demonstrates her competence to act as earth mother, as man's open-hearted and compassionate sexual comforter. In these two extracts it is neither extreme veneration nor extreme revulsion towards women that predominates but recognition and respect. Excitement is moderated by common sense. Ultimately it is a healthy regard for woman in all her complexions that distils from Byron's poetry and not a misogynistic compulsion to keep her – whether from exaggerated deference or inordinate repulsion – at arm's length.

Percy Bysshe Shelley (1792–1822)

There was one other domain of earthly endeavour whence the Romantic attended events which would transform the human soul: the field of revolutionary politics. The poet who displayed the most interest in the possibilities of change through social upheaval was Percy Bysshe Shelley.

Shelley's intellectual powers outshone those of the other Romantics. The complex of ideas and images enmeshed in 'Ode to the West Wind' and the philosophical dialectic of *Prometheus Unbound* display the control of a mind of extraordinary energy. The following discussion will limit itself to one of Shelley's shorter poems of social concern, while indicating that this was only one area, the political, among several others – philosophical, psychological, theological – over which Shelley stretched his considerable talents. Shelley was the Romantic poet most moved by the injustice of the British political system, which divided its constituents into rulers and ruled. 'The man of virtuous soul commands not, nor obeys', wrote Shelley in an early poem, 'Queen Mab', continuing to assert that

> obedience,
> Bane of all genius, virtue, freedom, truth,
> Makes slaves of men, and, of the human frame,
> A mechanised automaton.

Man sold not merely his body but his soul into slavery by agreeing to work for hire; and Shelley saw it as his life's duty to stimulate his less conscious brethren to throw off their chains. He desired nothing less than the abolition of the monarchy and the overthrow of religion: all life's evils stemmed from morality and the crippling effects its restraints engendered in the human spirit (Shelley's kinship with Blake's outlook and outrage is manifest). Once the tyranny of king and priest had been exterminated, Shelley affirmed, 'A garden shall arise, in loveliness / Surpassing Eden'.

Shelley's analysis of the origins of the social evils of his day underwent several revisions during his brief career, though his essential conviction that the existing structures played a primary role in generating those evils never wavered. The poems he produced at various stages in his life present no absolute solution or remedy, but rather constitute resting points in a tireless and ever-ongoing search for the source of human misery and hence its cure. In his maturity Shelley came to realise that the existing social framework was merely a mirror of man's own inward nature and that to reform the one he must first transform the other. The fundamental fault, that is to say, lay not so much in social forms and institutions but in the character of the men who had created those phenomena. So, in order for society to be revolutionised, the soul of man must first be reforged.

It was thus the duty of the poet and the artist to produce works of beauty, the contemplation of which would produce illumination and conversion in the hearts and souls of the less creative. Shelley remained profoundly assured of the poet's divine function as healer of social ills, despite his awareness that his own poetry extended to a readership that was so small as to be almost negligible. In his refusal to admit defeat and in his perseverance in doggedly perfecting his greatest works in the certain knowledge that only a few would read them, Shelley exemplifies what Dr Johnson called (in another context) 'the triumph of hope over experience'.

Shelley believed that man too readily bore the yoke of the traditions that were thrust upon him in his youth. 'Men of England, wherefore plough / For the lords who lay ye low?' begins one of his later poems ('Song to the Men of England'). In his own life Shelley had refused to compromise with traditional morality or to accept any injustice as ordained and therefore ineluctable. Sent down from Oxford after six months because he refused to retract a pamphlet on *The Necessity of Atheism*, which denied that the existence of God could be proved – a position he embellished in 'Queen Mab' by slating the Deity as 'A vengeful, pitiless and almighty fiend' – he went on to demonstrate his contempt for received moral tradition by putting into practice his beliefs about the bourgeois institution of marriage. Having run off with Mary Godwin, he afterwards invited his first wife Harriet to participate in the new ménage as a sister. His unorthodox matrimonial views assured Shelley of the antipathy of British upper-class society, attracting towards him an animosity that his suspected revolutionary political opinions could only reinforce. Like Byron, he was forced by the moral indignation of his peers to spend the last years of his life in exile.

Although he was 'sent down' from England, just as he had been expelled from Oxford, in punishment for remaining true to his personal convictions, Shelley never ceased to concern himself with the plight of his countrymen, particularly those 'bees of England' who drudged all their lives in pain and fear so that 'ungrateful drones' among the ruling class could 'drink their blood'. Although immured in exile abroad, Shelley was keenly aware of the troubles at home during the years that followed. The aura of repression that hung around the British government in the war years of the century's first decade and a half did not dissipate once its *bête noire* Napoleon had been despatched to the utter isolation of St Helena. For the fear remained throughout Europe that the French Revolution had spread a malignancy which, though it had been lanced by the Duke of Wellington at Waterloo, might lie dormant for years before eventually erupting with virulence, to the accompaniment of a crashing and crumbling of ancient thrones and gilded monuments. It therefore behoved all those with interests vested in the *status quo* to be very careful and supremely suspicious. For whenever two or three among the lower orders were gathered together on a street corner or in an attic room, conspiracy, it was feared, might well be afoot.

Discontent in the immediate post-war years of the second decade of the 19th century had two aspects: political and social. Political unrest was concentrated mainly among the middle class, many of whose members were newly rich in goods and property but anciently deprived, under the British constitution, of the right to vote and thus of any say in the running of the nation's affairs. The clamour for 'reform' of parliament became increasingly insistent after the return of peace, and was finally rewarded with the First Reform Act of 1832, which enfranchised the urban bourgeoisie and gave them the share in the direction of national policy that they had long sought. Social unrest was less easy to appease. Among the illiterate masses the concept of 'one man, one vote' was not so preposterous as it seemed to their 'betters'. But such hankerings after political power proved to be premature and the middle classes who had once encouraged these hopes among their proletarian counterparts turned against their erstwhile accomplices, dampening the flames they had previously fanned, once the 1832 Reform Act had given them what they wanted. Only the Chartist movement of the 1840s demonstrated, for those who had eyes to see, that the working classes would not always consent to their exclusion from the nation's parliamentary councils. But at the time the attention of the proletariat was centred on a more gnawing grievance: the problem of hunger.

The end of the Napoleonic Wars released an army of ex-soldiers onto an employment market that could not accommodate such an influx. To the misery of unemployment was added the intense hardship wrought among the poor by the Corn Law of 1815. Designed to protect the interests of the British landed gentry by prohibiting the importation of cheap foreign corn, the various Corn Laws effectively reduced the capacity of the working man to provide his family with sufficient bread. By 1819 unemployment and starvation were the spectres that haunted many a working-class family, uncushioned as they were by any social-welfare mechanism. The artificially high price of bread only augmented their anxiety and gave an edge to their awareness of the supreme unconcern of their parliamentary masters. It was at a meeting at St Peter's Fields, Manchester in 1819 that the

British army, ordered into reaction by the local authorities, perpetrated among the milling masses a slaughter which tarnished, at a stroke, the glorious reputation it had carried home from the Continent four years before. It was in ironic recognition that the same martial spirit which had inspired the victory at Waterloo was responsible for such savage repression at home that the tragedy in Manchester became known as the 'Peterloo' massacre. Triumph in foreign fields and butchery on home ground were recognised as being two sides of the same conservative coin. And it was against such a background that Shelley produced this piece of poetical polemic.

England in 1819

An old, mad, blind, despised, and dying king;
Princes, the dregs of their dull race, who flow
Through public scorn – mud from a muddy spring;
Rulers who neither see, nor feel, nor know,
But leech-like to their fainting country cling,
Till they drop, blind in blood, without a blow;
A people starved and stabbed in the untilled field;
An army, which liberticide and prey
Makes as a two-edged sword to all who wield;
Golden and sanguine laws which tempt and slay;
Religion Christless, Godless – a book sealed;
A Senate – Time's worst statute unrepealed, –
Are graves, from which a glorious Phantom may
Burst to illumine our tempestuous day.

Although 'England in 1819' is a sonnet, it follows neither the Petrarchan nor the Shakespearean archetype. There is no volta or change of direction in it, unless the uncertain hope expressed in the last one and a half lines be considered as such. The 14 lines are composed of one single sentence – with many interjections – of which the main clause does not appear until the penultimate line. 'These are graves' is the asseveration of this main clause and the poem's first 12 lines consist entirely of an exposition of what 'these' are that are leading so pointedly deathwards. The poet enumerates the diverse social abuses evidenced in the England of his day, piling image upon insufferable image, spewing forth the lava of his accumulated wrath. The sense of pent-up anger is reinforced by the abbreviated syntax in the subject catalogue, the omission of conjunctions and relative pronouns (' – mud from a muddy spring', ' – a book sealed', ' – Time's worst statute unrepealed'), as if the speaker were too enraged to bother with his gammar.

The technique of heaping one heinous example upon another until the whole top-heavy structure seems in danger of crashing down – indicative of the predicted end for his native country with its lopsided social structure – is rehearsed in the poem's opening line, where five pejorative adjectives are launched before the reader gains cognisance of the particular object of so much scorne: the 'king' himself, the senile and lunatic George III. Shelley begins his diatribe with the image of the demented king because it follows that a malady in the head of the realm must inevitably and adversely affect all the lesser members of the corporate state. All the subsequent images in the poem enforce this idea: once a malaise has set in at the top, the whole organism shudders and sickens. So the second line makes opprobrious reference to the king's heirs, indicating that one cannot hope for a purging or a rejuvenation of the old institutions from the forthcoming generation. The Hanoverian line of the monarchy, imported to Britain in 1714, is drained of any vitality it might once have possessed. Only the 'dregs', the leftovers of this German family which was never very sparkling to begin with (a 'dull race'), remain to poison its subjects. Shelley is probably alluding here to the Prince Regent, later George IV, a notorious *bon vivant*, loose in his morals and lax in his sense of public duty.

The insane monarch and his licentious heir, insensitive to the 'public scorn' that their antic behaviour triggers, seem the living examples of a system doomed to fall beneath the burden of its own decadence. The monarchy in 1819 is 'mud from a muddy spring': the origins of the divine institution are obscure enough, its present representatives and their right to enjoy the formidable power and privilege that headship of the realm invests them with are even murkier. Shelley extends his condemnation to the entire ruling class of Britain in the next three lines of his poem. The country's 'rulers' are discerned as insensate monstrosities paralysing the social body that they should theoretically animate. They cannot 'see' or 'feel' their subjects but are blindly ignorant of their needs. Parasitically they feed on their people, draining them of energy and life, 'leech-like' sucking the country dry until it faints anaemically from loss of blood. Although there may once have been a symbiotic relationship between rulers and ruled, a complementary and mutually self supporting cohesion between palace and people, the careless egotism of the present incumbents of the chambers of power, Shelley suggests, threatens the whole delicate fabric with the disintegration that had already been witnessed across the Channel thirty years before.

Shelley passes, in line 6, to the victims of this social inequity. What happens when the aristocracy neglects its duties towards the lower classes and merely bleeds where it should lead? The 'untilled' fields lie fallow, dearth succeeds to sufficiency and the people 'starve'. The untilled field is an image of the sterile kingdom that Britain has become, in Shelley's eyes, by 1819. But the phrase carries more connotations than this one simple idea. The people, after all, are not only 'starved' but 'stabbed', the alliteration reinforcing the point that the two crimes, visited on a hapless proletariat by a governing class hardened in its cruelty, are inseparably linked. The poem thus also seems to make allusion to the recently perpetrated massacre at St Peter's Field. That particular 'Field' is 'untilled' because it is in the heart of the city of Manchester and is not strictly speaking a field at all. Whether in the country or the town, Shelley implies, the labouring class finds itself deprived of nourishment and relentlessly harried to death by the class that in earlier, happier times acted as its patron and guardian. As for the military arm of the rulers, it is an army licensed to kill wherever it discovers a manifestation on behalf of freedom. But the practice of such 'liberticide' and the taste for slaughter it has fostered with the sanction of the authorities may, predicts Shelley, sharpen the army until it becomes 'as a two-edged sword' which, in Shakespeare's words, 'returns to plague the inventor'. Having accustomed itself to a legitimised 'prey' among the lower orders, the army's appetite may be whetted for richer pickings among the ranks of those who 'wield' or direct it.

Shelley now moves on in line 10 to define the legal realities of Britain in this era. He does so by using colour motifs: the laws are 'golden' and deep red ('sanguine'). There is a certain amount of irony in this device. The 'golden rule' is that of moderation; and 'sanguine' is synonymous with 'optimistic' or 'constitutionally hopeful'. But the application of the verbs 'tempt' and 'slay' to these statutes of prepossessing appearance indicates that they, like the army, have a double edge. The epithet 'golden' therefore suggests that the legal system can be bought with money and its 'sanguine' appearance thus takes on a more sinister hue: that of the blood of its ill-fated victims.

The fair exterior of the British constitution conceals a governing class, rich in power and privilege, working to suborn the law to its own ends of 'liberticide' and exploitation of the goldless masses.

If the lower classes are goldless, the upper classes are 'Godless', as line 11 makes clear. The Holy Word is locked up in a sealed book: no one is permitted to question the state's interpretation of the Bible. This is reminiscent of Blake's vision of the Church as simply another tool of oppression in the hands of the Establishment, the 'Chapel' with ' "Thou shalt not" writ over the door'. From the state religion Shelley moves to the state legislature: the 'Senate' or Parliament, which offers the spectacle of 'Time's worst statute unrepealed'. The institution of parliament, in Shelley's eyes, would have been better abolished long ago, since it serves only the interests of a selfish minority and not the needs of the entire nation.

With this glance at the seat of government Shelley's summary of the present state of his nation ends. At this point, in the final subsidiary clause of his sonnet sentence, Shelley admits a ray of hope with the vision of a revolutionary spectre which may arise from the ruins of the imminent catastrophe. The trochaic stress on 'Burst' and the subsequent caesura draw attention to the suddenness with which this new world might rise from the ashes of the old; but at the same time the vision remains conditional. It 'may' arrive; it is not certain. The present days are stormy, disordered and dark ('tempestuous') and though we are assured that such turmoil cannot last much longer, what will follow in its stead remains unclear. The 'Phantom' of liberty may be no more than that: an illusory hope which man continues to chase but which always eludes his grasp. On the whole, the unreliability of the final revelation scarcely lightens the overall atmosphere of doom that the previous 12 lines have combined to produce.

This quavering blend of hope and uncertainty is a suitable note on which to conclude this survey of the Romantic era. With the emancipation of the inner terrain, the eternally unfolding psychological landscape, as legitimate territory for poetical theme and inspiration, the young Romantics wrote in a fever of excitement in an attempt to body forth all the conceits, ideas and imaginings that had been left unsaid by generations of their predecessors. It was, to use an image from Keats's 'Ode to a Nightingale', as if someone had suddenly thrown open

> magic casements, opening on the foam
> Of perilous seas, in faery lands forlorn.

Although the inner journeys the Romantics subsequently embarked on – often sinking, like Shelley's Jupiter, 'Dizzily down, ever, forever, down' – were indeed 'perilous', threatening at times to unleash from some obscure dungeon of the mind a 'frightful fiend' like the one that causes Coleridge's ancient mariner to 'walk in fear and dread', they did not flinch before the challenge. It is no wonder that those Romantics who lived beyond the age of 30 give the impression of being by that time on the verge of mental exhaustion: their 'genial spirits fail', in Coleridge's words, and inspiration, having poured itself into the creation of some of the most enduring landmarks on the English literary scene, is spent for good.

The short time span of Romantic creativity represents a watershed in the history of English poetry. No poet has since been able to recapture that sense of unsophisticated self-assurance implicit in Wordsworth's 'first fine careless rapture', the exhilarating and unself-conscious spontaneity that enabled the Romantics to rise so effortlessly to heights of conceptual awareness and metrical accomplishment. 'Already with thee!' cries Keats in surprise when, in 'Ode to a Nightingale', he discovers himself, despite his earlier complaint that 'the dull brain perplexes and retards', uplifted painlessly from the sordid earth and transported, like his hero Endymion, to the company of the 'Queen-Moon . . . Clustered around by all her starry Fays'. For once in his history the poet had managed to wed himself, however temporarily, to the sacred source of his inspiration.

9 Victorianism: Arnold and Tennyson

'Victorianism' is an umbrella term covering the major part of the 19th century: a century unique in the diversity of its achievement and the boundless energy with which it pursued its goals. Queen Victoria ruled for a 64-year spell (1837–1901) which saw Britain transformed from a predominantly agricultural and slow-moving society into an uneven patchwork of forgotten fields and overcrowded industrial conurbations in which struggle, strife and rapid change were endemic. The 19th century witnessed the resuscitation of the austere Puritan work ethic of the 17th century – this time adopted with verve and vigour and applied with remorseless ingenuity to the technological possibilities set rolling by the steam-engine.

By the 1840s Britain was going through an irreversible process of industrialisation, the second stage of the Industrial Revolution that had begun with the introduction of steam power to cotton manufacture at the end of the 18th century. Now it was the railways, and the potential for instant communication and cheap transportation that they offered, that pushed the Industrial Revolution into its most dynamic phase. The wildfire growth of the factory system at home gave a new impulse to the colonial instinct and encouraged the exploitation of underdeveloped overseas lands (and their peoples) for their raw material and their market potential. By the end of the century, in consequence, Britain had acquired an 'Empire' of the first magnitude, over which Queen Victoria presided as its tight-lipped, indomitable empress.

The century, to those of an entrepreneurial bent, seemed an occasion of sterling possibilities. Fortunes were there for any who were industrious, or unscrupulous, enough to reach out and grasp them. In those spirits, though, who were less attracted by the golden glow of the stock market the Victorian period engendered much heart-searching and some inner turmoil. Where was God amidst all this scrabbling after the nuggets of Mammon? Had the smoke belching from the new factory-towns of Birmingham, Manchester and Leeds obscured the face of the Almighty and furnished a suitable screen for the nefarious activities of His restless creatures? Generally speaking, it was not the factory managers and entrepreneurs (the Bounderbys and Dombeys of Dickens's novels) who asked questions such as these but the writers, many of whom could not help admiring the achievements of their business-like brethren while at the same time nursing a deep uneasiness about where such 'Progress' might ultimately lead. The Victorian era is notable, among other things, for the shifting perspectives in its relationship with God.

Victoria's Britain, having demolished its tariff barriers by dismantling the Corn Laws and hoisting high the flag of Free Trade, ushered in the heyday of brute capitalism, gilt-edged and guilt-free. It also evidenced the peregrination of the evangelical spirit through every walk of life, observed the phenomenon of full churches and witnessed acts of parliament against the desecration of Sundays. It was an age of infinite variety. Never had women been so shielded from an awareness of the 'facts of life' as they were under the tutelage of a queen who refused to recognise the existence of lesbianism; but for the less privileged the awakening could be rude. A woman unfortunate enough to be born of working-class forbears might find herself drifting towards the prostitution maelstrom of the capital city, while her cosseted middle-class compeer would be practising arpeggios on a grand piano whose legs had been decently 'trousered'.

It is especially their sanctimonious attitude towards sex – as something relegated to the darkest corner of life – that has given the Victorians their reputation for hypocrisy. For, at the same time that the stereotype was being propagated of the Victorian woman as a self-sacrificing virtuous creature suffering sex as a matrimonial duty – the 'Angel in the House', as she was dubbed by the poet Coventry Patmore in 1854 – the brothels of London were proliferating and the practice of keeping an extramural mistress was becoming the rule rather than the exception among the upper classes. The received image of the Victorian father as a stiff-collared, dark-suited man, sternly disciplining his wife and children (the Mr Murdstone of Dickens's *David Copperfield*) is a stereotype, no doubt, but one to which many a 19th-century paterfamilias strove to conform. By compartmentalising his emotional life he could leave himself plenty of free time and surplus energy for the pursuit of his commercial interests. The Puritanism of the 17th century was reborn, wearing a frock coat and a top hat and rattling along on rails of iron at 50 miles an hour.

The age was rich in invention and creation and for sheer output it is without historical parallel. Fervent activity was generated not only in the industrial world but in the moral, religious, philosophic and artistic spheres as well. Victorian man was taking a deep breath and pulling himself up by his bootstraps. So the age that saw some of the worst exploitation of man by his fellows in human history also saw the first steps taken towards a truly democratic system of government, answerable to the needs and responsible for the welfare of all its citizens.

The development of a sense of social responsibility dates from the early years of Victoria's reign, and even earlier. Jeremy Bentham and the Utilitarians brought some of the 'enlightenment' of the 18th century into 19th-century Britain with their insistence that all social problems could be solved through the application of a rational outlook. Where they differed from their 18th-century forbears, however, was in the wider sweep of their purview. No longer was it considered sufficient to promote the well-being of the more fortunate classes while leaving the uneducated masses to fend for themselves or reap their reward hereafter but the 'greatest happiness of the greatest number must be preferred'. Thus while Victoria was yet uncrowned (Bentham died in 1832, five years before Victoria's accession) democratic motions were already being enacted. Slaves had been freed and the First Reform Act of 1832 had been passed. Once she assumed the throne, she presided over a wide range of reforming legislation – Factory Acts, Mines Acts, Education Acts, Parliamentary Reform Acts and many others – which bore witness to the underlying dynamic for amelioration of the British system which is one of the more praiseworthy facets of Victorian Britain. The evangelical impulse that drove the missionary David Livingstone to carry the Gospel light to the 'dark' African continent and that prompted Prime Minister William Gladstone to comb the London streets for prostitutes whom he might personally rehabilitate, lay behind much of the reforming legislation of the century.

The working-class populace which witnessed Victoria's funeral in 1901 was an urbanised community, irreversibly embarked towards the universal suffrage of both sexes that was to follow twenty years later: a literate world with its own newspapers and its own artists and writers (D. H. Lawrence, son of a miner, was to publish *Sons and Lovers* 12 years later). Victorian Britain, for all its deserved reputation for hypocrisy, had its redeeming features. It had a conscience that found expression not only in words but in Acts. 'Now that we have given them political power we must not wait any longer to give them education', said W. E. Forster, the Education Secretary, when the 1870 Education Act was passed to provide compulsory education for all Britons. Another Victorian imbued with evangelical zeal in the field of education was the poet and critic Matthew Arnold.

Matthew Arnold (1822–88)

Matthew Arnold was the son of Thomas Arnold, headmaster of Rugby School, and Matthew imbibed from his schooldays a sense of the educated man's responsibility and moral obligations to his culture and society. For culture and society, in Thomas Arnold's opinion, were interdependent: literary activity was the breath of social life. From his father's magisterial inculcation of the moral purpose in literature sprang Matthew's perception and promotion of the 'high seriousness' towards which all literature should aspire and for the want of which he castigated established literary figures such as Chaucer. In Arnold's view a writer could not afford to be frivolous, or even indulge his comic genius too much, for society depended on his exposition of the proper standards and decencies to hold it together.

The evangelical spirit was at work in Arnold. His father was one of the leading lights in the Broad Church movement and opposed the ideas and teachings of the High Church or Anglo-Catholic movement, founded in Oxford by John Henry Newman. Matthew himself held the job of inspector of nonconformist schools for 35 years. His evangelical enthusiasm is evident particularly in his prose works; such as *Culture and Anarchy* (1869), where he attacks the dominant English middle class (the 'Philistines') for their complacency, their obsession with material goals and their neglect of the spiritual or 'cultural' dimension. As a consequence of another of his prose works, *The Function of Criticism* (1864), it has often been claimed that Arnold raised literary criticism to the status of an academic discipline that it has enjoyed ever since.

His poetry tends to be more reflective, ruminative, even nostalgic than his prose: the hectoring tone is softened into a sad, sometimes whimsical melancholy. Because of his sense of the writer's 'mission', his belief that his own weightier purpose was to 'inculcate intelligence', Arnold abandoned poetry writing after ten years (in 1859) to concentrate on the highly serious activities of criticism and instruction. The poem of Arnold that follows is one of his earliest, written in memory of a girl he met in Switzerland in 1848. As an eminently respectable Victorian, endowed with a social purpose, Arnold soon conquered his passion for her and settled instead for the more 'sensible' proposition of marriage to a judge's daughter. Reason triumphed over instinct; but the possibilities of what might have been, the delights that might have been discovered along 'the road not taken' (in Robert Frost's words), may have continued to haunt Arnold beyond the year in which this poem was written (1849).

Arnold saw poetry as 'a criticism of life': a poem could present or re-present experience in an ordered and dispassionate manner, extracting meaning from one's contact with the incidents and accidents of life, so that one is 'no longer bewildered and oppressed by them'. Poetry operates as a balm, enabling both writer and reader to relax and unravel their tangled emotions and to live 'in harmony with them; and this feeling calms and satisfies as no other can'. Beneath Arnold's poems lies his theory of their therapeutic value.

To Marguerite – Continued

Yes! in the sea of life enisled,
With echoing straits between us thrown,
Dotting the shoreless watery wild,
We mortal millions live *alone*.
The islands feel the enclasping flow,
And then their endless bounds they know.

But when the moon their hollows lights,
And they are swept by balms of spring,
And in their glens, on starry nights,
The nightingales divinely sing;
And lovely notes, from shore to shore,
Across the sounds and channels pour –

Oh! then a longing like despair
Is to their farthest caverns sent;
For surely once, they feel, we were
Parts of a single continent!
Now round us spreads the watery plain –
Oh might our marges meet again!

Who ordered, that their longing's fire
Should be, as soon as kindled, cooled?
Who renders vain their deep desire? –
A God, a God their severance ruled!
And bade betwixt their shores to be
The unplumbed, salt, estranging sea.

There is no need of any knowledge of the first 'Marguerite' poem
('Isolation. To Marguerite') for an understanding of this, the sequel.
The four stanzas, permeated as they are with the binding image of the
archipelago of human individuals scattered haphazardly across the
immense ocean of life, render the poem as self-contained and as
'insular' as one of the human souls whose solitary fate it mourns. Thus
the abruptly startling 'Yes!' of the opening may be understood as
either the subsequent assertion following from a preceding argument
(in the earlier poem) or simply the eruption into speech of a
ruminative process that has hitherto been internal. In either case the
exclamatory monosyllable provides a sign that the poet is about to
voice a conclusive insight that he has just drawn from his experience
of human life.

The controlling image is that of the expansive sea punctuated by a
myriad of 'dot'-like islands. The place of humanity ('We mortal
millions') in this *mise en scène* is not revealed until the fourth line; a
tension of interest is set up by the preceding phrases until the delayed
main clause discloses that it is *we* who are the 'enisled' ones, marooned
in our individual selves amidst the mutely teeming ocean swell of
creation. Arnold, albeit unconsciously, seems to anticipate Darwin's
argument that human life has its origins in the sea. He even (in the
third stanza) foreglimpses the theories of geologists about the drifting
apart of the earth's continents ('surely once . . . we were / Parts of a
single continent'). At all events, his poem reflects another trace of the
evolutionist undercurrents of his day. Man has undergone some
change since the dawn of creation; and, whatever he might once have

been in a more primitive state, he is now securely locked into the fortress of his own insular ego-consciousness.

Arnold's poem, however, suggests a divine intervention in human development which is strictly absent from the hypotheses of the scientists. It is almost as if man's unhappy insularity has been decreed by an irascible Maker. Watery gulfs have been 'thrown' among human beings, severing them one from another according to the mystifying will (or whim) of a Creator (or Dictator). Arnold returns to this theme of divine culpability in his final stanza. Meanwhile he goes on to develop the ramifications of this 'enislement'.

The 'straits' that occur between us are 'echoing': the only response we hear to our cries is our own reverberated voice. We are like 'dots', almost invisibly insignificant phenomena amid the infinite vastness and supreme indifference of the sea of life that flows silently past. Our sheer numbers – an impression reinforced by the alliteration in 'mortal millions' – render us, as individuals, yet more insignificant. And life itself is unknowably 'wild', proceeding towards some unfathomable, 'shoreless' end. We, as individuals, can instinctively 'feel' a correspondence with our fellows, with whom we are prohibited from making any real contact. The 'sea of life' tantalises us by simultaneously encouraging and preventing traffic between us human islands: its 'enclasping flow' both embraces and enchains us. Our 'bounds' or limitations are 'endless' in time rather than in space: we seem destined never to escape from our island imprisonment across the inviting but alienating sea. Arnold's *cri de coeur* is the voice of spiritual estrangement, growing stronger in Victorian Britain as the Industrial Revolution advances: it is the impotent acknowledgement of an inexorable sundering from both God and fellow man.

The suggestion of an inward vacancy, of something unprovided in the heart of man, is elaborated in the second stanza. The islands have 'hollows', which are intermittently illuminated by the natural world, reminding mankind of what life used to be like at the dawn of its creation, when the nightingale 'divinely' uttered sounds of heavenly harmony, in the days before men had incurred God's displeasure and engineered their exclusion from such a paradisiac state of being. All was orchestrated into a symphony of love. Nowadays only the vestiges of such easy being-to-being communion remain; and they are activated, at best, spasmodically. The romantic imagery of 'the moon', 'nightingales' and 'starry nights' implies that such spasms may occur when the feeling of 'love' is stimulated in man's bosom. At such a moment he longs to unite, not just sexually with one, but spiritually with all of his fellow beings. On these rare occasions interpersonal communication may still occur, though it is restricted to a vocal act, the islands effusively babbling to one another from the bases of their seclusion:

> lovely notes, from shore to shore,
> Across the sounds and channels pour.

The exclamatory 'Oh!' that introduces the third stanza parallels the initial 'Yes!' The rational implications embedded in the latter, implying a logically-arrived-at assertion, are now abandoned for an ejaculation that is purely emotional. A longing from the 'farthest caverns', the most hidden recesses of the psyche, is provoked when the individual is reminded of the sterile inadequacy of his self-containment.

This yearning may express a political desire for the reversal of the industrialising process and a reversion to the simpler state of feudal England. However, the very inability of the poet and his 'islands' to put into exact words the nature of their craving suggests that it is not reducible to a simple 'romantic' desire for peasant life. The biblical myth of the loss of Paradise, the luscious garden where 'nightingales divinely sing', also informs the vision. In psychological terms, the contrast between the 'single continent' of the past and the small, scattered islands of the present suggests the process of *individuation* or progressing from a fluid state of semi-awareness towards full consciousness and realisation of oneself as a unique being. This is what the Adam and Eve story relates in a more picturesque way. Adam and Eve gain knowledge by eating the forbidden fruit; where hitherto they had wandered through the Garden of Eden in blissful ignorance, with no real sense of where their own identities ceased and those of the birds and flowers and trees began, henceforth (after the Fall) they possess a distinct and inalienable – though painful – self-consciousness. It is an irreversible process.

Man must bear the burden of his knowledge, the self-awareness that seems to be more of a curse than a blessing, to the end of his days. However strong his yearning to relapse into a simpler state of less conscious existence where his 'marges', the 'bounds' of his individual identity that he 'knows' so well, can 'meet' and mingle with other undefined and undefining beings, it is a futile wish. From its beginnings, in the first 'Marguerite' poem, in an expression of purely personal chagrin stemming from his inability to establish a permanent love relationship with a particular woman, Arnold's plaint, in 'To Marguerite – Continued', has broadened into a lament for the universal loneliness he perceives as man's inevitable lot in the hyperconscious state to which he has now evolved. 'No man is an island', John Donne had declared in the socially dynamic Britain of the early 17th century. Arnold, conversely, is suggesting that in the Britain of rampant capitalism, where only the cash nexus binds one man to another, Donne's proposition can no longer hold. Each man is an island. The singular 'sceptred isle' of Shakespeare's Britain has fragmented into a myriad of tiny consciousnesses.

The hope that is conjured in stanza 2 is soon lost in the 'despair' of stanza 3. The hint that communion might after all be possible is submerged beneath the monotonous 'watery plain' of daily life. What the moon ushered in as a tantalising promise at the start of stanza 2 subsides as an alliterated moan at the end of stanza 3:

Oh might our marges meet again!

The pattern of 'kindling' and subsequent 'cooling' is woven by the two central stanzas. Stanza 2 sets blazing the hope of an end to isolation, while stanza 3 immediately dampens this ill-considered optimism. The equation of the individual's 'deep desire' with 'fire' reinforces the sexual undertones of the poet's lament. It is, however, not merely sexual disappointment that the poet is bewailing, though that may have been the original spur to his intent. There is a broader malaise, physical and metaphysical. It is at this point that Arnold returns to the suggestion made by 'thrown' near the beginning of the poem, and implicit throughout, that man is not responsible for the position of cold insularity in which he finds himself. Arnold projects this hitherto half-suppressed resentment onto the surface of his poem by asking directly, 'Who ordered' this woeful state of affairs, 'Who renders vain their deep desire?' The switch from past to present tense in the interrogatives shows that this injustice was not simply perpetrated at some far-flung point in time but goes on being committed into the foreseeable future.

Having posed the question, Arnold loses no time in providing it with an answer:

A God, a God their severance ruled!

Not man, but man's Creator is responsible. God is the tyrant, decreeing 'severance', placing between men the curse of individual consciousness, forsaking them on the desert islands of their egos. The poet's spleen seems hardly able to contain itself and he repeats and emphasises the identity of the guilty One ('A God, a God . . . !') in bold blasphemy. Moreover, the extent of man's spiritual alienation is underlined by Arnold's use of the indefinite article to qualify the Almighty: He is no longer the one God, single and indivisible, of the Bible but merely 'a God', one among many, about whose identity the poet is uncertain.

In accordance with this God's incomprehensible but immutable bidding the gulf between men has come into being: the 'unplumbed, salt, estranging sea'. Man, in his isolation, is surrounded by the prolific world of nature, whose purpose he cannot fathom ('unplumbed') and whose otherness renders him bitter ('salt'). Having heaved himself onto the island strand of his ego-centred desires, he has cut himself off from his fellows and from the fount of life itself which the sea epitomises. It is not surprising that the image of the sea with which the poem so resoundingly closes should be rich in ambiguities. Rhetorically, the sea bears the brunt of the poet's immediate anger. Unable to pinpoint *the* God on whom to offload his sense of injustice, he focuses his hostility on the surrounding waters. At the same time he feels the promptings of a primaeval urge to abandon his hard-won consciousness and submit himself to the 'enclasping' arms of his once-native element; to feel the waves of unconsciousness once more lapping over him, soothing him into rest. The pull of the sea ('I must go down to the sea again, to the lonely sea and the sky', in the words of John Masefield's poem 'Sea-Fever') is perhaps, first and foremost, a desire to unshackle oneself from the burden of too much consciousness.

Therefore, the pejorative rhetoric with which the sea is charged in the poem's last line is only *verbally* negative. The bitter and disparaging suggestions contained in these three adjectives are considerably counteracted by, perhaps even drowned beneath, the rhythmical and musical beauty of the line: the assonance of 'unplumbed', its repeated 'ŭ' and nasal sounds reproducing the noise of the waves reverberating through hollow caves, the 's' alliteration in 'salt, estranging' and the long diphthong in the latter word suggesting the breaker crashing on the shore and its subsequent retreat to the accompaniment of many sucked-back pebbles. So sense is at odds with sound: the remonstration that the words carry semantically is offset by their musical quality. In this ambiguity rests the resolution of the poem. We are invited to respond to life's mysteries with more intuition, not to leave everything for analysis under the clear light of consciousness. Our response to experience must be more comprehensive, engaging all our faculties, those we have borne from the origins of our species (the Jungian 'collective unconscious') as well as those more recently acquired through the education of our minds.

Has what Arnold called the 'magic' of poetic style, the incantatory quality of rhythmic verse, enabled the reader to absorb and resolve the conflicting emotions that form the 'content' of the poem? It is impossible to determine whether the harmony and order implied by the verse and its organising sea image offer adequate compensation for the vision of a world governed by a vindictive or absent Godhead. The poem rests in precarious balance, swaying between the beauties and assurances offered by the unconscious or intuitive self, of which the sea is a perpetual remainder and reminder, and the doubts and demented depressions projected in the crucible of the over-refined intellect.

Alfred, Lord Tennyson (1809–92)

Alfred, Lord Tennyson became Poet Laureate upon the death of Wordsworth in 1850 and, because he consequently wrote poems for state 'occasions', he became mistakenly identified by the generation that succeeded him as an 'Establishment' poet: a man who might conjure up facile sentiment, might even don the mask of fashionable despair, but who was fundamentally 'safe' in his opinions. Even before his laureateship Tennyson was offering evidence of his orthodoxy in lines such as:

> Forward let us range,
> Let the great world spin for ever down the ringing grooves of change.

This advice, from 'Locksley Hall' (1842), seems to place Tennyson by the side of those other apostles of 'Progress' of the Victorian era.

Similarly, when the theories of the evolutionists burst upon an alarmed public, Tennyson seemed able, on the face of it, to absorb and adapt them to an optimistic vision of progress in which man would pass through ever more refined material states into a purely spiritual existence: a 'divine far-off event', the conception of which promised to restore clarity to the muddied waters of the soul stirred up by the Darwinists and their materialistic emphasis on the brutal origins of man ('the greater ape', scoffed Tennyson, in mimicking their reductive style and criticising their obsession with the physical).

The vision of Tennyson held by the Edwardian and Georgian writers who followed after him tended to be the simplified one of a man who pandered to the tastes and palliated the fears of his bourgeois paymasters. Harold Nicholson charged that Tennyson had been 'afraid of death, and sex, and God', and that therefore his poems, while recognisably musical in sound, were built on a spurious emotional basis. And later W. H. Auden, after admitting that Tennyson had 'the finest ear, perhaps, of any English poet', went on to assert, 'he was undoubtedly the stupidest'. This summary depreciation of Tennyson as a composer of tinkling verses devoid of any substantial content gained so much currency in the earlier part of the 20th century that it still encourages prejudicial views of him today, despite the trend of more recent criticism to rehabilitate him. Whenever the name of Tennyson is dropped it still, as often as not, summons up the image of a man of facile optimism, shallow emotion and fixed belief ('stiff in opinions', in Dryden's phrase): the image, in short, of the 'typical' Victorian gentleman.

Tennyson, as Poet Laureate, often gave his compeers what they wanted to hear, whether it were prophecies of the progress of a beneficent industrial empire or the glorification of British feats of arms in the service of this same empire:

> Right through the line they broke;
> Cossack and Russian
> Reeled from the sabre stroke
>   Shattered and sundered.

But Tennyson was not utterly dazzled by the pomp and splendour of Britannia in her heyday. For at the same time that Britain was spreading the fruits of her technological revolution to other parts of the world (railways to India, for instance) the scientists who had made such a revolution possible were beavering away at home and threatening to bring the Victorian social mansion crumbling about their heads. Tennyson's endeavours to assimilate the ideas of the evolutionists into an optimistic vision of mankind's development towards a completely spiritual state were not always successful. For, if what scientists were saying was true and man had indeed developed across vast aeons of time from primitive life forms, then the traditional view of a human species fashioned and implanted on earth by a concerned and almighty Creator was called into question. Tennyson was alert, like Arnold, to the implications of infernal loneliness that such a vision proposed for man, as the offshoot of an accidental rather than a deliberate genesis:

> There rolls the deep where grew the tree.
> O earth, what changes hast thou seen!
> There where the long street roars hath been
> The stillness of the central sea.

There is something disquieting about the 'stillness' of this 'central sea'. It may be from such a womb of static unconsciousness that man, along with other forms of life, has sprung, almost as an aberration.

Tennyson's ruminations on the possibility raised by his scientist contemporaries that God may have had no hand in man's creation, and therefore need feel no concern at his dissolution, carry him at times to depths of profound depression:

> He is not here; but far away
>   The noise of life begins again,
>   And ghastly through the drizzling rain
> On the bald street breaks the blank day.

Like the previous quatrain this comes from *In Memoriam*, a poem which Tennyson wrote in memory of his friend Arthur Henry Hallam, who died suddenly in his youth and with whom Tennyson had felt an intense kinship. The loss of Hallam, so unexpected and without any conceivable purpose in a divine schema, pushed Tennyson towards pessimism and at the same time provoked some of his most thoughtful poetry, while providing T. S. Eliot with enough ammunition later to charge Tennyson with harbouring 'emotion so deeply suppressed . . . as to tend rather towards the blackest melancholia'. In such a mood the poet can only see men as marionettes, obeying automatic and godless rhythms. And this 'darker' side to Tennyson's reflectiveness is never entirely absent from even his most apparently complacent statements:

> Follow Light, and do the Right – for man can half-control his doom.
> ('Locksley Hall Sixty Years After')

Man can, at best, 'half-control' but not fully direct his destiny; and it is the gloomier word 'doom' that Tennyson chooses to express the notion of fate.

Pessimism fuelled Tennyson's best poems and is never far from the surface of those often dismissed as too optimistic or chauvinistic. Behind the heart-stirring imperatives of 'The Charge of the Light Brigade' –

> Honour the charge they made!
> Honour the Light Brigade,
>   Noble six hundred! –

beneath the glittering splendour of the red-coated heroic dash for immortal glory, there is a surreptitious but resonant grumble:

> Someone had blundered.

The loss of Hallam gave a deeper dimension to Tennyson's poetry. Out of his grief grew his own qualified optimism to 'faintly trust the larger hope', the rather tentative Christianity that leavens much of his later poetry. More than for most other poets, the past for Tennyson is enshrined in an auroral glow and it is a past which throughout his poems he manages to evoke through the poignancy of simple diction and unaffected imagery:

> the tender grace of a day that is dead
> Will never come back to me.
> ('Break, Break, Break')

> Doors, where my heart was used to beat
> So quickly.
> (*In Memoriam*, VII)

Born apparently with no natural sensitivity to music, Tennyson learnt to discriminate the sounds of the English language to the point where Auden, so contemptuous of Tennyson intellectually, felt obliged to concede the exquisiteness of his 'ear'. This ear combined with Tennyson's intuitive rhythmic sense ('Half a league, half a league, / Half a league onward') to issue in some of the most unforced yet forceful 'sound pictures' in English poetry – the onomatopoeic effect of the harsh 'ă' vowel at the crisis of 'The Lady of Shalott', for example:

The mirror cracked from side to side.

In that 'cracked' we both hear and envision the splintering of the lady's world.

Tennyson stands out as the most eminently Victorian of the 19th-century poets in the consistent strain of his verse. A haunted though generally unspoken anxiety that human life may after all be no more than a brief flash in a cosmic darkness –

somewhere in the waste
The Shadow sits and waits for me –

(*In Memoriam*, XXII)

is assertively overridden by the poet's will rather than by his reason, to assure himself that mankind is striding forward to some God-directed higher purpose:

Evolution ever climbing after some ideal good.

('Locksley Hall Sixty Years After')

The latent pessimism that lurks near the heart of this Victorian poet and which might incline the man towards a life of listless inertia (the temptation succumbed to by his 'Lotos-Eaters') is overcome by a strenuous effort of the will, directing him to avoid the sin of sloth and to don the work habits of Christian endeavour. The idea of an instinctual struggle within man between dynamism and inertia was implicit in the theories of the evolutionists. A concept articulated by Sigmund Freud and expounded and developed later in the 20th century by Herbert Marcuse, this theory holds that man is torn between the regressive desire for rest, peace and oblivion (the

Thanatos or death-urge – the 'endeavour of all living substance to
return to the quiescence of the inorganic world', in Freud's words)
and the progressive impulse towards exploration, development and
fulfilment of the self (the *Eros* or life-instinct). The same conflict is
exhibited in one of Tennyson's early poems, 'Ulysses' (1842), in
which, typically, the sirens of pessimism and doubt are quelled, the
temptation towards supineness is spurned and the hero resolves,
despite his advanced age, never to abandon the quest for further
knowledge and wider experience, dedicating himself perpetually

> To strive, to seek, to find, and not to yield.

It is in this heroic resolution to keep working for, and believing in, a
noble end, despite the surrounding chaos in which man's little life is
located, that Tennyson seems so quintessentially Victorian.

Crossing the Bar

Sunset and evening star,
  And one clear call for me!
And may there be no moaning of the bar,
  When I put out to sea,

But such a tide as moving seems asleep,
  Too full for sound and foam,
When that which drew from out the boundless deep
  Turns again home.

Twilight and evening bell,
  And after that the dark!
And may there be no sadness of farewell,
  When I embark;

For though from out our bourne of Time and Place
  The flood may bear me far,
I hope to see my Pilot face to face
  When I have crossed the bar.

This poem was written in 1889, three years before Tennyson's death.
His familiar poetic gifts – judicious vowel choice and metrical finesse
– are in evidence: the long 'ō' and 'ãr' in 'moaning of the bar' suggest
the sound the sea makes when breaking along the sand bar at the

entrance to a harbour, and the last short line of each stanza suggests
the finality, and the peace, that death will bring after the long toil of
life –

>   And may there be no sadness of farewell,
>   When I embark.

The contrast in the poem is between the limitations of this life and the
'boundlessness' of the next: locked in by the land which he inhabits
and of whose clayey nature he perforce partakes, the speaker cannot
hope for a full knowledge or understanding until he is released from
his physical – and geophysical – prison, by death. The sea thus
signifies the medium which will carry him over to the greater liberty of
the next world. That Tennyson is still not overwhelmingly confident
that death is such a desirable end may be inferred from

>   And after that the dark!

Death is the last and the greatest adventure; but what succeeds it is
unknown and may, after all, be blank oblivion. The 'bar' at the
harbour mouth represents the limitations of physical life, which will
be crossed by death, an idea which is repeated more abstractly in the
fourth stanza:

>   from out our bourne of Time and Place
> The flood may bear me far.

'Bourne' means 'boundary' or 'limit': the somewhat archaic word is
probably chosen by Tennyson for its association with a speech in
Shakespeare's *Hamlet*, where the hero, contemplating suicide,
envisages death as

>   The undiscovered country, from whose bourn
> No traveller returns.

Both poets see death as a journey in which the human individual is
transmuted into something else: something 'dark' and, in this life,
unknowable.

Yet the general tenor of Tennyson's poem carries a conviction of
confidence, some might even say of complacency. The setting sun and

the evening star are both fading phenomena yet, since they will each be born again in ageless defiance of the limits of 'Time and Place', the sadness they initially prompt is moderated by a strong tincture of comfort. Like the poet's impending death, they prognosticate both an end and a beginning. The tone, established in the first stanza and undeviating throughout the poem, is that of an achieved serenity. There is no ambiguity about the 'one clear call' to which the poet is now responding. Whatever may have been his complaints, bewilderments and rebellions at earlier moments of his life, every faculty is now screwed up to the final duty of preparing himself to meet his Maker ('I hope to see my Pilot face to face'). In facing up to the last crisis of death all the previous inner conflicts are resolved: body and soul pull together as one, for the last time. The clarion call – the last trump of death – has the salubrious effect of galvanising the dissolute human soul into the act of organising itself into a state of readiness ('Shall I at least set my lands in order?' as T. S. Eliot puts it in *The Waste Land*). All other concerns are dismissed as irrelevant to this final, urgent errand of self-preparation.

On the one hand the poet sees death as the natural termination to a life that has been full of irresolution and frustration. Death is now the star by which to steer. Its function is natural and it is this natural aspect that Tennyson stresses at the close of each stanza, referring to the soul as if it were lent to earthly flesh for a brief spell before being recalled to its spiritual source:

> that which drew from out the boundless deep
> Turns again home.

It is this perception of death as the veritable outcome of life that bestows upon the poem its serenity of composure and its sturdy injunction against post-mortal grief ('may there be no sadness of farewell').

On the other hand, despite this bold determination to meet death with equanimity, the acknowledgement of 'after that the dark!' is never far away. The poet cannot avoid confessing that all his experience has hitherto been gained through his bodily senses – landlocked firmly in this fallen world – and that death, for all of his courageous endeavour to neutralise its sting and render it innocuous, remains an adventure utterly untried and unknown:

> The flood may bear me far.

So the poem exemplifies to the end Tennyson's 'Victorianism'. His awareness, as he said elsewhere, that there are 'thoughts that arise' in him which defy linguistic expression bubbles up again here. Ultimately all of life's manifestations – its sunsets and evening stars, its twilights and tolling bells – are engulfed in the unfathomable deep of death.

10 Other Victorians: Browning, Hopkins and Hardy

Robert Browning (1812–89)

While Tennyson felt duty-bound to celebrate Britain's providential destiny and affirm his faith that the expansion of Empire and the performance of God's will were one and the same thing, his fellow poets, free of the burden of the laureateship, did not labour under the necessity of resolving all the contradictions of Victoria's buccaneering empire.

Robert Browning preferred to occupy himself in probing the more secular motives behind human behaviour. Unlike Tennyson, Browning seldom seems to have concerned himself with what the passing fashions of public taste demanded. He never wrote with one eye on the marketplace and to such phenomena as the burgeoning jingoistic sentiment of Victoria's reign he apparently remained indifferent. Even when, later in life, his early reputation for obscurity was finally giving way to public recognition, he was still – in 1871 – only selling 2500 copies of a poem ('Balaustion's Adventure') in five months whereas Tennyson at the same time was receiving advance orders for 40 000 copies of an unpublished poem (part of *Idylls of the King*). Ever since his first poem, 'Pauline', had been attacked as 'morbid' and narcissistic by John Stuart Mill, Browning had paid more heed to the sage opinions of erudite criticism than to the sensual appetites of the masses. He also learnt to conceal himself and his feelings behind a variety of masks and assumed identities.

Browning resembles more recent poets in his deliberate eschewal of public acclaim and in his conscious cultivation of 'obscurity', in the certain knowledge that such practice would prohibit him from ever reaching a wide audience. In Browning one can see the beginnings of poetry's present retraction – from the arena of the marketplace, by way of the 'Tower' in which W. B. Yeats penned his wrathful laments for the passing of the era of aristocratic patronage, down to the present day when new volumes of verse seldom find a readership outside literary reviews and university libraries. The poet is speaking to an ever-shrinking circle of auditors and Browning seemed aware of this.

If Browning's poems, however, seemed to run counter to public taste and to be bafflingly opaque on their first appearance, they are not necessarily so now. Today the reader is more willing to credit the secular motives that prompt the Renaissance bishop to order for himself a sumptuous tomb of jasper, 'One block, pure green as a pistachio nut' ('The Bishop Orders His Tomb at Saint Praxed's Church'), to nod corroboratively at hearing (in 'Soliloquy of the Spanish Cloister') one monk confess his poisonous jealousy of another ('If hate killed men, Brother Lawrence, / God's blood, would not mine kill you!') and to acknowledge the verisimilitude of the madnesss that impels Porphyria's lover to strangle her with her own luxurious hair and afterwards to comment:

> And thus we sit together now,
>   And all night long we have not stirred,
>   And yet God has not said a word!
>
> ('Porphyria's Lover')

Browning's revelations of the cynicism that lies behind the masks, manners, customs and costumes of social and ecclesiastical conformity strike an answering chord that Tennyson's 'nobler' visions of man and his destiny often fail to move. Through the dark catalogue of characters speaking out of his poems Browning displays a vivid realisation of the proliferation of evil in the world. 'That hoary cripple, with malicious eye' that leers upon the hero in the first stanza of 'Childe Roland to the Dark Tower Came' is reincarnated a hundred times, in a hundred forms, in Browning's oeuvre. Taken as a whole, the declaimers of his dramatic monologues weave a 'warped' tapestry, as richly 'negative' in its way as Chaucer's inventory of the Canterbury pilgrims is 'positive'. If there is a religious vision informing the works of both these poets, in Browning it has become many shades darker, the humour several grades more acidic, than is evident in his illustrious predecessor.

Browning's 'dramatic monologue', the device of having his poems spoken by a participant in their events, is one of the most obvious ways in which he has influenced more recent poetry. Having been taken to task for exposing too much of himself in his early work 'Pauline', Browning recoiled, turned his back on Romantic tenets about the poet's self being the fittest subject and most fertile seedbed of poetry and proceeded to produce poems whose protagonist, and exponent, is a character other than the author himself. Browning, in other words, took to hiding behind a persona. He remains effectively concealed behind the screen in front of which his mouthpieces discourse and act; his own feelings in the matter can only be discerned obliquely or obscurely, if at all. In 1842, with the publication of his *Dramatic Lyrics*, an early collection of monologues, Browning stated emphatically his renunciation of the Romantic mode, claiming for himself in these poems the detachment of a dramatist towards his puppet characters and disclaiming all personal involvement with any of the speakers or the sentiments they expressed. A reader can be familiar with Browning's poems without ever becoming familiar with Browning himself. He remains a poet of blurred identity, inaccessible.

Such detachment from his work as Browning aimed at has been much admired and imitated in the 20th century, particularly since the revulsion of feeling against Romanticism in the early decades. T. S. Eliot, for example, strove after a similar severance between the poet and his object. Like Browning, he used speakers – middle-aged buffoons, commercial travellers on the search for prostitutes – who obviously could not be identified with the poet himself. This endeavour to dampen the ardent fires of Romanticism, to reintroduce the factor of distance, or dissociation, between the artist and his opus, has become a hallmark of much modern writing. Today's work of art has an organic existence of its own, from which, once it is made, its creator remains supremely detached, 'indifferent' – in the words of James Joyce's aspiring artist, Stephen Dedalus – 'like the God of creation . . . paring his fingernails'.

Browning's approach to his *métier* is secular, urbane. Poetry is not a shrine to be venerated by writer and reader alike; it is a craft like any other. For a man allegedly secure as a rock in his religion, Browning's poems seem singularly devoid of any sacerdotal atmosphere. Even his religious characters – like Fra Lippo Lippi, with his attraction towards 'that white smallish female with the breasts' – savour more of this world than the next. The earthiness of Browning ensures that his work will find a receptive audience in the present agnostic age, though the deeper concern of his later poetry with religious issues is less likely to meet with sympathy.

In technique, tone and content Browning anticipated most of the 20th century's preferences and preoccupations. There are, nonetheless, some areas in which he remains indisputably Victorian. The sheer volume of his work bears witness to his enormous energy, a characteristic which he shared with so many of his countrymen in all walks of life. There is also about many of his monologues just a tinge of the Victorian proclivity towards melodrama which is absent from the self-deflating monologues of T. S. Eliot's personae, ensuring that the reader can never mistake the work of one poet for that of the other (Browning's 'hoary cripple, with malicious eye', for instance, has his counterpart in Eliot's seedier 'Jew' who 'squats on the windowsill'). A barely perceptible tendency towards exaggeration and occasional bombast marks Browning's monologues as decidedly 'dramatic'. His characters seem to hug the limelight. And they deliver their opinions in full voice from centre stage, instead of whispering them *sotto voce* from the wings in the manner of Eliot's apologetic J. Alfred Prufrock.

In the poem which follows, the speaker, a 16th-century Italian aristocrat, has received the agent of a fellow nobleman, whose daughter's hand he is soliciting in marriage. The reader is permitted to eavesdrop on their conversation as they pass through the gallery; until, as they descend the staircase, their voices fade out of earshot.

My Last Duchess

FERRARA

That's my last Duchess painted on the wall,
Looking as if she were alive. I call
That piece a wonder, now: Frà Pandolf's hands
Worked busily a day, and there she stands.
Will't please you sit and look at her? I said
'Frà Pandolf' by design, for never read
Strangers like you that pictured countenance,
The depth and passion of its earnest glance,
But to myself they turned (since none puts by
10   The curtain I have drawn for you, but I)

And seemed as they would ask me, if they durst,
How such a glance came there; so, not the first
Are you to turn and ask thus. Sir, 'twas not
Her husband's presence only, called that spot
Of joy into the Duchess' cheek: perhaps
Frà Pandolf chanced to say 'Her mantle laps
Over my lady's wrist too much,' or 'Paint
Must never hope to reproduce the faint
Half-flush that dies along her throat:' such stuff
20 Was courtesy, she thought, and cause enough
For calling up that spot of joy. She had
A heart – how shall I say? – too soon made glad,
Too easily impressed; she liked whate'er
She looked on, and her looks went everywhere.
Sir, 'twas all one! My favour at her breast,
The dropping of the daylight in the West,
The bough of cherries some officious fool
Broke in the orchard for her, the white mule
She rode with round the terrace – all and each
30 Would draw from her alike the approving speech,
Or blush, at least. She thanked men, – good! but thanked
Somehow – I know not how – as if she ranked
My gift of a nine-hundred-years-old name
With anybody's gift. Who'd stoop to blame
This sort of trifling? Even had you skill
In speech – (which I have not) – to make your will
Quite clear to such an one, and say, 'Just this
Or that in you disgusts me; here you miss,
Or there exceed the mark' – and if she let
40 Herself be lessoned so, nor plainly set
Her wits to yours, forsooth, and made excuse,
– E'en then would be some stooping; and I choose
Never to stoop. Oh sir, she smiled, no doubt,
Whene'er I passed her; but who passed without
Much the same smile? This grew; I gave commands;
Then all smiles stopped together. There she stands
As if alive. Will't please you rise? We'll meet
The company below, then. I repeat,
The Count your master's known munificence
50 Is ample warrant that no just pretence

Of mine for dowry will be disallowed;
Though his fair daughter's self, as I avowed
At starting, is my object. Nay, we'll go
Together down, sir. Notice Neptune, though,
Taming a sea-horse, thought a rarity,
Which Claus of Innsbruck cast in bronze for me!

Browning has captured perfectly the tone of effortless urbanity and unremitted egocentricity of this representative of the genteel world. The Duke exhibits his treasures to his visitor with a natural ease, as if implicitly stating that one of his social caste has an unquestionable and inherent right to the good things of life. He is the centre of his own universe; all lesser mortals orbit around him. If art is created, it is made to please *him*: the sea-horse sculpted by 'Claus of Innsbruck' was 'cast in bronze for me!' The second word of the poem is 'my', its last word is 'me' and the first-person pronoun occurs frequently throughout the speech, underlining the importance which the speaker attaches to himself. Indeed, he scarcely seems to interest himself in what his interlocutor might have to say but merely uses him as a convenient peg upon which to hang the trappings of his egregious self-esteem.

The portrait of his previous wife hangs on the wall of the gallery and he invites his visitor to inspect it. His phrasing suggests his assumption that his late wife, though dead, has become a permanent part of his collection, one *objet d'art* among many. She is 'painted on the wall', as if embedded there, 'looking as if she were alive'. The Duke's attitude towards people, as towards things, is that of the collector: she is '*my* last Duchess'. Moreover, his attitude towards those whom he commissions to work for him is equally imperious. The painter Frà Pandolf, who has wrought this miracle – the man whose 'hands / Worked busily a day' at the Duke's behest – is regarded as a superior sort of servant (like Claus of Innsbruck later); and it is the Duke's critical judgement of the finished product ('I call / That piece a wonder') that counts, not anyone else's.

The smoothness of his discourse, the graceful polish of his syntax, is enhanced by the ease with which the Duke glides over the rhyme words without pausing to draw attention to them. The poem is written in rhyming couplets but, unlike those of Pope, Browning's couplets flow fluidly into one another, pursuing the rhythms of speech so faithfully that one might well remain unaware that the poem has any rhymes at all. Browning achieves this by running a 'natural' sentence across what would, in Augustan verse, be the end-stopped second line of the couplet ('I call / That piece a wonder'; 'I said / "Frà Pandolf" by design') so that the rhyme passes undetected by the ear. In this he is probably indicating the 'artfulness' that lies beneath the Duke's easy manner. There is more to the Duke than meets the eye (or ear). He has developed a pose of unquestionable authority, so much so that he probably himself by now believes in the myth of his own indestructibility. The slightly larger-than-life aspect of the Duke's arrogance and vanity gives this poem the very faintest tinge of melodrama. His absolute authority ('none puts by / The curtain I have drawn for you, but I') and the timorous subservience to which he is accustomed among his guests (who 'seemed as they would ask me, if they durst') are made clear. It is no wonder that the agent apparently ventures no remark but listens in obsequious silence.

The Duchess's portrait depicts, in contrast to her husband's controlled and icy demeanour, a 'depth and passion' in her 'earnest glance': and these strong emotions could not possibly have been elicited, the spectator feels, by such a man as her spouse. The Duke openly admits as much ('Sir, 'twas not / Her husband's presence only called that spot / Of joy into the Duchess' cheek'). Frà Pandolf apparently capitalised on the opportunity of his sittings with the Duchess to practise the courtly as well as the painter's art. The spontaneous warmth of the lady's character ('the faint / Half-flush that dies along her throat'), called forth first by the painter's words before being committed to canvas, contrasts sharply with the Duke's rigorous self-control. Browning suggests the displeasure that the discovery of such an artless disposition in his young wife must have caused him. Now, having fixed her where he wanted her, in a frame of his own devising, he can dispassionately anatomise her failings, which he duly proceeds to do.

His wife, he proclaims, provoked in him such irritation as eventually became intolerable. There is no mistaking the mixture of scorn and jealous wrath that must have possessed him during their marriage. Now that she is gone or, as it were, embalmed in the preservatives from Frà Pandolf's palette, the Duke can analyse her character with cold, aristocratic aloofness:

> She had
> A heart – how shall I say? – too soon made glad,
> Too easily impressed.

It is not only the lady's love of life (as opposed to his own preference for petrified art objects) that angers the Duke but the lack of discrimination she shows in bestowing her affection ('she liked whate'er / She looked on, and her looks went everywhere'). She rates everything equally, whether it be the Duke's love-making, the sight of a sunset, a present from an admirer ('some officious fool') or the 'white mule' she keeps for exercise. The implicit equation between the beast of burden and the Duke himself, in that the Duchess displays – to his suspicious eyes – exactly the same quantity of affection for each (''twas all one'), must have been especially infuriating for one of the Duke's aristocratic outlook and temper ('as if she ranked / My gift of a nine-hundred-years-old name with anybody's gift').

He had taken as his bride, evidently, someone who could not be bent to his will: a woman whose natural graces contrasted and conflicted with the Duke's highly-trained elegance and *savoir-faire*. An assurance of his innate superiority prevents the Duke from bending to correct or reprimand what he dislikes in his wife's behaviour ('I choose / Never to stoop'). The irritation inaugurated by her 'trifling' and, in itself, innocuous misconduct widens into an irreparable breach. The couple drift into an estrangement. The Duke is too proud to admit to his wife that her behaviour is capable of displeasing and even 'disgusting' him. He can only express his disapproval by withdrawing further into his tower of aristocratic *hauteur*.

Despite the Duke's regal assumption that his auditor will share his interpretation of the affair, the visitor's silence might itself proffer an implicit criticism of his conduct. The Duke's next revelation can only stun the listener into a trance of deeper immobility, so that the Duke has to prod him out of his reverie ('Will't please you rise?'). The understatement of the Duke's confession, the casual way in which he discloses that he ordered his wife's dissolution ('I gave commands; / Then all smiles stopped'), gives a sinister outline, if any were needed, to the unsavoury shades of his character already revealed by his conversation. And to what does he refer in 'This grew'? To his wife's supposed infidelity or to his own creeping paranoia? To the Duke, it is all the same: he was annoyed and that was enough. He used his god-like prerogative to obliterate from the range of his vision whatever displeased him: in this instance, his previous Duchess. 'There she stands / As if alive', he remarks unfalteringly, without a trace of remorse; and follows this with an invitation to join 'the company below', passing suavely from reminiscences of his late wife, whose death he decreed, to a celebration of the marriage contract with his new one.

An unabashed cynicism betrays itself in the Duke's subsequent bestowal of priority on the material benefits that will accrue from his projected marriage ('The Count your master's known munificence / Is ample warrant that no just pretence / Of mine for dowry will be disallowed'); though for form's sake he adds the hollow codicil that 'his fair daughter's self' is, after all, his prime object. All is couched in the glib terminology of aristocratic diction, which, like the 'glozing' words of Milton's Satan, covers a core of rampant self-centredness with a veneer of politeness. So the Duke passes from our hearing, soliciting his guest's admiration for another 'rarity' among his collection of trophies: this time, a sculpture of 'Neptune . . . taming a sea-horse', which no doubt casts a reflecting glow on the Duke's own vanity at having subdued for ever the warm-blooded spontaneous creature, the 'sea-horse' that he had taken as his last Duchess.

The power of Browning's poem is drawn from what is missing as much as from what is present. The late Duchess, though removed from the scene by her husband's imperious will, establishes herself as a powerful presence in the halls of his castle. She haunts with mute reproach the gallery where her husband is describing her shortcomings so eloquently. The silence of his captive audience, the go-between from his next bride, endorses the reader's own reservations about the Duke's disquisition. The Duke barely bothers to exculpate himself. Secure in the hierarchical position conferred upon him by his 'nine-hundred-years-old name', he makes no excuses. It is in the interstices of his argument that the callous reality of the Duke's character looms, darkly threatening, arrogant, autocratic and implacable.

Although Browning remains mute while his protagonist lays down the law, he implicitly shares the same moral horror that his poem induces in his audience. Yet the final judgement remains vague. What sort of world is it in which such people as the Duke are allowed to trample roughshod over any who oppose them, without ever being called to account? Browning's poem, although written as early as 1840, seems already at the threshold of 20th-century artistic vision, wherein vice escapes unscathed and unpunished in both this world and the world to come.

Gerard Manley Hopkins (1844–89)

The poetry of Gerard Manley Hopkins was unpublished in his lifetime and remained unknown until its first appearance in 1918. Because of its unorthodox techniques, Hopkins's poetry seemed unusually 'modern' and un-Victorian to the post-Great War generation who discovered it. The compressed vocabulary of his verse – devolving from the expressed intention of his poetic paradigm, Keats, to 'load every rift with ore' – together with the nervy texture of his rhythms and the unabashed exposure of his religious feelings gave Hopkins a distinctive voice to the critics and poets of the 1920s who were busy rejecting so much else in Victorian poetry. Perhaps it was the sense of impending religious crisis ('I wake and feel the fell of dark, not day') that lingered below the surface of even his brightest poems that secured Hopkins's verse so sympathetic an audience 30 years after his death. Certainly the vitality of his pressure-cooked lines, the associative technique by which one image leads to or blends with another – and the corresponding demands for a vigorous intellectual effort on the part of the reader to decipher the grammar and disentangle the thought processes – stimulated later writers and critics. Thus Hopkins, although the roots of his imagery lie in Keats and the origins of his 'innovative' techniques of rhythm and diction lie much further back – in the alliterative metre and picturesque 'kennings' (such as 'whale-road' instead of 'sea') of Anglo-Saxon poetry – was hailed as the true upholder and reforger of the poetic craft, while his contemporaries were being dismissed as hacks churning out the doggerel of a debased tradition.

This initial verdict has undergone several reappraisals since. Hopkins is now seen as more of a 'traditionalist' than was at first thought, the quality of his intellect has suffered some denigration ('his thinking about beauty, man, and Nature is unimpressive', says an otherwise sympathetic critic, Austin Warren) and the work of his late-Victorian contemporaries has conversely undergone some rehabilitation. Nevertheless, the startling effect of Hopkins's visions and his undeniably unique way of expressing them remains one of the main links between the poetry of this century and the last. Hopkins's verse constitutes both the injection of a new vitality into the form of poetry and a revival of immediacy and intimacy in the relationship between man and God not heard since Herbert's day. The Victorian public who could nod approvingly at Tennyson's deference to God as 'my Pilot' would scarcely have greeted Hopkins's reference to Christ as 'my dear' with equal aplomb. Such frankness would have been deemed vulgar. Perhaps the 20th century senses a kindred soul in Hopkins because of his intense individualism: his awareness that man is either alone with God or alone without Him, but always alone and unique. Where other Victorians were extolling the 'greater whole' of the communal life or the Imperial idea, Hopkins was exploring the sanctity of the isolated individual and lauding the peerless identity of each particle of creation, in a manner redolent of Blake's primary proclamation that 'every thing that lives is Holy'.

Hopkins, like Blake, was able to 'see a World in a Grain of Sand'. He had a microscopic eye for the small particulars of nature which Tennyson ('A million emeralds break from the ruby-budded lime / In the little grove where I sit') also displayed, though without the religious insight afforded by Hopkins's perspective. This fascination with the finer details of the natural world finds its outlet in the sketches and writings of Hopkins's notebooks and reappears in his poems. Such delight in the phenomena of nature seemed, to the devout Catholic that Hopkins had become at an early age, at odds with the proper end of all devotion: God Himself. It seemed to express too strong an attachment to the things of this world. Hopkins was able to circumvent the problem through his discovery of the writings of the mediaeval Catholic philosopher Duns Scotus.

Scotus, a Franciscan monk, claimed that each genus, or natural species, was composed of a myriad of individuals, each with its own distinctive form (*haecceitas* or 'this-ness'). Once one had grasped the general pattern (*quidditas* or 'what-ness') that lay behind the individual form, one had a direct insight into the comprehensive divine plan that governed all the unique instances of creation. Hopkins seized on Scotus's formulation with gratitude, seeing in it a validation of his own fascination with the created object. And in his poems 'Harry Ploughman' and 'Felix Randal' the individual working man is fleshed out in concrete epithets ('big-boned' and 'hardy-handsome'; 'Back, elbow, and liquid waist') only as a step along the road of Hopkins's ultimate purpose: the glorification of the Creator who has moulded such fine figures of men.

Hopkins focused his gaze on the individual forms – or as he preferred to call them, the 'inscapes' – not only of men but of birds, beasts and plants. The intensity of his perception and the blacksmith-like labour through which he forged his rhythms combined to body forth images of natural life that were apt and true. So the coloured dots on a trout's back are presented as 'rose-moles all in stipple upon trout that swim' (colour, texture and distribution of markings are all succinctly evoked); elsewhere the dynamic dancing movement of tall poplar trees on a breezy summer's day is conjured by repetition, alliteration and a strongly-stressed rhythm:

My áspens déar, whose áiry cáges quélled,
Quélled or quénched in léaves the léaping sún;

('Binsey Poplars')

and on another occasion the poet, observing the flight of a falcon in the early morning sunlight ('the fire that breaks from thee . . . !'), is caught up in the 'ecstasy' of the bird's earth-disdaining career and shares the exhilaration of its soaring arabesque movements ('My heart in hiding / Stirred for a bird'). Hopkins found myriad instances of beauty in the world around him; a short country walk would yield countless occasions for glorifying the Creator who had devised it all.

Hopkins's espousal of the Catholic faith and the demands for self-abnegation and submission that the Jesuit order imposed on him entailed enormous sacrifice. It seems that the poet-Hopkins was inevitably in a state of permanent warfare with the Jesuit-Hopkins, despite the sanction that Duns Scotus's writings had seemingly given to the former. An individualist and a perfectionist who refused to alter one word of his poems to compromise with the tastes or opinions of others (as his letters to his friend and first editor, Robert Bridges, testify), Hopkins was at the same time aware that to court fame as a poet – even the limited fame attracted by a writer of 'obscure' and 'difficult' verse such as his – would be at odds with the self-obliteration which his religious order demanded. In his lifetime Hopkins as poet was never permitted to have the last word over Hopkins as priest; hence the long interment of his poetry before its surprising resurrection after the First World War.

Hopkins made heavy sacrifices, and not only artistic ones, in the assumption of his priesthood ('I am a eunuch', he said, 'but it is for the kingdom of heaven's sake') and often, in consequence, in the middle of a poem a shadow falls across the brilliantly sparkling vision that has been evoked. In the midst of his eulogy on the 'growing green' of the Binsey poplars Hopkins suddenly remembers the vulnerability of the 'sleek and seeing' human eyeball, which a mere 'prick will make no eye at all'. Sometimes this darkness was more than a mere flicker across an otherwise scintillating screen. Like most mystics, Hopkins seems to have experienced at least one 'dark night of the soul', when the light of God's presence seemed to have been altogether withdrawn from him. Then he wrote his so-called 'terrible sonnets', in which, 'pitched past pitch of grief', he is unable to conceive of man as anything more significant than a puny insect clinging desperately to the surface of a spinning, God-forsaken globe, awaiting only the annihilation of death:

O the mind, mind has mountains; cliffs of fall
Frightful, sheer, no-man-fathomed.
. . . Nor does long our small
Durance deal with that steep or deep. Here! creep,
Wretch, under a comfort serves in a whirlwind: all
Life death does end.

('No Worst, There Is None')

Such profound depressions seem to operate as painful but inevitable stages on the spiritual journey, ultimately serving to recast, and reinforce, the relationship between the individual and his God; and it is a Hopkins in a happier state of mind that speaks in the following poem.

God's Grandeur

The world is charged with the grandeur of God.
 It will flame out, like shining from shook foil;
 It gathers to a greatness, like the ooze of oil
Crushed. Why do men then now not reck his rod?
Generations have trod, have trod, have trod;
 And all is seared with trade; bleared, smeared with toil;
 And wears man's smudge and shares man's smell; the soil
Is bare now, nor can foot feel, being shod.

And for all this, nature is never spent;
 There lives the dearest freshness deep down things;
And though the last lights off the black West went
 Oh, morning, at the brown brink eastward, springs –
Because the Holy Ghost over the bent
 World broods with warm breast and with ah! bright wings.

For all the apparent obscurity of some of the expressions in this poem, its theme is fundamentally simple and is summed up in the first line. 'The world is charged with the grandeur of God': 'charged' both in the sense of loaded or primed – as if the world were brimfull of God's glory, which pulsates through every vein of it like a thrilling electric current – and in the sense of bearing the responsibility, being 'charged' with the duty, of revealing the divine splendour of the Maker to earth's human inhabitants. The rest of the poem develops this simply stated theme, as if Hopkins were presenting a text and then expounding it in the manner of a sermon. Beneath the unusual diction and telescoped syntax lies a bedrock of Christian conformity.

Nor are the rhythm and the form of the verse itself so altogether extraordinary as they might at first appear. The poem has the orthodox sonnet structure, with the standard division between octave and sestet. As for Hopkins's famed 'sprung rhythm', it draws its inspiration (like much of his vocabulary) from Old English poetry, where it is the number of stresses (or 'beats') in a line, rather than the number of syllables, which determines its length. Even this 'rule' Hopkins tends to interpret liberally, so that the first line has four stressed syllables ('The wórld is chárged with the grándeur of Gód') while the last line bears a probable seven ('Wórld bróods with wárm bréast and with áh! bríght wíngs'). The accretion of stresses here has the effect of moving the poem from an initially poised solemnity to an enthusiastic outpouring which spills over the containing walls of the sonnet in imitation of the emotions of the convinced Christian, whose 'cup runneth over' with joy. The main effect of Hopkins's rhythmic variations is to reproduce the stresses and strains of the poem's unfolding intellectual argument.

In his attempt constantly to vary his line-rhythms and to fit metrical stress to mental stress – to blend metre and matter – Hopkins was undoubtedly a precursor of 'free verse' exponents of the 20th century, at the same time that he was reaching back to the infancy of the English poetic tradition and reviving its flexible metres, its alliterative effects and its unsophisticated, concrete-clear vocabulary ('With swift, slow; sweet, sour; adazzle, dim'). To scan a Hopkins poem properly, the reader needs to take into account the twists and turns, the flights and descents of its developing argument. Hopkins himself asserted that it was the *overall*, not the line-by-line, rhythm of the poem – or in longer poems the stanza – which counted, since a poem, like any other emanation of God's glorious creation, had organic wholeness. Thus, as Hopkins put it, 'the scanning runs on without break from the beginning . . . to the end and all the stanza is one long strain, though written in lines asunder'.

In this poem Hopkins goes on to elaborate his initial assertion. God's grandeur will 'flame out, like shining from shook foil'. One of the startling things about Hopkins's poetry – and in this he is again a precursor of the 'moderns' – is his juxtaposition of ancient and modern, of ecclesiastical and secular images. So here God's glory 'flames out', in the manner of the burning bush that amazed Moses, at the same time that His splendour seems, in the poet's eye, to be reflected by the glittering of something so trivial as tinsel ('Shaken goldfoil', Hopkins wrote in an explanatory note to Bridges, 'gives off broad glares like sheet lightning'). The coupling of imagery from the everyday or 'scientific' world to the deepest emotions is reminiscent of the practice of Donne. In his use of imagery, as in his methods of metre and syntax, Hopkins casts backwards at the same time as he anticipates more recent developments.

The third line, with its employment of alliteration ('gathers to a greatness'), again seems to hark back to Old English poetry, an impression which is reinforced throughout the poem by Hopkins's obvious preference for the Anglo-Saxon monosyllable over its less concrete Latin equivalent ('reck' for 'recognise' or 'consider', for instance). Hopkins seems to be recalling a simpler age, when raw, unsophisticated man saw his Creator in the rocks, trees and stars with which he was in much closer and more constant contact than his 19th-century successor. So he draws an image of God's glory from the homely vocabulary and earthy activity of the peasant: it is like the 'ooze of oil' yielded by grapes at the end of an arduous but successful harvest. The monosyllables 'ooze' and 'oil', with their prolonged vowels, suggest perfectly the slow, steady accumulation – the 'gathering' – of experience and evidence from life before God's glory bursts upon the consciousness like fine wine striking the palate. The individual is like a vessel being filled, drop by drop, with consciousness of God and increasing in well-being as God's grace seeps into him. The ambiguities of the Christian covenant are also touched upon:

> It gathers to a greatness, like the ooze of oil
> Crushed.

The forcefulness of that emphatic and fully stopped 'Crushed' right at the start of a new line is brutal both semantically and metrically. We are forced to pause and recognise that man's assurance of salvation only came about through the 'crushing' of Christ on earth. Joy has been bought with pain. The caesura which must follow the full stop after 'Crushed' allows Hopkins, skilful preacher that he is, to change his tack swiftly and strike home with a question aimed at his congregation's callous complacency: 'Why do men now not reck his rod?' The image of God with His corrective cane is almost folkloric in its simplicity and directness.

Hopkins answers his question by proceeding to show how man's apprehension of God has become blurred with the passing centuries. The repetition in 'have trod, have trod, have trod' suggests the mindless automatism to which man has been reduced. Hopkins may be thinking specifically of the detrimental effects on human consciousness of the Industrial Revolution, as he goes on to cite three various ways ('seared', 'bleared' and 'smeared') in which 'trade' and 'toil' destroy the sharpness of the faculties, burning and branding the psyche with the lust for material acquisition. Man's 'smudge' both begrimes and befogs the glories of the created world, at the same time as his 'smell' is infiltrating everywhere. Hopkins is aware that the pollution that man's industry has emitted corrupts both the natural, God-given environment and his own, God-given soul. 'The soil is bare now' has sterile implications premonitory of Eliot's *The Waste Land*, and man, in insulating himself from direct contact with his habitat, is perversely restricting his resources of spiritual contact with his Creator: 'nor can foot feel, being shod'.

Having laid down his diagnosis of man's spiritual shortcomings, Hopkins proceeds in the sestet to declare that, after all, nature is sempiternal and God all-forgiving. Whatever violation of his earthly freehold man may commit, 'nature is never spent' and can be counted upon to renew itself, for its source is God: 'There lives the dearest freshness deep down things'. The sap, the juice of life that refreshes and revives all things – what D. H. Lawrence was to evoke as the 'living flood' of the 'great force' of life and Dylan Thomas to define as 'the force that through the green fuse drives the flower' – is qualified as 'dearest', most precious because it emanates from Christ, who through His sacrifice guaranteed that life should be eternal ('never spent').

In the sestet Hopkins is able to draw again the spiritual sustenance that he has seen thinning out in the octave. Thus, 'though the last lights off the black West went' – 'black' as a result of both industrial pollution and inner obfuscation, clouding the light of heaven – Hopkins feels able to prophesy a new dawn with confident ecstasy ('Oh, morning'), 'springing' (both with joyful sprightliness and as a fount of refreshment) from the 'east' which is both the birthplace of each day's new sun and the scene of the nativity of the Son of God. All is not so hopeless as the octave had implied. Why not?

> Because the Holy Ghost over the bent
>   World broods with warm breast and with ah! bright wings.

As with the earlier exclamatory 'Oh', the 'ah!' of the last line, an even stronger and more syntactically disruptive interjection, indicates in the poet an exuberance that is hardly to be repressed. The compassion ('warm breast') of God, as well as His capacity to lift man out of his troublous trappings, assures Hopkins that, however corrupt ('bent') the world has become, God's mercy is infinite.

God, in the form of the Holy Ghost, 'broods' over the world. There may be a suggestion in that of a certain sullen displeasure on the Creator's part: He is meditating morosely on what His creatures have made of their earthly abode and perhaps manufacturing an appropriate punishment. Thus this may be an appearance of that shadow which sometimes falls across Hopkins's verse in its most illuminated moments. Yet the dominant associations are of 'warm breast' and 'bright wings': of 'brood' in the sense of guarding and fostering with affectionate creative love. It is predominantly on a note of hope that Hopkins's poem ends.

Thomas Hardy (1840–1928)

More famous in his own time for his novels, Thomas Hardy has been steadily acquiring a reputation as a poet, to the point where his poetry now seems the more significant achievement. An architect by profession, Hardy began writing poetry in his 20s but switched to novel writing as a more certain way of getting into print. His last novel, *Jude the Obscure* (1896), was so savagely mauled by the critics – offended no doubt by its relentless indictment of the English social and educational establishments – that Hardy, his reputation as a novelist by now secure, turned his attention back to his first love, poetry. He continued to produce poems until shortly before his death in his 80s. Like Wordsworth, Hardy wrote many of his poems from personal reminiscence, but the fire did not die out in him as he grew older. On the contrary, the passion seemed to grow stronger and the sense of loss – never far from the surface of Hardy's poetry – deeper with the passing years. The speaker who bares his soul in much of Hardy's verse is not ashamed to admit past failures and weakness. There is a simple heroism – unintellectual but honest – in the vulnerability exposed in these poems. Wordsworth would have taken more care to cover the traces of character flaws.

Hardy's novels and poems are rooted in the countryside of his native 'Wessex' (the counties of Dorset, Hampshire, Wiltshire and Somerset). The glamour of the cities that so appealed to many of his 'modernist' contemporaries held no attraction for him. The landscape in his work has a primaeval quality and is sown with reminders – pagan ruins at Stonehenge, a Roman amphitheatre, a Norman church – of the presence of the past. Indeed past and present interact intimately in Hardy's works; the cows, for instance, in one of his novels shelter from the heat in a ruined church and cool 'their thirsty tongues by licking the quaint Norman carving, which glistened with moisture'. So ancient, even archaic, does the landscape of Hardy's poems and novels seem that it comes as a surprise when the occasional steam train wheezes across it. Mechanical invention sounds the knell to the old agricultural way of life, as the clanking and belching threshing-machine disturbs the rural tranquillity in *Tess of the d'Urbervilles*.

The people in Hardy's works – and, in his poems, this includes Hardy himself – are powerless to prevent the intrusion of technology and the break-up of their traditional rhythms. Hardy sings an elegy for an age that is already over; and his works are overladen by a sense of tragic doom. People are in the grip of a destiny that manipulates them malevolently and against which struggle is futile. This hostile fate comes partly from outside them but is also partly invited by character traits within them.

'Whose is the child you are like to bear? –
His? After all my months o' care?'
God knows 'twas not! But, O despair!
  I nodded – still to tease,

recounts the woman who has unwittingly goaded her lover to murder, in 'A Trampwoman's Tragedy'. Hardy perceives humanity to be in the hands of a 'Vast Imbecility', a Deity either indifferent towards His creatures or actively destructive of them:

'The Earth, sayest thou? The Human race?
By Me created? Sad its lot?
Nay: I have no remembrance of such place:
Such world I fashioned not.'

('God-Forgotten')

With this impersonal 'Will' individual human nature often cooperates perversely to promote its own downfall. Hardy's works are pervaded first and last by a sense of waste. At the same time, a poignant beauty coexists with this feeling of desolation. The underprivileged Jude and the downtrodden Tess fighting against their unconquerable destinies exhibit beauty in the nobility of their struggles – in the clash of will and Will. The beauty also derives, more concretely, from Hardy's presentation of nature.

Steeped from birth in an agricultural tradition (unlike Keats, the 'Cockney' poet), Hardy's first-hand acquaintance with nature was raw and unillusioned. Nature in his work has a brute power – unmediated by the writer, uninformed by God – which looks forward, in some ways, to Ted Hughes's more recent presentation of it. Hardy's familiarity with the rural rhythm – the seed-sowing time and harvest festivities – ensured that the folklore of song and dance entered his consciousness at an early age. His poetry exercises common-sensical control on often distraught subject-matter and presents all with the elegant unforced metaphor of the countryman:

The flowers we potted perhaps are thrown
   To rot upon the farm.
And where we had our supper-fire
May now grow nettle, dock and briar,
And all the place be mould and mire
   So cozy once and warm.

('Tess's Lament')

The poems prompted by the unexpected death of his first wife Emma Gifford – 'Never to bid good-bye, / Or lip me the softest call' – reveal the consciousness of emotional neglect towards her in later years when she was 'weak and lame' and 'had changed from the one who was all to me'. His poems confess that human love, no matter how firmly pledged, cannot be sustained and will turn sour in time; then mutual accord turns to mutual reproach:

> Your eyes on me were as eyes that rove
> Over tedious riddles of years ago;
> And some words played between us to and fro
>   On which lost the more by our love.

('Neutral Tones')

Hardy's poetry has a tone of pained sincerity that is rare in any age. The poem which follows is less personal, more general in its source; in it Hardy speaks for mankind as well as for himself.

The Darkling Thrush

I leant upon a coppice gate
    When Frost was spectre-grey,
And Winter's dregs made desolate
    The weakening eye of day.
The tangled bine-stems scored the sky
    Like strings of broken lyres.
And all mankind that haunted nigh
    Had sought their household fires.

The land's sharp features seemed to be
    The Century's corpse outleant,
His crypt the cloudy canopy,
    The wind his death-lament.
The ancient pulse of germ and birth
    Was shrunken hard and dry,
And every spirit upon earth
    Seemed fervourless as I.

At once a voice arose among
    The bleak twigs overhead
In a full-hearted evensong
    Of joy illimited;
An agèd thrush, frail, gaunt, and small,
    In blast-beruffled plume,
Had chosen thus to fling his soul
    Upon the growing gloom.

So little cause for carolings
    Of such ecstatic sound
Was written on terrestrial things
    Afar or nigh around,
That I could think there trembled through
    His happy good-night air
Some blessèd Hope, whereof he knew
    And I was unaware.

The date which Hardy appended to this poem was 31 December 1900: in other words, the poem commemorates the end of the 19th century and was, in fact, first titled 'By the Century's Death-bed'. The poem impresses by the darkness of its overall tone – from the 'darkling' of its title to the prevailing overcast atmosphere conjured by such diction as 'desolate', 'bleak', 'gaunt', 'blast-beruffled' and by references to 'the weakening eye of day', 'the cloudy canopy' and all the accumulated implications that the end of the 19th century coincides with an exhaustion unto death of all terrestrial life.

The theme is late Victorian: gone is the heady confidence of Tennyson's patriotic surges, to be replaced by a more hesitant and introspective attitude and a reacknowledgement that man at his keenest moments sees, in St Paul's words, 'through a glass, darkly'. The metre, on the other hand, is 'light'. It trips effortlessly along in the age-old ballad pattern of alternate four and three-foot iambic lines. Much of the poem's haunting effect comes from this contrast, or tension, between theme and metre, between the content and its vehicle. The metre is itself an instrument of time, swinging the poet irresistibly into the new century that he is so reluctant to enter. In addition, its associations with the oldest poetic expressions in the language (ballads derive from an oral folk-tradition of almost complete illiteracy) cannot help but suggest that the poet's present experience of deep despondency is by no means unique but is as timeless as the ballad metre itself.

The metre, in other words, conveys an implicit and comforting reassurance that belies the profound pessimism of the theme. It insinuates a sense of order which is ostensibly denied by what the poet sees and hears around him. This underlying conviction of a governing order to the world, intangible but inherent, is reinforced by the way the poem splits structurally into two stanzas of 'fervourless' lassitude and gloom followed 'at once' by the spiritual uplift lent by the thrush's 'ecstatic' warblings. 16 lines of dejection are exactly counterbalanced by 16 lines of consolation. At the same time Hardy intersperses his verse with occasional archaic diction replete with antique resonance: such as 'coppice', 'afar or nigh', 'shrunken', 'carolings' and the 'darkling' of the poem's title. Such diction links the poem with its predecessors in the language and subtly undermines the speaker's claim of utter isolation by intimating his continuity within a developing poetic tradition.

'Darkling' is a word with poetic reverberations. It means 'surrounded by dark'; though, in the context of the poem, it becomes apparent that it is the poet himself who is 'darkling' and not the bird, who rather chooses 'to fling his soul / Upon the growing gloom'. Hardy has probably taken this epithet from Keats's 'Ode to a Nightingale', where the poet ('Darkling, I listen') harkens to the voice of the night bird and experiences in consequence a kind of transfiguration beyond the terrestrial plane. Keats's bird has associations with Greek mythology (Philomela was transformed into a nightingale after being raped by her brother-in-law Tereus) but Hardy's ordinary English thrush, 'frail, gaunt, and small, / In blast-beruffled plume', has no such grandiose connections. It is a bird plain and simple, and its scruffiness is irrefutable; which makes its 'full-hearted evensong / Of joy illimited' perhaps even more an act of defiant heroism than is the 'plaintive anthem' sung by its consciously mythologised predecessor, the 'light-winged Dryad of the trees' of Keats's ode.

Hardy's poem, penned when the twilight was falling on Romanticism at the same time that the curtain was closing on the 19th century, is more earthbound in its awareness of the natural world. The sun is not the glorious dynamic star, whose 'flaming robes streamed out beyond his heels', of Keats's 'Hyperion'; it is dropsical and ageing, the 'weakening eye of day'. Nor do natural phenomena carry any assurance of a supernatural life to come: the bine-stems, 'tangled' and confused as the poet, 'score' or scratch the face of the heavens rather than seeming to point the way towards them and suggest to the speaker the discordancy of 'broken' lyre strings instead of the comprehensive harmony of created nature that a Romantic might have caught from the scene.

The opening stanza carries an overall impression of withdrawal. The insipid sun is retiring from life, heaven is receding from earth and 'all mankind' is turning inwards to extract what comfort it can from its scattered 'household fires'. Only the poet is abroad and he seems to be wandering in a world of ghosts: the frost has endowed all objects with a shroud of 'spectre-grey', the earth seems dead, forsaken even by the ghost-like men who previously 'haunted' it. This vision of the earth as a corpse wrapped in its shroud beneath an indifferent and inaccessible heaven is further developed in the second stanza. Meanwhile the poet is reduced to a state of dispirited inertia, leaning against the gate of a wood in death-like immobility. In the dead of winter the blood of life has deserted the face of the land, whose 'features' are 'sharp', angular, devoid of the fleshy rotundity that nature lends it in summer. What the poet observes around him furnishes him 'naturally' with the perfect image for what he feels within him. An era has ended, never to be revived, and the landscape in which all sparks of life have been extinguished reinforces the despondent cast of his mind. There is even a pun on 'outleant', implying 'out-lent', hence suggesting not simply that the dead body of the 19th century is displayed, or 'leaning out', for all to see in this emblematic demonstration by a mortified nature but also that the century has gone on too long anyway: it has outrun its lease.

It may be inferred from this that the confidence of Tennyson's tenure as laureate has expired, along with the belief in Britain's divinely-appointed imperial fate. The turn of the century marks a final turning-point in the thinking man's attitude to empire. In some indefinable and no doubt irrational way the change of century seemed to bode the end of Britain's world hegemony. The intoxicating sense of purpose and destiny that had impelled Tennyson to cry 'Forward, the Light Brigade!' has faded with the waning of the century and only the 'dregs' are left for the poet bitterly to mull over. And the 'land' over which he sees nature to have cast so heavy a pall is the England which Tennyson had earlier enthused about in very different terms:

Shout for England! . . .
George for England!
Merry England!
England for ay!

('English Warsong')

There is no hint in Hardy of England's eternity: the clouds provide the canopy for the crypt and the moaning wind supplies the death lament, for both the century's passing and England's. There is a finality about this raw winter scene which suggests that sap and vitality will never return ('The ancient pulse of germ and birth / Was shrunken hard and dry'). There is a premonition in the poet that the turn of the century coincides with the turning of a page in the history of his native land, as if he already heard in his prophetic ear the 'Channel Firing' he was to write about 14 years later.

The experience he recounts is not, after all, one of unrelieved gloom. At the nadir of the poet's meditation, on this dark night of his soul, some evidence does reach him that all around is not so utterly 'fervourless' as he; and the last two stanzas of the poem constitute an attempt to alleviate the ominous warnings offered in the first two. The song of the diminutive thrush is flung out in defiance of nature's overwhelming hostility. Such a display of totally unwarranted rejoicing defies all rational explanation and the poet is at a loss to comprehend it ('So little cause for carolings / Of such ecstatic sound / Was written on terrestrial things'). Since there is no physical justification for such an outpouring, the motivation can only be metaphysical. The bird must be inspired by 'some blessèd Hope' which eludes the poet, blindfolded by his scepticism. The references to Christian music implied by 'evensong' and 'carolings' and the religious ecstasy suggested in the 'joy illimited' of the thrush's hymn indicate that the most precious relic that is being buried with the old century is a sense of religious assurance: the serene confidence that comes from feeling that man is ever in his Maker's eye. The unsophisticated thrush, evidently, still carries this blissful, intuitive assurance. The poet can only listen in astonishment to the unsolicited expression of such 'Hope' amid the 'growing gloom' of his own speculations.

Unlike his precursor Keats at the beginning of the century ('Already with thee!'), Hardy is incapable of being lifted out of himself by the bird's song and transported to a more timeless and ecstatic state of being. His feet remain firmly planted on the ground, his mind stays anchored to 'terrestrial things' and though he might admire and envy the bird for the facility with which it is able to ignore its earthly prison and communicate with its Creator uninhibitedly, that is a communion from which he knows himself to be excluded. And in this Hardy's poem is a precursor of the 20th-century artistic predicament.

11   The Early 20th Century: T. S. Eliot

Beneath a superficial semblance of harmony, peace and concord there were many strains developing in the artistic fabric of Victorian Britain. The poets were homogeneous in appearance only. A closer inspection reveals a far greater range of doubt, scepticism and revolt than is normally associated with Victoria's reign. Even the queen's favourite poet, Tennyson, confessed now and then to 'faltering where I firmly trod'. It is only from the promontory of the present age – when, teetering on the brink of mutually assured destruction, man casts his eyes back to those halcyon days – that Victoria's Britain assumes the faint luminosity and the granite durability of one of its civic statues. The past solidifies only in retrospect. To those who actually lived in it, it seemed fluid and mutable enough.

Nevertheless, 19th-century poetry does possess something which is singularly lacking from that of the present day. For all their carping, writers under the old queen still believed in the values that tradition had sanctified. But the battlefields of the Somme, Passchendaele and Verdun sent those values spinning off beyond the stratosphere. 'Things fall apart; the centre cannot hold', as W. B. Yeats put it in a poem written just after the Great War. With an entire generation of European manhood all but wiped out in the cataclysm, a feeling of resentment hardened against the traditional leaders of the country. The old paternalistic values, the cores of stability around which British society spun – the class system and the Church of England – were discredited, perhaps irredeemably. A generation had marched to its death, blithely believing in the patriotic slogans and military judgement of its leaders. It was a battered Britain that picked itself up, once the smoke had cleared from the European battlefields, to resume the labour of living.

This is not to suggest that everything was rosy before the Great War broke up the dream. There were many unsettling influences at work to disturb the belief in the supremacy of Britain and British institutions. Indeed, the premonition of some impending catastrophe can be found as far back as the mid-19th century with Arnold's vision in 'Dover Beach' of a 'darkling plain . . . / Where ignorant armies clash by night'. The murmur of poetic voices prophesying war continued throughout the century and gathered to a crescendo with Hardy's fevered but futile warning in 'Channel Firing' – 'All nations striving strong to make / Red war yet redder. Mad as hatters' – six months before the outbreak of hostilities in 1914. As the imperial war-machine, after a sluggish start, began gathering momentum during Victoria's reign and after, a cautionary note was sometimes sounded from poetic quarters, even the most ostensibly 'patriotic' ones:

> If, drunk with sight of power, we loose
>   Wild tongues that have not Thee in awe . . .
> Lord God of Hosts, be with us yet,
> Lest we forget – lest we forget!

This sage reminder of the dangers inherent in self-glorification was issued by Rudyard Kipling in 'Recessional' on the occasion of Queen Victoria's Diamond Jubilee. Such warnings passed unheeded.

Britain and Kaiser Wilhelm's Germany were competing with each other to produce bigger battleships and longer-reaching guns, each country convinced that it was advancing under God's special favour and protection. At the same time, the revelations of psychology were casting similar doubts to those of the poets on man's innate sanity. Here again, prophecy was rife. In 1913 Carl Gustav Jung had a dream, recalled in his posthumous *Memories, Dreams, Reflections* (1964), of Europe weltering under a sea of mud and blood –

> I saw a monstrous flood covering all the northern and low-lying lands between the North Sea and the Alps. . . . I saw the mighty yellow waves, the floating rubble of civilisation, and the drowned bodies of uncounted thousands. Then the whole sea turned to blood –

a vivid augury of the trench warfare that was shortly to follow. This in turn lent validity to the serious study which the practitioners of psychiatry accorded to the fantastic activities of the unconscious mind. Here it was Sigmund Freud who led the way. His *Interpretation of Dreams* (1900) attempted to show – and, by so doing, to jolt European society out of its complacency – that the surface behaviour of human beings conceals a wild mêlée of longings, urges and all sorts of devious desires, which break out to find their expression in dreams and, from time to time, in actual conduct. Freud took the lid off the simmering pot of Victorian repression even more effectively than had Charles Baudelaire and the French Symbolists – and their British imitators, Algernon Swinburne and Oscar Wilde. This was to *épater la bourgeoisie* – to shock the middle classes – with a vengeance. Beneath the polished manners of the genteel Austrian society that formed his clientèle, Freud revealed a seething snake pit of unexpressed desires. Polite society never forgave him for it. Another chink in the mental armour of pre-Great-War Europe was exposed. But, unperturbed, the leaders of the nations continued to gird themselves for the coming catastrophe, convinced of the rightness of their cause and unwittingly illustrating the soundness of the King's caveat in *Hamlet*: 'Madness in great ones must not unwatched go'.

Traditional religion exerted a waning influence on rulers and ruled alike. In the 1890s' poetry of Wilde and the 'decadents', God ceased to be the inimical spoiler of Arnold's vision and became merely superfluous. Freud himself, in his essay 'The Future of an Illusion' (1927), placed the religious urge at a more primitive, less 'civilised' stage of human development. Not only has religion faltered at the threshold of the technological age but art, too, has proved inadequate. The Futurist Manifesto of Filippo Tommaso Marinetti, published in 1909, exhorted artists in all media to take cognisance of the importance of the machine, the new dynamic, and to centre their art around it. The consequences of such an 'ideal' can be witnessed in the cold, rigid, machine-like human beings that inhabit the paintings and the novels of Wyndham Lewis, an early disseminator of the Futurist ideals in their English form of 'Vorticism'.

The 20th century has not fostered one sustained movement and its offshoots, as the 19th century nurtured Romanticism, but has rather encouraged the fragmentation of the artistic consciousness into many single splinters. If this has been the age of the atom in science, it has been the age of the 'ism' in art. As well as Futurism and Vorticism, the early years of the century gave birth to Cubism, Imagism, Dadaism, Surrealism, Fauvism, Primitivism and many others, all of which are often blanketed under the term 'Modernism'. Many of the adherents of one particular 'ism' have, at various times, been at war with the apostles of another. The consensus in the artistic consciousness has broken down and the effect is much like what one observes in an ant hill if the queen ant is removed: a scurrying hither and thither, devoid of cohesive purpose. Movement beomes a multi-linear foraging at cross purposes instead of a circular orbit around a fixed centre. The fixed centre, the 'queen ant' that no longer imposes its subordinating pattern is the sense of religious conviction which has, by and large, gone out of art in the 20th century.

Of the many movements spawned in the early years of the century, the influences of two have continued to the present day: Imagism and Surrealism, the one emphasising the supremacy of consciousness, the other placing its trust in the infallibility of the unconscious. Neither movement places much confidence in God, scarcely heeds Him indeed. Imagism, developed by T. E. Hulme and Ezra Pound shortly before the Great War, is basically an anti-Romantic revolt. Instead of involving himself, the artist now rigorously excludes himself from his work and concentrates on moulding clear, hard, dry images which must stand alone, once formed, with no umbilical cord linking them back to their creator. They must not be given a human 'face'. Such fancies as that of Keats towards the bees – 'they think warm days will never cease' – would be anathema to the Imagists, since bees, in reality, cannot possibly 'think'. The Imagists wanted to see, and to represent, the object as it was in isolation, unconnected with man, an ontological phenomenon – or item of existence – abiding by its own physical laws.

In Imagism an attempt was made to shift the focus of attention away from the 'subjective' inner world of the artist to the 'objective' outer world which continues to be, whether or not the artist is there to record it. Yet the use of such 'objects' always serves a distinct purpose in the artist's plan. The 'Image', as Pound expressed it, 'presents an intellectual and emotional complex in an instant of time'. An example of this is found in T. S. Eliot's 'Gerontion':

> Vacant shuttles
> Weave the wind.

This image establishes at once a sense of purposeless activity. The process of weaving is conducted with an empty shuttle and an insubstantial loom ('the wind'). The 'intellectual' response, which Eliot intended to be simultaneous with the 'emotional' reaction, is strengthened if the image sets reverberating in the memory the words on which it is based, from the Book of Job, written at a time of much greater spiritual vitality: 'My days are swifter than a weaver's shuttle, and are spent without hope. O remember that my life is wind: mine eye shall no more see good' (vii. 6–7). Eliot's practice of Imagism was highly conscious. Each image was carefully chosen and expressly sculpted to communicate an instantaneous matrix of impressions, intellectual and emotional. The image was what Eliot termed the 'objective correlative', by whose means he conveyed simultaneously, and quicker than words could manage, a complex 'statement' involving both thought and feeling. In Imagism the artist's own personality, his particular 'psychic mould', remains in abeyance and has, in theory, nothing to do with the work of art he fashions.

Surrealism, on the contrary, denies the artist his right to impose an order, by conscious effort, on the chaos he beholds around him. To the surrealist the only 'valid' art comes as a direct, uncensored expression of the unconscious. Surrealism as a movement was not 'officially' formulated until 1924 in Paris, with the publication of André Breton's 'Manifeste du surréalisme'. But several earlier movements had already pointed the way. The most notable of these was Dadaism, founded in Switzerland by Tristan Tzara in 1916, when the war was locked in a devastating stalemate all along the Western front, from the North Sea to the Swiss frontier. The daily evidence of wholesale attrition, the recurrent news of heroic but pointless self-sacrifice on battlefields such as the Somme, convinced the Dadaists that life itself must be absurd if its most civilised societies could thus senselessly destroy one another. The dominant feeling the Dadaists sought to convey was disgust. The Great War had blasted the 19th-century myth of human 'progress' to smithereens and all the fragments were, to the Dadaists, of equal importance (or unimportance), to be pasted together haphazardly, uninhibitedly, without any attempt by the intrusive human consciousness to impose an order or pattern. The collage became a favourite genre among the Dadaists, one of their number, Kurt Schwitters, compiling his miscellanies from litter gathered on the streets.

Artistic responses to the crisis tended to divide into one of two camps. Either the artist grasped the mane of Imagism and determined to ride onward, whatever might hap, guided by the power of his own imagination and intellectual energy, if by nothing else: at the worst, he could be his own Creator. Or he fell in with the Surrealists, deciding that the old battles were no longer worth fighting and that nothing short of a revolution in artistic aims and methods would be adequate to cope with the new situation. The 'imagists', in other words, tended to be conservative, attempting to rehabilitate traditional values wherever possible and believing that the artist's role was to struggle heroically to construct some kind of order from the prevailing instability; while the 'surrealists' held that the old ways and beliefs were totally discredited and that only a revolution − artistic, social and political − could hope to salvage anything from the wreck. Surrealism was, artistically and politically, anarchistic. The havoc of the First World War had been wrought, it believed, by man's overriding ego. It was time, therefore, that the unconscious be given a chance to express itself and redress the balance. All forms of order were rejected, everything had equal value: a theory of egalitarianism which had parallels in the left-wing political movements with which Surrealism became associated.

Such a break with the past as the Surrealists desired proved, in practice, to be impossible. After all, the painter still had to mix the same pigments as his predecessor and the poet had to wield the same words. The Surrealists attempted to get round this problem by plastering image to image and word to word in bizarre juxtapositions: such confusion was held to reflect the disorder of existence itself and therefore to be valid. Even so, the Surrealists were unable to effect the complete break with the past that they wanted. Much of their work had been anticipated, in various forms, by 19th-century artists: it was not the Surrealist painter Salvador Dali, but the Symbolist poet Charles Baudelaire, who first raised excrement to the pitch of art.

The 'imagist' poet tends to undertake the heroic task of attempting to fashion some kind of shape and system out of the prevailing disintegration ('Shall I at least set my lands in order? / London Bridge is falling down falling down falling down', remarks Eliot in *The Waste Land*). He believes that life can yet be a noble affair and that the human being is still capable of achieving dignity through sacrifice. Such a writer, given the inability of contemporary Christianity to support him, will often attempt to erect a more potent mythology of his own (as Yeats did) which will validate the idea that there is a spiritual plane to human life and a continuing purpose from one generation to the next. He may even try to resuscitate the inert body of the old religion by blowing some of his fire and zeal into it, as Eliot and, later on, W. H. Auden did; or he may, like D. H. Lawrence, seize upon the discoveries of psychology to suggest that man can find personal 'order' by following the directives of his 'darker' self. Whatever the source of their conviction, the 'imagists' maintain a steadfast belief that man is not a mere accidental animal but is acting out the decrees of an obscure but noble purpose.

The 'surrealist', on the contrary, has no such faith to keep him going. To him the universe is absurd and pointless and man is merely one among many incidental excrescences, a pimple on the face of the material world, and of no intrinsic merit. The 'surrealist' will hence tend to debase rather than exalt the value of the human beings he introduces and will emphasise the absurdity of life by showing how absolutely without control over their environment his characters are. Evelyn Waugh's satiric novels are in this mould, as are some of the poems of Louis MacNeice:

The Laird o' Phelps spent Hogmanay declaring he was sober,
Counted his feet to prove the fact and found he had one foot over.
Mrs Carmichael had her fifth, looked at the job with repulsion,
Said to the midwife 'Take it away; I'm through with
    overproduction'.

('Bagpipe Music')

In this example neither the aristocracy (the 'Laird o' Phelps') nor the ordinary folk ('Mrs Carmichael') have dignity or even humanity (the Laird finds he has an extra limb and the mother is repelled by the new life she has spawned); at the same time the over-repetitive, mechanical rhythm of the long lines, sounding like a fairground carousel, suggest how people in the technological age 'ride' through life without giving much thought to it. To the 'imagist' human life can still attain to dignity; to the 'surrealist' it is ludicrous beyond redemption.

In the 19th century art had usually striven to keep up with the discoveries of science: Tennyson's approving nod at the railway age – 'Let the great world spin for ever down the ringing grooves of change' – though deficient in its physics (trains, contrary to what Tennyson supposed, do not run in grooves) is optimistic in its faith that scientific progress will always be for the better. The Victorian belief in progress has given way in the 20th century to the nightmare perspective of a driverless train speeding towards a dark destination, the rhythm of the wheels indicating not – as it had done to Tennyson – concordance with some divine plan but merely the monotonous drone of a world without spirit or spiritual hope:

> The damned are the damned are the damned are the damned are
>   the
> The World to come the Atom Plan the World of Man the Atom
>   Bomb the
> Coming Day the Biggest Bang the Wrath of God the Atom Age the
>   Day of Wrath.

Thus David Gascoyne, in the Train-Wheels Chorus of his poem 'Night Thoughts', expresses the sense of helplessness and defeat felt by many a modern poet.

The 20th century displays a nervous mixture of faith and despair, of firmness and insecurity, of belief in order and disbelief in anything beyond the present moment (the basic tenet of Existentialism). While some poets (the 'imagists') are energetically constructing artifices which will superimpose a sense of order on the muddle of modern life, others (the 'surrealists') are working to undermine those structures and bring them crumbling to earth. At various times in his career – and even, perhaps, within a poem – the same poet may act as both builder and demolition squad. Disunity and fragmentation in the work of art are endemic to this disordered century, where all values have been in a state of flux and instability since the First World War, and even before. A poet who had begun registering this shift of consciousness before the war broke out was the 'anti-romantic' Thomas Stearns Eliot.

T. S. Eliot (1888–1965)

By 1914 Romantic intensity had degenerated into thoughtless cliché, an example of which offers itself in Rupert Brooke's sentimental vision of the English soldier killed in overseas action:

>   there's some corner of a foreign field
>   That is for ever England.
>
> ('The Soldier')

In the wholesale slaughter that was shortly to follow in the 'foreign fields' of France and Belgium Brooke's public-school outlook on death and glory would come to seem painfully callow. The 'war poets', Wilfred Owen, Siegfried Sassoon and Isaac Rosenberg among others, were not slow to supply the corrective lenses and introduce the 'realistic' image, plain and unadulterated, of death in battle ('A man's brains splattered on / A stretcher-bearer's face'). And on the home front T. S. Eliot was undertaking a comparable mission to shock the bourgeois poetry-reading public out of its complacency.

Eliot's technique, learnt originally from the French Symbolist poet Jules Laforgue, was to present constant shifts of perspective, to juxtapose sublime with incongruous images and thereby dislocate the reader and set working in him a variety of different responses. Eliot's poetry perplexed its early readers (and many later ones) by its refusal to guide them through its mercurial transitions of mood and viewpoint and also by its interjection of untranslated Greek and Latin phrases and by its constant echoes of earlier European literature, some teasingly half-familiar, some obstinately obscure. Here is the difference between the poet in Eliot's day and the poet in Keats's. Keats can refer to earlier literature, to Greek mythology, to Christian story, in the certain knowledge that his reader will pick up the reference. Eliot, writing in an age of cultural barbarism – despite, paradoxically, the implementation of compulsory education for all Britons since 1870 – flaunts his own erudition before his readers and upbraids them for their cultural illiteracy. The explanatory notes he appended to *The Waste Land* on its first publication in 1921 were an ironic underlining of the low expectations Eliot had of his readers' capacity for extracting all the veins of richness from his poetry unaided.

Eliot began writing 'The Love Song of J. Alfred Prufrock' in 1910 and it was published in 1917, two years after he came from America to settle in England (he subsequently became a naturalised Briton). The title itself foreshadows one of the methods Eliot employs in this and later poems: the technique of bathos. The 'romantic' expectations set rolling by 'Love Song' are halted abruptly by the rectangular name, 'J. Alfred Prufrock', lifted by Eliot from a company of furniture wholesalers in his native St Louis and redolently suggestive of its protagonist's two most salient – and reprehensible – characteristics: prudishness ('Pru-') and effeminacy ('-frock'). Throughout the poem the 'romantic' pretensions of its speaker – who is ostensibly on his way to propose marriage to a woman he admires – are consistently undercut by the intruding 'reality' of his self-perceptions ('a bald spot in the middle of my hair'). Similarly, passages of great poetic beauty are succeeded by clippings of utter banality, while other flights of rhetoric are brought promptly to earth by the insertion of a most 'unpoetic' remark or image ('how should I begin / To spit out all the butt-ends'). All this helps to 'characterise' its speaker, Prufrock, who is obviously incapable of a sustained effort of the imagination. At the same time, Prufrock's failed chivalry is partly a product of his environment: the contemporary 'knight', surrounded as he is by the material comforts and securities of bourgeois society ('I have measured out my life with coffee spoons'), is insidiously deflected from his aim of achieving something extraordinary, of enduring merit. Read the opening section of the poem.

This first part sets the scene for the crucial encounter – the inevitable anticlimax – around which the poem is woven. Prufrock girds up his loins and sallies forth on his mission: to interview the lady and pop the 'overwhelming question'. The serpentine course he traces through the winding streets 'that follow like a tedious argument' suggests the reluctance with which he undertakes his task. He would rather circumvent a direct confrontation with the lady, if he could. The initial image gives some indication of Prufrock's state of mind: the sunset he notices on his journey appears, in his eyes, 'like a patient etherised upon a table', reflecting his own feeling of numbed impotence when called upon, for once in his life, to take an initiative. In a wider sense, the image reproaches modern man with a loss of sensitivity. The romantic expectations aroused by 'When the evening is spread out against the sky' are rudely jolted by the clinical simile of the subsequent line. This is a technique Eliot uses frequently, setting two contrary emotional responses twanging against each other.

The ensuing images convey the seediness and isolation endemic to urban existence: the 'restless nights in one-night cheap hotels', and the 'sawdust restaurants'. Prufrock, anaesthetised though he is by his acceptance of the unadventurous role society has cast him in, is half-aware of a dissatisfaction, a 'restlessness'. The streets themselves wickedly mirror this half-formed discontent and bring it to his consciousness. As the poem progresses, it becomes evident that Prufrock's intended proposal necessitates a wider reformation in the character of the speaker. It involves turning upside-down the 'safe' received picture of the world that Prufrock has hitherto held.

Henceforth he would begin to live more dangerously, more excitingly, more heroically. To present himself as a serious suitor to the lady means breaking out of the shell of impotence in which society has enclosed him. It involves a revolution of the whole man; and Eliot is implying that the whole of Western manhood needs such a regeneration if it is not to atrophy entirely. Thus, although Prufrock does have a tendency towards self-dramatisation, his claim that this is an 'overwhelming question' is not altogether exaggerated.

Yet Prufrock always shies away from answering the question and his initial approach, after leading circuitously up to this interrogative point, in lines of various lengths, metres and rhythms indicative of its speaker's tortuous and evasive mental processes, peters out timidly in a jingling rhyming couplet:

Oh, do not ask, 'What is it?'
Let us go and make our visit.

After such a feckless conclusion, not much doubt is left as to how the 'visit' itself is likely to terminate. Both question and quest bear the seeds of their own abrogation. Marking Prufrock's arrival at his destination, the subsequent couplet (lines 13–14), which will echo later on in the poem as a refrain of the futility of Prufrock's hermetically-sealed social circle, further jars on the 'aesthetic' sense by its coupling of the great Renaissance artist Michelangelo with the society women who 'come and go' in idle, purposeless prattle. Michelangelo, as opposed to Prufrock, was one who did have the courage to look the universe in the face and comprehend it with nothing but his own unaided faculties, all conventional filters removed. Unlike Prufrock, who merely wonders 'Do I dare?', Michelangelo did have the boldness to disturb the universe. Now he has been reduced to a topic of conversation at bored 'society' gatherings. The jog-trot rhythm and rhyme of the couplet add emphasis to this degradation.

Prufrock, however, has forfeited his right to be linked to Michelangelo. He has plumped for the security of clinging to accepted beliefs rather than run the risk of challenging them. Thus inured in his coffee-spoon world and conscious that to launch out with opinions of his own after so long a time of meek acquiescence risks courting ridicule ('They will say: "How his hair is growing thin!" '), it is unlikely that Prufrock will be able to summon and sustain the necessary energy. It is an energy akin to that involved in artistic commitment and there are signs throughout the poem that Prufrock is something of an artist *manqué*. But artistic commitment demands a sure sense of, and reliance on, one's own vision and inner resources. As Bernard Bergonzi remarked, 'Eliot . . . regarded poetic creation as . . . a surrender to possibly terrifying forces'. It is just such a surrender – a leap into the dark – of which Prufrock reveals himself to be incapable through his many hesitations. He prefers to take refuge in self-mockery and self-denigration.

The texture of the poem is impressionistic; it follows Prufrock's thoughts, in flitting about from one stimulus to another. Having recorded the precise tone of the chitchat about Michelangelo, Prufrock turns his bored gaze (lines 15–22) to the weather outside the house. Here, to add to his sense of helplessness, an all-encompassing fog seems to be bringing another blanket to help extinguish the light of his feeble, fluttering genius. The fog is seen as a friendly dog but it also represents an influence which effectively prevents Prufrock from launching out confidently on the vehicle of his own self-expression. The fog which 'curled once about the house, and fell asleep', seemingly stopping Prufrock from leaving, reminds him of how the affectionate tolerance of his hosts actually immobilises him from fully expressing, and being, himself ('corporal friends are spiritual enemies', as Blake observed).

This section, with its over-extended metaphor of the fog-dog and its dwelling on distinctly unpoetic phenomena ('the pools that stand in drains'), also indicates Prufrock's spasmodic creative urge at the same time as it illustrates his inability to see anything but the more insanitary and insalubrious aspects of creation (the dominant colour of his 'etherised' but unethereal imagination is a urinary 'yellow'). In the fog-enshrouded drawing room Prufrock's resolution already begins to wilt. He begins to justify procrastination (lines 23–34) and one senses surely that his earlier determination to make his declaration – of love but also of his own poetic response to the universe – is irretrievably slipping away. 'There will be time', he twice repeats, while still harping on his animated fog conceit; he seems to nourish a secret, autoerotic delight in the latter, which, the more he elaborates it, the less likely it is that he will ever share it with anyone else. If Prufrock does have his moments of artistic vision, he enjoys them – as he enjoys everything else in life – in private, so that they, like him, are doomed to sterility.

His quintessential cowardice is revealed in his attempt to bolster an argument for delay. He deludedly assures himself that, at some future time, it will be appropriate for him to 'murder and create' – to assume his artistic mantle and shock everybody's expectations of him: to destroy ('murder') his old self and 'create' a new. The application to his unassuming self of such bold verbs as 'murder' and 'create' and such solemn-sounding endeavour as is implied in 'all the works and days of hands' is, one suspects, mere posturing. Prufrock cannot sustain a grand illusion for very long. Like his image of the fog which soon descends to the 'pools that stand in drains', Prufrock's inflated dream of his own significance finishes up, anticlimactically, on his 'plate'. With him, the abstract very quickly gravitates to the concrete: to the bourgeois household objects, the plates, coffee spoons, marmalade, teacups and trousers, which are the landmarks by which Prufrock flounderingly navigates his voyage through life.

The whole passage draws an ironic undertone from implicit comparison with its model, the Book of Ecclesiastes. Prufrock's adaptation of these insights to vindicate his own cowardice starkly illuminates the gap between the ethos of his own milieu and that of earlier days. The dignity of the original is soon destroyed by the ludicrous intrusion of the dinner plate into Prufrock's stream of thought. The gaucherie of Prufrock's style, his meandering between the incipiently sublime conception and the baldly prosaic image, his distortion of the slow seasonal rhythm of life as beheld in Ecclesiastes into a kaleidoscopic quick-change dance rhythm ('Time for you and time for me') shows to the reader what a pale imitation of a proudly lived existence modern life has become. The blasé enumeration of visions – moments of profound insight – by the hundred shows what little value after all Prufrock attributes to such epiphanies; and this is followed by the ironic pun in 'revisions' (re-visions), suggesting that the moment of insight is in itself of so little significance that it can be 'revised', altered, a hundred times under the cold light of the intellect. Prufrock is devaluing his own intuitive insights. 'Would it have been worth it, after all?' he asks himself periodically. It is much easier to lapse into the safe routine of middle-class ritual: the 'toast and tea' are accorded equal importance, in Prufrock's scale of values, with the 'visions'.

In the remainder of the poem, not given here, Prufrock's hesitancy increases. His self-doubt grows, abetting his lethargy instead of abating it. Even the lady whom he had earlier intended to 'overwhelm' with his question seems no different from all the other comatose beauties he has known. He barely visualises her at all, noticing only the 'arms' that 'lie along a table', as if devoid of life. She becomes one with the 'etherised' patient stretched upon the table in line 3: someone without soul or animal vitality. So he lets the critical 'moment' – the opportunity both for proposing to the lady and for revealing his insights into the social hell they all inhabit – go by with an ironical shrug and a lame excuse: 'I am no prophet'. His is the 'love song' of the silent majority, the middle-of-the-road, mid-Atlantic male, who can only follow the cues of others but never initiate his own actions.

Prufrock and his confederates, rather than acknowledge that the mind, as Hopkins said, 'has mountains' and that a life lived perilously can carry one from the heights of exhilaration to the depths of despair and back again, opt for a routine of humdrum predictability, cushioning themselves from all unpleasantness behind a bulwark of material objects that act as obstacles to any inroads of the spirit. Auden was to return to the same idea – the theme of childhood innocence protracted perversely into adulthood – two decades later in '1st September 1939':

The lights must never go out,
The music must always play,
All the conventions conspire
To make this fort assume
The furniture of home;
Lest we should see where we are,
Lost in a haunted wood,
Children afraid of the night
Who have never been happy or good.

Or, as Eliot put it in *Murder in the Cathedral*, 'Human kind cannot bear very much reality'. Yet a life lived 'safely', behind the protection of the conventions, is a life lived mechanically and therefore soullessly. This is the awareness that Prufrock teeters on the brink of reaching throughout his 'love song', without ever managing to break through to it. An irreproachable inmate of America, Prufrock is presented as a paradigm of Western man in this century: choosing his words and guarding his conduct so as to offend nobody, ever ready to roll out the rhetorical platitude yet at heart a motley character, leaving no distinct impression, no stamp of his own personality. Having lingered a while in the anterooms of the imagination, Prufrock returns to the drawing room that constitutes his earthly prison, withdrawing into it like a snail retiring into its shell.

The vision of 'Prufrock' is bleak and does not augur well for mankind under modern democracy. The bleakness in Eliot's poetry was to be mitigated somewhat by his subsequent espousal of Anglo-Catholic doctrine and ritual, by a faith in what had been established by past tradition rather than a hope for anything good that might emerge from a technological present.

12   The Last Romantic: W. B. Yeats

Prufrock's self-denigration disguises an innate slothfulness, an unwillingness to accept that great ends are commensurate with the immense expenditure of energy and self needed to attain them, a collapse in the belief that had hitherto held sway in previous, more unwaveringly Christian centuries: the belief that through commitment, effort, discipline and self-sacrifice man could transcend the infirmities of his nature and win through to a worthy goal. This belief underlay in particular the endeavours of the Romantic poets, who held that through a concentrated output of imaginative energy the individual could break through to a higher self, a clearer reality and 'leave the world unseen' far behind or beneath him. Such faith was common to most 19th-century poets, writing in the shadow of the Romantic mountain range that had miraculously pierced the clouds in the early years of the century. But Prufrock remains nonplussed at the prospect offered by such creative endeavour, merely muttering, 'And would it have been worth it, after all?'

W. B. Yeats (1865–1939)

One poet whose voice rings out in splendid isolation amid the general air of glum defeat of the 20th-century poetic fraternity is William Butler Yeats. Helped no doubt by being severed from the English mainstream through his Irishness, a separation enhanced by his retreat in 1917 and periodically thereafter to the Norman tower he purchased at Ballylee, Yeats never ceased to affirm his belief that the poet's was a highly serious calling and that the poet deserved to be in the forefront of civilisation's leaders (a belief made concrete by Yeats's admission to the new Irish Senate in 1922). Yeats was the last in a tradition going back to Blake (whom he edited) and beyond, according to which the poet was a seer, more gifted than his fellows, able to penetrate the veils of the material world.

Yeats spoke out from behind a variety of masks and in many different moods throughout his long life but always with a lucid sureness, an exhilarated certainty, that poetry-making was among the world's most vital, and vitally needed, professions. In his unswerving conviction that the poet's function was of the utmost importance – his belief, with Keats, that the poet 'is a sage;/A humanist, physician to all men' – and in his unfailing ability to turn over the stones of day-to-day existence and discover the jewels embedded there, Yeats is pre-eminent among those he called 'the last romantics'.

Other aspects of his poetry further disclose Yeats's Romanticism. The two poems below, written at opposite ends of his career, bear witness to Yeats's continual yearning for a place where the creative intellect might thrive in peace, unshackled from the cruder demands of the body which houses it. Yet, conversely, few poets have had a greater awareness than Yeats of the vital interdependence of spirit and flesh. And, although his poems might conjure various earthly paradises – Innisfrees, Coole Parks and Byzantia – where the artistic soul, having shed the earthier demands of the body, may wander and create at will, there is always an implicit admission by Yeats that the soul relies on the experiences of its attendant body to nourish its activity. Art needs life, in all its miry confusion, if it is not to produce mere empty rhetorical artefacts. 'Fair needs foul', as the speaker in 'Crazy Jane Talks with the Bishop' declares, seeing that 'Love has pitched his mansion in / The place of excrement'.

Yeats was continually looking within himself and weaving new material out of what he found there. In his belief that his individual life and the changes and developments that occurred in the course of it were of general significance and worthy of transmutation into verse, Yeats again illustrates his Romantic tendency. Unalloyed Romanticism is most particularly evident in his earlier poems. But as Yeats grew older and became more embittered by the inability of the woman he loved, Maud Gonne, to return his love, the 'romanticism' is tempered by a hard realistic edge. From the suffering and disappointments of his private life Yeats fought through to a reforging of his experience into poetry. His faith in intensely-lived experience and in the rejuvenating properties of love never wavered. In a poem written after he was 70, here is Yeats affirming that all political events and intellectual activities wilt in insignificance beside the beauty and promise contained in a young, nubile girl:

Politics

How can I, that girl standing there,
My attention fix
On Roman or on Russian
Or on Spanish politics?
Yet here's a travelled man that knows
What he talks about,
And there's a politician
That has read and thought,
And maybe what they say is true
Of war and war's alarms,
But O that I were young again
And held her in my arms!

The old man's irritation and irascibility at the political chitchat he is forced to endure, colloquially expressed in the first ten lines, are suddenly transcended by the heartfelt lament of the last two: an entreaty which, in its suggestion that the 'inner man', or soul, remains perpetually young while its bodily casing grows increasingly decrepit, is a shout of simultaneous pain and exultation.

Unlike Wordsworth, who early withdrew from involvement in urban life to remain fixed behind the one 'pantheistic' mask and whose poetic mine was fairly well exhausted by his 33rd year, Yeats interspersed his periods of retreat and meditation with bouts of activity in the theatrical and political circles of Dublin, continually reforging a new 'mask' for his poetic personality (the 'I' of his poems) and avoiding the pitfalls of repetition and complacency right up to the time of his death at the age of 73. The first poem below, however, voices – from Yeats's 'early' period – a straightforward Wordsworthian impulse towards flight from the city into a world of pure pastoral delight.

The Lake Isle of Innisfree

I will arise and go now, and go to Innisfree,
And a small cabin build there, of clay and wattles made:
Nine bean-rows will I have there, a hive for the honey-bee,
And live alone in the bee-loud glade.

And I shall have some peace there, for peace comes dropping slow,
Dropping from the veils of the morning to where the cricket sings;
There midnight's all a glimmer, and noon a purple glow,
And evening full of the linnet's wings.

I will arise and go now, for always night and day
I hear lake water lapping with low sounds by the shore;
While I stand on the roadway, or on the pavements grey,
I hear it in the deep heart's core.

The theme needs little elaboration. The speaker, bogged down in his civilised routine, wishes to 'arise', to take wing like the linnet of stanza 2, and fly to a refuge of 'peace'. This haven for which the poet yearns is 'Innisfree': an island known to Yeats in County Sligo, bearing a name particularly apt for his purpose. The 'freedom' implied by Innisfree is a release not only from the restraints of urban society but from the demands, especially sexual ones, made by his own body. The poem proclaims the urge to recapture the lost innocence and the luscious fullness of response to life of childhood. Innisfree is a 'lake isle', insulated from any contact with fellow men by the shielding, 'lapping' waters.

There is a remarkable preponderance of 'womb' imagery in the poem. The poet wishes to ensconce himself in a 'small cabin' constructed with the earthy materials of 'clay and wattles'. The overhanging 'glade' where he plans to do this is itself a sort of protective womb, sheltering him in his 'alone'-ness; his only companions are the bees, themselves nestling within the womb-like 'hive' of the poet's provision. There are wombs within wombs. And, as befits this vision of prenatal existence, it is sounds rather than sights that strike the speaker's awareness. The glade is 'bee-loud', buzzing with the business of its insect occupants but not identified by any pictorial characteristics: the flutter of the linnet's wings 'fills' the twilight while the bird itself remains unseen and the 'low sounds' of the lake water are 'heard' while the lake itself is unvisualised.

Such light as does come to the poet has been filtered through many layers, dropping through 'the veils of the morning'. So diffused is this light, and so blurred the objects which come within the poet's visual range, that there seems to be little to distinguish midnight from midday ('There midnight's all a glimmer, and noon a purple glow'). The poet can here indulge in reverie to his heart's content. There will be no intrusive voices, or ocular reminders of other responsibilities, to call him out of his brown study. As well as the sound-image of the waves gently caressing the shore of his island retreat, the word 'lapping' conveys further associations, for it also means 'drinking up milk'; and there may be an additional pun intended from its third meaning of 'enfolding', 'wrapping around'. In other words, the poet, enveloped by the warm, nourishing womb-like waters of his imagined refuge, will be able to think his way back to his earliest origins, to rediscover the roots of his pre-existence and to recompose the internal harmony and ecstasy that prevailed when, in Wordsworth's words, 'The earth, and every common sight, / To me did seem / Apparelled in celestial light', before there was any clear 'I' or ego-awareness.

Thus the overall impression emerging from Yeats's early poem is a kind of effusive vagueness, an enthusiasm for a goal which remains unconceptualised except insofar as it is a flight from the concrete of the 'roadway' and the 'pavements grey' of the city. The practicality initially suggested by the poet's concern with his building materials ('of clay and wattles made') and by his clear-cut assertion of the exact extent of his cultivation ('Nine bean-rows will I have'), indicating that he intends to set about his experiment in self-sufficiency with the same hard-headed efficiency of Henry Thoreau (whose 19th-century withdrawal to the American 'wilderness' is described in *Walden*), soon peters out in 'romantic' sounds and shadings. The activity originally promised by the poet's projected building and planting is soon overshadowed by the feeling of luxurious passivity, the poet doing nothing, just resting immobile the livelong day – 'morning', 'midnight', 'noon' and 'evening' – and allowing the 'peace' which 'drops' with infinitesimal 'slowness' to seep into his consciousness: a consciousness which, having shed all adult responsibility and recaptured the child's sense of wonder at, and oneness with, the created world, may once more float free in absolute receptivity, lying open, in Tennyson's words, 'all Danaë to the stars'. 'Realism', in other words, is soon supplanted by 'romanticism'.

Or is it? For all the urgency expressed, there remains a suspicion that the poet knows that his dream is unrealisable, that Innisfree will remain forever out of reach. This is evident when one compares the openings of the first and third stanzas. Despite the note of decision on which the first stanza abruptly opens ('I will arise and go now'), by the opening of the last stanza the speaker has not yet budged. His actions contradict his words. He is willing himself into motion at this juncture ('I *will* arise and go now'), yet his feet remain firmly planted where they are ('While I stand on the roadway'), stubbornly refusing to follow the directives issuing from the poet's fugitive fancy. The poem thus displays a dichotomous split between the two distinct 'I's inhabiting the same poetic soul: one of these identities yearns inconsolably for a life of milk and honey in an earthly paradise ('I shall have some peace there'), while the other self knows that such an attempt to dodge the complications of adult existence would in the end be futile and that 'real' life, however dismal, must be borne with dogged and heroic patience ('While I stand on the roadway, or on the pavements grey'). This is something else that the poet also admits 'in the deep heart's core', although it is implicit rather than avowed in this poem. As Yeats's poetic career extended, and as his life unfolded, he set about the task of reconciling the two impulses – towards the realm of the imagination and the domain of reality – that are posited in this early poem.

The following poem, written in Yeats's 63rd year, takes up the theme again, though with an added irony acquired by age.

Sailing to Byzantium

I

That is no country for old men. The young
In one another's arms, birds in the trees
– Those dying generations – at their song,
The salmon-falls, the mackerel-crowded seas,
Fish, flesh, or fowl, commend all summer long
Whatever is begotten, born, and dies.
Caught in that sensual music all neglect
Monuments of unageing intellect.

II

An aged man is but a paltry thing,
A tattered coat upon a stick, unless
Soul clap its hands and sing, and louder sing
For every tatter in its mortal dress,
Nor is there singing school but studying
Monuments of its own magnificence;
And therefore I have sailed the seas and come
To the holy city of Byzantium.

III

O sages standing in God's holy fire
As in the gold mosaic of a wall,
Come from the holy fire, perne in a gyre,
And be the singing-masters of my soul.
Consume my heart away; sick with desire
And fastened to a dying animal
It knows not what it is; and gather me
Into the artifice of eternity.

IV

Once out of nature I shall never take
My bodily form from any natural thing,
But such a form as Grecian goldsmiths make
Of hammered gold and gold enamelling
To keep a drowsy Emperor awake;
Or set upon a golden bough to sing
To lords and ladies of Byzantium
Of what is past, or passing, or to come.

The poet is once more speaking in the first person. But whereas in the earlier poem Yeats establishes his own importance in the scheme from the very first word, so that the details of 'Innisfree' are painted in as subordinate items to the all-important 'I' in the foreground, in the later poem it is the qualities of the desiderated refuge, the paradise lost, which assume pride of place, the poet hovering in the background and not presenting himself directly until almost halfway through the poem ('therefore I have sailed . . .'). Furthermore, the whole presentation of 'I' is coloured by a blend of earnestness and self-mockery, the kind of mixture of seriousness and self-deprecation that a mature man adopts as his mask – his persona – before the world, simultaneously revealing and concealing the complex inner workings of his 'heart'.

The poem throughout carries an undertone of irony, indicating various levels of disparity between the poet's declarations and his real intentions. What had lain buried in 'The Lake Isle of Innisfree' is brought into the light of day by the deployment of a more richly ironic tone: the soul might cry 'arise and go' but the body, and perhaps the mind as well, will advise 'stand' and stay where you are. Such a 'bifocal' vision, announcing a split between impulse and performance, is further encouraged by the obvious unattainability of 'Byzantium'. The poem is constructed around the basic contrast between Ireland – the 'That' of the first line, the world of nature and natural instincts – and 'the holy city of Byzantium', an ideal world where the artist can flourish unimpeded by the calls of the flesh. Yeats wrote elsewhere of Byzantium – an oriental Christian civilisation that had perished several centuries earlier – that it represented for him an epoch when the artist and his audience had been closer together than at any time before or since, a time when 'architect and artificers . . . spoke to the multitude and the few alike'. In that era, as he envisioned it, there had been between art and life a symbiotic partnership which had since split into a dichotomy. In a social climate so conducive to mental pursuits the artist could set about erecting the monumental works that proved so difficult to create in the cloying, clawing sensual world of 20th-century Ireland.

Since Byzantium is obviously impossible of literal attainment – it is long gone in the recesses of time – Yeats can only be referring to a figurative Byzantium: a paradise of the mind or the imagination, where the creative genius can forge unhampered its 'monuments of unageing intellect'. Yet the audaciousness of this phrase, with its implicit claim for the eternal quality of the poet's own work and for the extraordinariness of his intelligence, suggests that the poet has penned it with his tongue in his cheek. He is laughing at his own pretentiousness, even while he clings with the utmost seriousness to the conviction that a communal structure in which art plays no major role is merely brutal. Such is the complexity of the mature Yeats's attitude to art and life.

It is a complexity which is developed further by the contradictory images of the first stanza, and indeed the whole poem. The world on which the poet is explicitly turning his back – it is 'that' country not 'this' – is an irrefutably attractive one. It is a world of love ('the young / In one another's arms'), joy ('birds in the trees . . . at their song') and the teeming sexual vitality suggested by its shoals of fish ('The salmon-falls, the mackerel-crowded seas'). All this is rejected, ostensibly, in a fit of pique from one of the 'old men' towards the younger generation that is supplanting him. The disgruntled sarcasm of 'at their song', applied to both the birds and the young lovers in their smiling insouciance, is an attempt to disparage what he can no longer enjoy. The same may be said of his summation of all this fertile, procreative activity from which he feels excluded as 'those dying generations'. By reproducing himself, the implication is, man, along with his fellow animals, is engendering not only new life but new death – his own. He is caught in the unceasing round of 'whatever is begotten, born, and dies' – what Eliot's Sweeney calls the cycle of 'birth, and copulation, and death' – from which the poet–artist wishes to extricate himself.

Yet at the same time that he is casting aspersions on this 'natural' life lived according to the instincts, the speaker is painting it in arresting terms, using images brimming with life and vitality, the very opposite of the austerity the poet is promising himself in his Byzantine exile. Moreover, the choice of the terminology 'fish, flesh, or fowl!' associates this rejected 'country' with the world at its moment of fresh creation, before death had come into it ('and God said unto them, Be fruitful and multiply . . . and have dominion over the fish of the sea, and over the fowl of the air': Genesis, i. 28), adding to the blend of disdain and regret in the poet's attitude. The attractions of physical life are glimpsed in the ambiguous reference to 'that sensual music'. It may be disarmingly appealing but it is also the siren song that lures man away from his higher destiny, immuring him within his body and its appetites:

Caught in that sensual music all neglect
Monuments of unageing intellect.

Sexual desire obscures the clarity of the artistic vision and weakens the urge to communicate it; yet at the same time such desire is an indispensable element in the creation of the artistic monument, from its inception to its completion ('What else have I to spur me into song?' asked Yeats elsewhere).

The ageing poet, viewing himself with honest irony, stands exposed as of no more account than a scarecrow, a 'tattered coat upon a stick'.

This image expresses Yeats's sense of the anticlimax of life, if calibrated simply on a carnal scale: flesh falls, energy wilts, the old man performs a grotesque parody of his once vigorous acts, frightening away the 'birds in the trees' and, no doubt, the 'young' of his own species. And yet man can counter the effects of inevitable physical debility by nurturing that part of himself – the 'soul' – which is not eroded by the passage of time. In fact, the further the body deteriorates, the more unimpeded becomes the expression of the ageless spirit which inhabits it. The 'song' of the weather-beaten, world-pummelled scarecrow soars in triumph across the earthly fields, growing stronger with each new manifestation of physical decrepitude ('louder sing / For every tatter in its mortal dress'). Thus Yeats expresses his belief that the perishable poet has tapped an underground source of perennial consolation.

What exactly this source is escapes particular description. Only by 'studying / Monuments of its own magnificence', by contemplating the created legacy of other artists, will the individual soul discover the spring of its own immortality. Hence the expressed desire of the poet to abandon a world where art is diluted, and sometimes overwhelmed, by nature:

And therefore I have sailed the seas and come
To the holy city of Byzantium.

Sailing the seas represents a break with his past life – impure because immersed from time to time in the needs of the body – and the assumption of a new and 'holy' discipline: henceforth the only calls he will heed are artistic ones. Byzantium is an anteroom to eternity; here the poet intends to hone his spirit for the work it will accomplish once he has succeeded – through death – in completely discarding his mortal shell.

How sincere Yeats is in turning towards a static world of artistic 'monuments' and in his rejection of the dynamic world of 'whatever is begotten, born, and dies' remains matter for conjecture. His humorous portrayal of his ageing self in the guise of a scarecrow suggests an affection for his body which does not entirely square with his apparently contemptuous dismissal of it as 'a dying animal'. There is a fully-conscious element of posturing in Yeats's plea to be 'consumed' by the 'sages', the artist-prophets of earlier times. Yeats formulates his desire to live what is left of his life in a kind of museum where his senses will be fed only by the music and mosaics of earlier artists, while implicitly acknowledging that such a rarefied existence would be unsatisfactory. His request to the sages in stanza 3 to be the 'singing-masters' of his soul is both serious and wistful. The poet apparently clamours for a state of being which he knows is impossible. The human eye pieces the sages together from their suggested form in 'the gold mosaic of a wall'. They inhabit another sphere, an eternal one ('God's holy fire'), and yet they depend on the cognitive and deductive powers of the observant and 'animal' eye to endow them with cohesive identity and 'being'. Without this dynamic, organic and physical reaction, they would remain merely a myriad of fragments of inanimate matter.

The poet asks them to descend from their eternal sphere to his temporal one. 'Perne in a gyre' is an imperative, calling on the dead sages to spin down from their static world into the poet's generating and degenerating sphere of being ('perning' is a spiralling movement facilitating concourse between spiritual and earthly planes). He demands to be taken by them out of the imperfect, dying world of nature and into the perfect, undying state of infinite being of which he has already been vouchsafed glimmers by the harmonious yet immobile presence of great works of art. The sages are beseeched by the poet to step down momentarily and lift him out of his soiled and sullied bodily state – in which, despite his advanced age, he finds himself still as 'sick with desire' and as insufficient in self-knowledge ('It knows not what it is') as any fledgeling adolescent – into a state of being ('Byzantium') in which he need no longer heed the body's demands on his higher abilities.

Yet, when one considers the immobility of the sages, 'standing' perpetually in 'God's holy fire', burning without consuming, and contrasts their state with the teeming activity of the first stanza, one can scarcely avoid the inference that Yeats's plea to be rid of the flesh carries certain unspoken reservations. Wrenched from the 'dying animal' of the body which houses it, the soul might have little left to sing about. Dead poets write few poems. Eternity itself is an 'artifice', a concept of the time-bound, earth-borne mind, without any tangible identity. The word 'artifice', meaning a forge for creative work but also something artificial and spurious, sets warning bells ringing in the mind. In consequence, the reader approaches the poem's final stanza thoroughly alert to the layers of irony that may be deposited beneath the speaker's declared intent.

In the poet's ideal world all natural objects – birds or boughs – are 'gold' or 'golden' and all humankind is purged of its lower orders: nothing but the aristocracy, 'lords and ladies', promenades at leisure through the gold-bespangled precincts of Byzantium. Yet there are paradoxes in the presentation of this dream world, suggesting that the poet is undermining his El Dorado even while constructing it. All the elements that go into the making of Byzantium seem to have been copied from the 'fallen' world of nature, 'those dying generations'. The 'birds in the trees' of the first stanza find their counterparts here, though moulting feathers and peeling bark have been given a coat of 'gold enamelling' to render them permanent. The vitality of the natural kingdom seems to have been reduced to something clockwork, mechanical and repetitive. The number of times (four in four lines) that the word 'gold' and derivatives of it occur in this stanza emphasises the monotony of this perfected world. No wonder its Emperor is 'drowsy'.

Not only does Byzantium emerge as a uniform world of bored inhabitants, artificially imitating the 'natural' world it has banished from its purlieus; it is not even a zone where the artistic impulse, ostensibly Byzantium's *raison d'être*, seems able to flower. Byzantium is a place of craft – of hammering and enamelling – but not of art. Uprooted from its soil amid the dying generations and transplanted among the pavements of a city of 'artifice', the creative urge wilts and dies. Scratch off the 'gold enamelling' and there is nothing in Byzantium that could not be found, to better purpose, in the world of 'nature' that the poem seems so assiduous in rejecting. Even the 'lords and ladies of Byzantium' need to be entertained with news of 'what is past, or passing, or to come': in their 'golden' world there can be no flux – no past, present or future – yet they desire to hear songs about temporal changes.

The speaker – the 'I' – of 'Sailing to Byzantium' seems intent on rushing to an idealised location where he can shrug off his ageing bodily shell and release the creativity of his 'unageing' intellect. The irony – unremarked by the 'speaker' but deftly manipulated by Yeats – is that only in the fallen world of animal sensuality and pervasive death can the 'monuments' erected by the artistic sensibility have any meaning or purpose. 'Once out of nature', the artist is cut off from his source and will find himself singing, like a clockwork canary, to no end. Prophets are needed in this world, not the next; it is of little avail to sing to those who inhabit eternity of 'what is past, or passing, or to come'.

Yeats's poetic career, like this particular poem, exemplifies a heroic resignation to being human, based on an understanding that all of mankind's finest accomplishments find their source in man's maverick disposition as a mongrel creature, half angel and half beast. As Yeats declared in 'The Circus Animals' Desertion', when describing the perennial and unmodified tactic of his search for inspiration:

> I must lie down where all the ladders start,
> In the foul rag-and-bone shop of the heart.

13 War and its Aftermath: W. H. Auden

The splendour of Britain's imperial progress in the 19th century and the success, by and large, of her armed forces blinded most of her poets to the technological revolution that had been going on in the weapons and methods of warfare and rendered them unfit to make the kind of black and ominous prognostications of impending Armageddon that had been issuing from the pens of their Continental (particularly German) confrères since the 1890s. The Prusso–Austrian War of 1866, with its demonstration of the ruthless efficiency of the new needle-gun, had made European poets outside the British Isles much more susceptible to the tremors of a world war. While Continental poets were prophesying this dire event, British poets, with few exceptions, went on trilling notes of pastoral roundelay until the outbreak of hostilities in 1914.

> About the woodlands I will go
> To see the cherry hung with snow,
>
> *(A Shropshire Lad*, II)

sang A. E. Housman in 1896; and Rupert Brooke was blithely hoping, in imagery more prophetic than he knew of the coming trench warfare, that the God of the Victorians was still sitting behind the screen of this world, covertly working his purpose out:

> One may not doubt that, somehow, Good
> Shall come of Water and of Mud;
> And, sure, the reverent eye must see
> A Purpose in Liquidity.
>
> ('Heaven')

Only after the successive shocks of repeated slaughters and two winters in the trenches did English war poetry shed its inherited forms and begin to find its own personal voice: the splintered rasp of 20th-century consciousness, its dreams and beliefs hopelessly shattered, groping its way through no-man's-land, its only goal survival.

Wilfred Owen was the most accomplished of the young officer-poets of the Great War; the apocalyptic vision that the war soon provoked in him was personally fulfilled, tragically enough, by his own death in action a week before the Armistice. Although he was never *technically* 'modern' in the way that his contemporary T. S. Eliot was, Owen's modernity exists in the straightforward, matter-of-fact way he recorded, free from any 'poetic' or 'romantic' veil, the horrors he witnessed on the battlefield:

> If you could hear, at every jolt, the blood
> Come gargling from the froth-corrupted lungs,
> Obscene as cancer.
>
> ('Dulce et Decorum Est')

Owen's poetry registers a widening gap between society's institutions and its intellectuals; as the war, and his service in it, was prolonged, the mood of his poetry became more recriminatory, embittered and alienated.

During the 19th century the division between the 'poet' and the 'state', so commonplace in France at the time, had seldom been apparent in Britain; in fact, quite the contrary. Wordsworth and Tennyson were elevated to the level of national institutions in their lifetimes; Arnold, Dickens and many another 'major' Victorian writer regarded the role of the literary creator as indispensable to the healthy functioning of the social organism. However critical they may have been of their country's practices, they seldom doubted that society's ills could not be healed by a little wise guidance and correction from their own muscular intelligence. Only with the end of the century, through the imprisonment of Oscar Wilde and the increasing gloom of Hardy's poetic voice, did the gap between society's institutions, which by their static character tend to ossify, and its poets' imaginations, which by their dynamic nature tend to worry and chafe at the restrictions imposed by the social framework, begin to seem unbridgeable.

W. H. Auden (1907–73)

Wystan Hugh Auden is, perhaps, the most salient example of the mutually detrimental relationship between nation and poet that has subsisted since the Great War. Acclaimed by reviewers as a most promising poet when his first volume of verse was published in 1930, when he was only 23, and acknowledged by subsequent critics to be the natural successor to Eliot, Auden never rose to the eminence expected of him. Brilliant as his verse is – at times ironic, at times laconic, at times lyrical, and marvellously deft at moving between serious and colloquial tones with a sense of balance that seldom falters – Auden's poetic legacy, viewed entire, remains a medley of diverse moods and themes, a motley material that cannot be gathered into the coherent fabric that a unified vision, or even a belief in his own essentiality as a poet, might have created. In the middle of his poignant elegy in memory of Yeats, for example, Auden drops the disclaimer that 'poetry makes nothing happen' – as if he were deliberately repudiating Yeats's belief that literature could alter the behaviour of men, expressed in Yeats's poem 'The Man and the Echo':

> Did that play of mine send out
> Certain men the English shot?

The difference between Yeats's conception of the poet's heroic significance and Auden's acceptance of his practical nonentity could hardly be greater.

The several alterations of viewpoint and commitment in his personal life – from Marxism to orthodox Anglicanism, a stint of ideological left-wing service with the Republican forces in the Spanish Civil War being succeeded by withdrawal to exile in the United States just as Fascism was casting a darker, more menacing shadow over the whole of Europe – have their counterpart in the variety of Auden's oeuvre. He was, at different times, a polemical playwright, a creator of light and of serious verse, an opera librettist, a producer of political poems in his youth and of meditative quasi-religious poetry in his maturity. All adds up to an impression of energies scattered outwards, not orbiting around a common centre. Despite the gusto with which he threw himself into each new poetic task, there hangs over Auden's poetry an awareness of its inconsequence. Such a vision stops short of being tragic only as a result of Auden's modesty, sense of humour and unerring gift for comic timing:

> As I listened from a beach-chair in the shade
> To all the noises that my garden made,
> It seemed to me only proper that words
> Should be withheld from vegetables and birds.
>
> ('Their Lonely Betters')

There is a subtle air of self-mockery here, a feeling of self-deflation behind Auden's image of himself idling away an afternoon in his collapsible (and unpoetic) 'beach-chair' listening to the noises of 'vegetables and birds'. The use of the word 'vegetables' rather than the more appropriate 'trees' gives exactly the slightly pompous tone that Auden seeks. The poet, pontificating in diction a little too dignified for its subject-matter ('It seemed to me only proper that words / Should be withheld'), emerges as a somewhat ludicrous figure. And yet, for all its deliberate self-puncturing, the same poem can offer glimpses of the depths to which the poet's vision might reach if only he thought he would be taken seriously:

> We, too, make noises when we laugh or weep,
> Woods are for those with promises to keep.

Auden has a lot of the clown about him. Afraid to take himself too seriously, for fear of attracting laughter rather than tears, he often slips a tragic 'telegram' into a poem which opens on a note of comic burlesque. Thus in one poem the reader is entertained with the vignette of a couple of rather low drinking establishments:

> At Dirty Dick's and Sloppy Joe's
>   We drank our liquor straight,
> Some went upstairs with Margery,
>   And some, alas, with Kate.
>
> ('The Sea and the Mirror')

The poet positions himself into a closer, more precise relationship with the characters he describes by his interpolated 'alas'. He has already experienced these dives and these women, one gathers, and his verdict on one of the latter is far from favourable. If these are low characters, the poet does not scruple to include himself among their number. Again he is clowning, deliberately deflating his dignity. Yet a few lines afterwards comes a reference, in simple lyrical language, to the universal tragedy involved in being human:

> The nightingales are sobbing in
>   The orchards of our mothers,
> And hearts that we broke long ago
>   Have long been breaking others.
>
> ('The Sea and the Mirror')

Auden can move his audience from guffaws to tears at the drop of a jester's hat.

Elsewhere in his poetic canon Auden keeps up a sustained comic voice against which the tragic is rarely permitted to make itself heard; but frequently a solemn resonance can be detected in even the most ostensibly 'comic' of statements:

> The village rector
>   Dashes down the side-aisle half-way through a psalm;
> The sanitary inspector
>   Runs off with the cover of the cesspool on his arm –
> To keep his date with Love!
>
> (*The Ascent of F6*)

The incongruous pairing of vicar and sewerage engineer seized in the midst of their professional duties and borne away by an irrepressible lust is simultaneously ludicrous and serious, suggesting as it does that service to a stronger passion than that inspired by the ordinary vocation is the correct choice, even if dignity and social responsibility have thereby to be abandoned. Auden, more than Eliot, had an ear for the colloquial and the ability to incorporate it into the integral structure of his verse and theme. His adroitness with rhythm enabled him to slide colloquialisms into his lines so that they seldom, if ever, draw attention to themselves by disrupting the established metric pattern. Auden also had the ability to compress an insight within the boundaries of an epigram.

> Those to whom evil is done
> Do evil in return,

he writes in '1st September 1939', encapsulating in a nutshell the sociological – though not the moral – justification of violent revolution.

Auden's undoubted gifts as an entertainer seem sometimes offset by an irrepressible urge to startle and shock:

> Financier, leaving your little room
> Where the money is made but not spent,
> You'll need your typist and your boy no more;
> The game is up for you and for the others.
>
> ('Consider This and in Our Time')

The overall image that emerges of Auden himself – and in this he is a representative modern figure – is that of the poet as vagabond, outcast 'upon the skirts of human-nature dwelling' (in Keats's words). The poet's place is no longer at the centre of society, as it had been in Arnold's and Tennyson's day. The poet now is excluded from society's rituals and wanders around on its periphery playing sometimes the role of amusing buffoon and sometimes the role of unregarded prophet. The indelible conviction of the artist's insignificance, of his redundancy amid the machinery of modern life – and, indeed, of the superfluity nowadays of all individual acts of high or heroic endeavour – is everywhere evident between the lines (and sometimes within them) of Auden's multifarious verse.

Musée des Beaux Arts

> About suffering they were never wrong,
> The Old Masters: how well they understood
> Its human position; how it takes place
> While someone else is eating or opening a window or just
>   walking dully along;
> How, when the aged are reverently, passionately waiting
> For the miraculous birth, there always must be
> Children who did not specially want it to happen, skating
> On a pond at the edge of the wood:
> They never forgot
> 10 That even the dreadful martyrdom must run its course
> Anyhow in a corner, some untidy spot
> Where the dogs go on with their doggy life and the torturer's
>   horse
> Scratches its innocent behind on a tree.

In Brueghel's *Icarus*, for instance: how everything turns away
Quite leisurely from the disaster; the ploughman may
Have heard the splash, the forsaken cry,
But for him it was not an important failure; the sun shone
As it had to on the white legs disappearing into the green
Water; and the expensive delicate ship that must have seen
20   Something amazing, a boy falling out of the sky,
Had somewhere to get to and sailed calmly on.

This poem amply demonstrates Auden's belief that actions calling for supreme artistic or heroic exertion, what Shakespeare called 'enterprises of great pitch and moment', pass wholly unheeded by the world at large. He takes as his cue a painting executed in the 16th century by Pieter Brueghel, showing thereby that the undervaluation of artistic energy is a common failing of mankind at all times and not a myopia which is peculiar to the 20th century. The picture referred to – and which he describes in some detail in the latter part of the poem – depicts the fall of Icarus; who according to Greek legend followed the example of his father Daedalus, the inventor, and made wings for himself, fixed to his shoulders by wax, but on flying too close to the sun discovered that the wax was melting, whereupon he plummeted into the sea and was drowned. Both father and son, Daedalus and Icarus, are sometimes taken as types of the artist who aspires, by his imagination and ingenuity, to lift himself above his mere animal nature.

The point of Brueghel's painting, as Auden makes clear towards the end, is the indifference of Icarus's fellows to his remarkable achievement ('something amazing') and tragic end (he dies when still a mere 'boy'). Brueghel's canvas is dominated by the other activities that Auden describes – the 'ploughman' plodding methodically along behind his team, the galleon with 'somewhere to get to' dipping through the waves – while Icarus's 'white legs', disappearing into the sea, occupy an inconspicuous corner of the whole, like the peripheral role which Auden recognised as the artist's lot in the social drama. And even Brueghel's painting is hidden away, out of the public eye, mummified in a museum.

The conversational tone of Auden's language admits the reader at once to his discourse. He is at the reader's side, nudging him with his elbow and encouraging his acquiescence with a wink and a nod. He does this with consummate ease, moving deftly from the high seriousness of the 'dreadful martyrdom' (Christ's crucifixion) to the low comedy of the 'doggy' lives and the horse's 'behind', so that one scarcely notices any incongruity. The poetry does not call attention to itself as poetry, the disclosure of its theme is deceptively casual. Yet the variation of the line-lengths and the well-placed pauses have all been skilfully contrived to punctuate the development of Auden's argument in a precise, though unobtrusive, manner. The pause after 'human position', for instance, in the third line, makes the reader halt momentarily and absorb Auden's topic – the place of individual suffering within the community at large – before plunging into the long fourth line with its implications that the momentum of life's routine prevents anyone from displaying more than a passing concern for another's pain, which 'takes place'

> While someone else is eating or opening a window or just walking
> dully along.

As well as Auden's virtuosity with rhythm and varying line-lengths, the poem's tone, with its fluctuations between the tragic and the casual so that nothing ever jars, bears further witness to the poet's quiet artistry. In the fifth line, for instance, the expectations of the old from the new life after death promised them through the 'miraculous birth' of Christ are subtly augmented in their intensity by the addition of a second, stronger adverb:

> the aged are reverently, *passionately* waiting.

Their original, calmer feelings of religious 'reverence' are superseded by more 'passionate' emotions; it might be thought, therefore, that their desire to be renewed in the body is more ardent than their desire to be renewed in the spirit (a most unChristian priority). Then, from the mention of the 'miraculous birth', Auden switches at once to more colloquial language – the children 'did not specially want it to happen' – and a more commonplace image: 'skating / On a pond at the edge of the wood'. In the context of the poem this crystal-clear image (which seems to be straight out of one of Brueghel's paintings of outdoor activities in a Flemish winter) assumes other shades. The skating represents people's propensity for self-indulgence and amusement, regardless of the tragedies by which they are surrounded and of the dark fate which awaits them: the 'edge of the wood' beside which they cavort in blithe oblivion may be the 'haunted wood' of Auden's '1st September 1939'.

The end of the poem's first section sees a return to Auden's blend of the comic and the tragic. The specific reference may be to Christ's crucifixion on the hill of Calvary but the generic reference is to all instances of cruelty between man and man. Even while the dreadful deed is being done, the dogs are pursuing their 'doggy life' in absolute indifference and the horse on which the 'torturer' sits is more concerned with ridding itself of a bothersome insect than with the solemn scene that is unfolding before its uncomprehending eyes. Auden here emphasises the comic at the expense of the tragic: it is not the 'martyrdom' that takes the attention but the horse's attempt to soothe its irritation. Auden accentuates the comic yet further by transferring the epithet 'innocent' from the horse itself (which is not to blame for what its rider perpetrates) to the most fundamental part of its anatomy. The very mention of an 'innocent behind', so irreverent in the neighbourhood of the 'dreadful martyrdom', might seem liable to topple the poem's tone irretrievably into the realm of earthy burlesque. Yet, so adroitly does Auden interchange the two masks through which life may be viewed that the equilibrium between tragedy and comedy is unfalteringly maintained.

This mixing of 'funny' and serious references reflects the diversity of life and demonstrates that an event which is one man's tragedy may be another man's delight or chance for profit. The same perception, that self-centred man is too concerned with glutting his own needs to spare more than a cursory thought for the distress of one of his fellows, emerges from the mixture of 'tragic' events and 'comic' characters in Shakespeare's plays, if one follows the reading of Dr Johnson (in *The Preface to Shakespeare*):

> Shakespeare's plays are not . . . either tragedies or comedies, but compositions . . . exhibiting the real state of sublunary nature . . . and expressing the course of the world, in which the loss of one is the gain of another; in which, at the same time, the reveller is hasting to his wine, and the mourner burying his friend.

The 'comprehensiveness' of Shakespeare's vision re-emerges in Auden's poem. And Auden, by choosing a painting from the Renaissance as prime illustrator – indeed, motivator – of his theme, is acknowledging that the *separateness* of the individual life has been noted in eras very different in time and temper from his own.

The casual unconcern, the self-absorption that prevents man from participating in the triumphs and catastrophes of his fellows is depicted in several images located at various parts of Brueghel's canvas. As Auden comments, 'everything turns away / Quite leisurely from the disaster' of Icarus's downfall. A lifetime's aspirations, efforts and ingenuity are reduced in the mind of the multitude – insofar as it gives the matter any thought at all – to 'a boy falling out of the sky'. Auden singles out three aspects of Brueghel's painting which emphasise the world's indifference to the individual life (and death). The ploughman 'may have heard the splash', but 'for *him*', wholly bound up in his appointed task and following the furrows of his own concerns without deviation, Icarus's débâcle 'was not an important failure'. The men on board the ship are similarly unable or unwilling to divagate from their course to go to the aid of a suffering fellow. So much are they the slaves of their ship's commercial schedule – their vessel's vassals, as it were – that the boat has usurped the use of their own manly functions: it is the ship, not the sailors, that has 'seen' the falling Icarus and that makes the inhuman decision to ignore his 'cry' and 'sail calmly on', its crew cabinned and confined in the roles of serviceable automata. And over the whole scene, 'the sun shone / As it had to'. Even the gods of Icarus's world are indifferent to his fate. There is also a link with the 'dreadful martyrdom' alluded to in the earlier part of the poem, for Icarus's 'forsaken cry' recalls the desolate shout of the crucified Christ, deserted by man and abandoned by God: 'My God, my God, why hast thou forsaken me?' (Mark, xv. 34). Under the casual manner of Auden's delivery serious questions are being ushered in.

Auden's tone is deceptively and deliberately offhand, as if he realised that his society has reached such a state of atheism and self-indulgence that solemn envoys must present themselves in comic garb if they are to obtain an audience. Thus the casual way in which the 'Old Masters' are introduced and the manner in which a masterpiece of the Renaissance art world is slipped into the discourse as an apparent afterthought ('In Brueghel's *Icarus*, for instance') constitute an attempt by the poet to sugar the pill of his moral lesson in an age when the 'Old Masters' – the artists and the prophets – are given scant attention and accorded small significance by the people *en masse*.

From Brueghel's painting Auden picks out and emphasises the 'centrifugal' aspects – the flight from a common centre to a disparate periphery where nothing coheres. Instead of men congregating around a common core, they appear to be drifting ever further apart. Auden's poem, like the painting that inspired it, has no focal centre around which the less significant elements are organised; its most important event occurs in its outskirts, 'by the way' as it were. Auden does not fulminate against his fellows for electing to follow the easiest, most thoughtless course in life; in fact, by associating them with the children skating unconcernedly beside the wood he seems to absolve them of all blame. The sun shines as it has to and man must follow his incorrigible nature. Nevertheless, for all the charm of the scene and the excuse offered by its tolerant interpreter, Auden's poem carries an apocalyptic undertone. Must not so much disregard *vis-à-vis* the acts of high courage and monumental achievement undertaken by others meet one day with the punishment it deserves? If men displace such endeavours to the edge of their vision, the very brink of their consciousness, if they relegate the finest accomplishments of their species to the status of museum pieces and if they neglect their religion until it performs a merely perfunctory role in their lives, will they not ultimately foster the return of the Chaos 'of Tumult and Confusion all embroiled, / And Discord with a thousand various mouths' depicted in Milton's *Paradise Lost*? Questions such as these constitute the sub-text of the poem, which Auden prods the reader into formulating despite the unpropitious mood of modern times.

14 Poetry in the Nuclear Age: Ted Hughes

In recent years it has become increasingly difficult for a young writer to pledge himelf, as Auden had done in his undergraduate days, to a career as a poet. The days when poetry was accorded high significance among the social mores – the times when the young Keats could make the romantic gesture of abandoning a profitable career in medicine to plunge himself into the serious but uncertain business of sculpting poems – are long since gone. The years when new instalments of verse-narrative were awaited avidly by a public for whom there was no alternative mode of amusement – when a fledgeling poet like Lord Byron could 'awake one morning and find himself famous' – seem unlikely to return. The aspiring poet nowadays knows that his slim volumes of verses might attract a trickle of sales and a notice in the Sunday newspapers at most.

Aware of the paucity of reward and the dearth of 'feedback' to be anticipated from poetry, today's budding writer is more likely to turn to the more lucrative field of drama. As for those who, despite the unfavourable conditions, elect to pour their talents into the poetic mould, their fate seems less assured. Today's poet must often subsidise his costly creative urge by taking on a full-time job, like the late Philip Larkin, who worked for many years as librarian of Hull University. Or he must, like Thom Gunn, divide his energies between writing and university-teaching (a combination that is not often compatible). He might even, in an age when everything, even culture, seems easily disposable, take the terrifyingly 'logical' step of throwing his own life away, as Sylvia Plath did.

In recent years man's nervousness, doubt and uncertainty – registered so lucidly in Owen's response to the battlefields of the First World War – have been further augmented by the invention of the nuclear bomb and by the realisation that this is, indeed and at last, the weapon that will undo us all. The Western world, already fragmented intellectually and spiritually, now languishes in the knowledge that it may fragment itself physically into the bargain. In the shadow of such a threat the poet does indeed assume the pitiful dimension of a still small voice crying in the wilderness. Yet perhaps even so small a voice, if heeded, may deter mankind from using the 'dreadful darts' with which, like Milton's Death, he is making such menacing gestures.

The writer cannot help but provide a renewal of faith in the better inclinations of mankind's common disposition. The act of writing is in itself an indication that all hope has not been abandoned; the mere fact of 'doing', of 'making' or creating, is a pledge of an irrepressible positivity within the human spirit. Despair knows no action and cannot stir itself from listless immobility, for it can conceive of no possible beneficial consequences. Edmund Spenser, during the Renaissance, personified despair as a man of unkempt appearance sitting on the floor of a dark, damp cave, bereft of vision and lacking even the motivation to feed himself:

> Musing full sadly in his sullen mind;
> His griesie locks, long growen, and unbound,   (greasy)
> Disordered hong about his shoulders round,
> And hid his face; through which his hollow eyne   (eyes)
> Lookt deadly dull, and stared as astound;   (bewildered)
> His raw-bone cheekes through penury and pine,   (starvation)
> Were shronke into his jaws, as he did never dine.   (shrunk)
>
>   (*The Faerie Queene*, I. ix. 35)

However desparate the spiritual condition of man might be, he will not be conducted to the pole of absolute negativity represented by Spenser's Despair so long as he is possessed, and moved, by the impulse to write, to 'pour forth his soul abroad' like Keats's nightingale and dispel for a time the shadows of the circumambient darkness.

Ted Hughes (1930–)

One poet who manages to keep despair at bay is Ted Hughes, who wrote a series of poems celebrating, albeit through the unflattering figure of an unprepossessing, scavenging bird, 'Trembling featherless elbows in the nest's filth', the indomitable will to survive. Hughes published his *Crow* poems in 1971, and in them he depicts a scraggy creature, devoid of conventional morality and lacking a sense of beauty or any regard for traditional religion. One can see in Crow an adumbration of post-nuclear man. The world which Crow inhabits seems to have been overwhelmed by a holocaust of catastrophic proportions:

> the trees closed forever
> And the streets closed forever
>
> And the body lay on the gravel
> Of the abandoned world
> Among abandoned utilities
> Exposed to infinity forever
>
> Crow had to start searching for something to eat.
>
> ('That Moment')

Oblivious to the apocalyptic implications of his environment, Crow, unlike Spenser's Despair, applies himself to the immediate task of satisfying his stomach. Spiritual and aesthetic considerations, existential questionings, can wait; physical demands are more urgent, as becomes apparent in another poem, where the basic driving urges of the irreverent and earthbound Crow, whose formative years have been passed 'under his mother's buttocks', are contrasted with the more visually pleasing and airier activities of other birds:

> While the bullfinch plumped in the apple bud
> And the goldfinch bulbed in the sun
>
> And the wryneck crooked in the moon
> And the dipper peered from the dewball
>
> Crow spraddled head-down in the beach-garbage, guzzling a
> dropped ice-cream.
>
> ('Crow and the Birds')

In rhythm, verb, image and association Crow's 'line' is categorically separate from those of his fellow fowl. Perhaps this suggests that man must follow a radically new direction, eschewing earlier aesthetic, moral and religious guidelines, if he is to survive his present crisis. Certainly, little respect is paid by Crow (or by Hughes) to a conventional religious myth in the following poem.

A Childish Prank

Man's and woman's bodies lay without souls,
Dully gaping, foolishly staring, inert
On the flowers of Eden.
God pondered.

The problem was so great, it dragged him asleep.

Crow laughed.
He bit the Worm, God's only son,
Into two writhing halves.

He stuffed into man the tail half
With the wounded end hanging out.

He stuffed the head half headfirst into woman
And it crept in deeper and up
To peer out through her eyes
Calling its tail-half to join up quickly, quickly
Because O it was painful.

Man awoke being dragged across the grass.
Woman awoke to see him coming.
Neither knew what had happened.

God went on sleeping.

Crow went on laughing.

Crow is always immanently true to his nature as a 'crow'; he is not plagued by any identity problems. Hughes remarked that the animals in his poems are 'in a state of energy which men only have when they have gone mad'. He is perhaps conceiving of 'madness' in the way that Blake saw it: as a stripping away of all the layers of conditioned responses imposed by society's various 'education' systems, to leave simply the 'poor, bare forked animal' of 'unaccommodated man' (as Shakespeare expressed it in his exploration of the ambiguities of 'madness' in *King Lear*). Such madness, such freedom from social taboo or restraint of any sort, leaves Crow with an abundance of energy to devote to his main task of survival. Crow is born unhampered by tradition, community or conscience and nothing extraneous is permitted to intrude on his identity. He is himself alone and takes evident delight in it. His freedom from inherited constraints even allows him a superfluity of energy to spend on amusing himself with the kind of practical joke related in 'A Childish Prank'.

God and His creations, Adam and Eve, are relatively inactive when compared with the superabundant dynamism of the playful Crow. Man and woman lie supine amid 'the flowers of Eden', soullessly staring into space in a stupefied manner reminiscent of the 'deadly dull' gaze of Spenser's Despair. And God, having created His paradise and its occupants, seems at a loss to know how to animate it. This 'problem was so great, it dragged him asleep'. A heavily 'ponderous' and ultimately bored Creator becomes first indifferent and then somnolent. It is left to Crow to fill the man and woman with 'soul' and to bring life and vitality – not to mention humour – into the garden; and to 'crow' over his achievement.

While God sleeps, Crow cackles; and gets busy with his scheme. He snatches 'the Worm' and bites it into 'two writhing halves'. This is a reinterpretation of the serpent-myth of Genesis. The snake who tempted Eve is traditionally identified with Satan but here Hughes brands the reptile as 'God's only son', a radical reassessment of the Bible narrative. In this view the devil, the serpent and the Saviour are all fused into the slimy skin of the writhing 'Worm'. Crow is unceremoniously taking a religious symbol of longstanding affective power and turning it inside out. He behaves similarly in another poem in the series, 'Crow Communes', when, finding himself perched on 'God's shoulder', he 'tore off a mouthful and swallowed': a profane parody of the Eucharist, for Crow 'eats' not to satisfy his spiritual hunger but solely to gratify his body's greed. Nothing is sacred in the land that Crow inhabits.

Crow's perspective on man's creation takes one right back to the starting-point – both of the Bible and of the inherited notion of man's dichotomous nature as part body, part soul. The stress here on the physical aspects – and the 'Worm' is even earthier than the serpent, since it crawls not only on the earth but in it – coupled with Crow's habitual disregard for anything that cannot be exploited for carnal profit and delight suggests that there is nothing ever very refined or spiritual in man's nature or the conduct of his affairs, however he might like to delude himself to the contrary.

Crow is debunking not only the Christian view of man as an angel–animal hybrid but the pre-Christian ideas of Plato which similarly etherealised some of man's basic desires. Plato held that each man or woman was a split half of a complete whole and that the search (usually unsuccessful, and therefore unrelenting) for the 'ideal' partner was a quest for the primordial 'other half' of his or her entity. 'Platonic love' hence celebrates the non-sensual, or 'spiritual', aspects of male/female relations and demotes the significance of, or even the need for, physical motives. Crow certainly gives short shrift to this refinement. Man's search for his 'opposite number' is simply the urge of the worm to reunite with its other segment. The worm's phallic signification is obvious, as is the suggestion that the only nexus binding man and woman together is the genital one. The repetition of the verb 'stuffed' not only emphasises the crude haste of Crow's surgical operation but draws attention to the sexual act to which mankind will be permanently condemned by Crow's prank. The 'pain' of love, so long celebrated by poets of many civilisations, is here revealed as nothing more than the two halves of the severed worm crying out for their 'wounds' to be healed by reunification, 'Because O it was painful'. The woman's eyes, through which in the courtly love tradition the woman's soul and the essence of her finer nature make themselves known, here communicate nothing 'holier' than an insatiable yearning for phallic repletion: a 'deep' and instinctive urge that cries out to be satisfied, 'quickly, quickly'.

Reflected in Crow's unglazed eye, man's claims to spirituality are made to look ridiculous in the light of his subjection to his body's demands ('Man awoke being dragged across the grass'). Rather than being uplifted or impelled in response to any finer feeling sown in him by God, man is merely possessed and animated by a sexual desire of whose roots he remains ignorant ('Neither knew what had happened') and which he misinterprets as an urge for spiritual union with 'God's only son'. On this reading, all human behaviour, including the practice of religious devotion, is reducible to the instinct for sexual satisfaction and any apparently non-sexual activity would be simple sublimation of this fundamental desire. Crow is obviously a Freudian.

At the poem's end God continues sleeping, a sleep that will presumably endure till doomsday. The indifference subsisting between Creator and created in modern societies seems permanent. A point has been reached where it is becoming more and more difficult to accommodate God. There is no room either within the inn or without it. Perhaps the 'natural' end of a congregation so spiritually adrift will be the kind of universal cataclysm that is understood to have ushered in the topsy-turvy landscape of the *Crow* poems. Yet, despite the bleak vision of the future displayed in Hughes's *Crow* poems, all is not despair. After such debunking and mockery as God is treated to by Crow's mischievous antics, can any residual respect for religious values remain? What Hughes may be inculcating is a purge, a thorough-going clean-out of all the vestigial lumber in man's religious consciousness, all the piled-up obsolete symbols accumulated from earlier centuries (the 'flowers of Eden', Adam and Eve, the serpent), in order for man to reappraise, perhaps even reactivate, his relationship with God. Only by such a 'shocking' irreverence as Crow displays towards the Almighty in these poems could so necessary a 'purification' be effected. This having been done, a revitalised spirituality might ensue and mankind be once more able to behold a creation 'Speechless with admiration', like Crow in 'Crow Goes Hunting'.

Crow, in the end, is the force of life itself, the Eros-instinct, the determination to survive, adapt and endure at all costs. At the same time he never deviates from his quintessential identity as crow. Even when he uses his imagination, he does so in a way that conforms entirely to his inherent nature (digging up worms). Crow survives through energy, imagination and fidelity to intuition. The poet exercises similar faculties; and even if the world around him is falling to pieces, the strength of mind he evinces in taking up his pen and filling an empty sheet of paper with words, images, associations, combinations and music is a pledge of hope, a witness that so long as the poet endures the human spirit is not yet interred for all time.

Chronological Table

	Historical and political events	Literary and cultural events
1554		Sidney born.
1558	Succession of Elizabeth I to throne (until 1603).	
1564		Shakespeare born.
1572		Donne born.
1578	Drake begins voyage round the world (completed in 1580).	
1586		Death of Sidney.
1587	Settlement of Raleigh colony in Virginia; execution of Mary Queen of Scots.	
1588	Defeat of Spanish Armada.	
1590		Publication of Spenser's *Faerie Queene* (Books I–III).
1591		Publication of Sidney's *Astrophel and Stella*.
1593		Herbert born.
1600	Charter granted to East India Company.	
1603	Reign of James I (until 1625).	
1605	Failure of Gunpowder Plot (to blow up parliament).	
1609		Publication of Shakespeare's *Sonnets*.
1611		Publication of King James (Authorised) Version of Bible.
1616		Death of Shakespeare.
1620	Arrival of Pilgrim Fathers in Massachusetts.	
1621		Marvell born.
1625	Reign of Charles I (until 1649).	
1629	Dissolution of parliament (until 1640).	

	Historical and political events	*Literary and cultural events*
1631		Death of Donne; birth of Dryden.
1633		Death of Herbert; publication of Donne's *Poems* and of Herbert's *Temple*.
1642	Start of Civil War.	Closing of the theatres (until 1660).
1649	Execution of Charles I; abolition of monarchy; Protectorate of Cromwell.	
1651		Publication of Hobbes's *Leviathan*.
1658	Death of Cromwell.	
1660	The Restoration: monarchy of Charles II (until 1685).	
1662		Royal Society chartered.
1665	Great Plague of London.	
1666	Fire of London.	
1667		Publication of Milton's *Paradise Lost*; Swift born.
1671		Publication of Milton's *Samson Agonistes*.
1678		Death of Marvell; publication of Bunyan's *Pilgrim's Progress*.
1681		Publication of Marvell's *Miscellaneous Poems*.
1684		Publication of Dryden's 'To the Memory of Mr Oldham'.
1685	Reign of James II (until 1688); Duke of Monmouth's rebellion crushed at Sedgemoor.	
1688	Landing of William of Orange in England; flight of James II.	Pope born.
1689	Joint accession of William and Mary to throne (until 1694).	
1690	Defeat of James II's Irish army by William at Battle of the Boyne.	
1694	Death of Queen Mary; reign of William III (until 1702).	
1698		Publication of Collier's *Short View of the English Stage*; end of Restoration-drama revival.
1700		Death of Dryden.
1702	Reign of Queen Anne (until 1714).	

	Historical and political events	*Literary and cultural events*
1707	Union of Scotland and England.	
1709		Publication of Swift's 'Description of the Morning'.
1713	Treaty of Utrecht, ending War of Spanish Succession.	
1714	Reign of George I (until 1727); start of Whig Oligarchy (until 1760).	Publication of Pope's *Rape of the Lock*.
1716		Gray born.
1721	Sir Robert Walpole's Prime Ministership (until 1742).	
1722		Publication of Defoe's *Moll Flanders*.
1726		Publication of Swift's *Gulliver's Travels*.
1727	Reign of George II (until 1760).	
1740		Publication of Richardson's *Pamela*.
1744		Death of Pope.
1745	Jacobite rebellion in Scotland,	Death of Swift.
1746	stamped out at Culloden.	
1749		Publication of Fielding's *Tom Jones*.
1751		Publication of Gray's 'Elegy'.
1756	Start of Seven Years' War with France.	
1757	Clive's defeat of French in India.	Blake born.
1759	Wolfe's victory over French at Quebec.	
1760	Reign of George III (until 1820).	
1764	Discovery of steam power by Watt; invention by Hargreaves of the spinning jenny.	
1765		Publication of Johnson's *Preface to Shakespeare*.
1768	Cook's first voyage to Australia and New Zealand.	Foundation of Royal Academy under Joshua Reynolds.
1770		Wordsworth born.
1771		Death of Gray.
1775	American War of Independence (until 1783).	
1776	American Declaration of Independence.	Publication of Volume I of Gibbon's *Decline and Fall of the Roman Empire*.
1781		Publication of Rousseau's *Confessions*.

Historical and political events	*Literary and cultural events*
1788	Byron born.
1789 Start of French Revolution.	Publication of Blake's *Songs of Innocence*.
1792	Shelley born.
1793 Louis XVI of France executed; start of Reign of Terror; France and Britain at war.	
1794 Fall of Robespierre and end of Reign of Terror.	Publication of Blake's *Songs of Experience*.
1795	Keats born.
1798	Publication of *Lyrical Ballads* (by Wordsworth and Coleridge).
1799 Pitt's Combination Acts, banning trades unions.	
1801 Union of Great Britain and Ireland.	
1802	Publication of Wordsworth's *Preface to Lyrical Ballads*.
1804 Napoleon declared Emperor of France.	
1805 Defeat of French navy by Nelson at Trafalgar.	
1807 Slave trade abolished.	End of Wordsworth's 'fertile' period.
1809	Tennyson born.
1811 George III declared insane; Prince George's regency (until 1820).	
1812	Publication of Cantos I and II of Byron's *Childe Harold's Pilgrimage*; Browning born.
1813	Publication of Jane Austen's *Pride and Prejudice*.
1815 Defeat of Napoleon at Waterloo; Holy Alliance agreed among reactionary powers of Europe.	
1816	Publication of Coleridge's 'Kubla Khan'.
1817	Publication of Coleridge's *Biographia Literaria* and Keats's 'Chapman's Homer' sonnet.
1819 'Peterloo' massacre in Manchester.	Keats's 'miraculous year' of poetic creation; Shelley's 'England in 1819', 'Ode to the West Wind' and Act III of *Prometheus Unbound* written.
1820 Reign of George IV (until 1830).	

Historical and political events	*Literary and cultural events*
1821	Death of Keats in Rome.
1822	Death of Shelley in Italy; Arnold born.
1823	Publication of Byron's *Don Juan*.
1824	Death of Byron in Greece.
1825 Stockton and Darlington railway opened.	
1827	Death of Blake.
1830 Reign of William IV (until 1837).	
1832 First Reform Act passed, extending vote among middle classes.	
1833 Slavery abolished; Oxford Movement launched by Keble, Newman and Pusey.	First part of Tennyson's *In Memoriam* written.
1837 Reign of Queen Victoria (until 1901).	Publication of Dickens's *Oliver Twist*.
1839 Chartists' petition rejected by parliament.	
1840	Hardy born.
1842	Publication of Browning's 'My Last Duchess'.
1844	Hopkins born.
1845 Great Famine in Ireland.	
1846 Repeal of Corn Laws.	
1847	Publication of Emily Brontë's *Wuthering Heights* and Marx's *Communist Manifesto*.
1849	Arnold's 'To Marguerite – Continued' written.
1850	Death of Wordsworth.
1851 Opening of Great Exhibition in London.	
1854 Start of Crimean War against Russia (until 1856).	
1857 Indian Mutiny.	
1859	Publication of Darwin's *Origin of Species*.
1860 Unification of Italy.	Publication of Dickens's *Great Expectations*.
1865	Yeats born.
1867 Second Reform Act passed, extending vote to urban working classes; Dominion of Canada established.	Publication of Marx's *Das Kapital*.

Historical and political events	*Literary and cultural events*
1868 Gladstone's reforming ministry (until 1874).	
1870 Forster's Education Act passed, providing primary education for all.	
1871–2	Publication of George Eliot's *Middlemarch*.
1874 Work of social reform continued by Disraeli's ministry (until 1880).	
1876 Designation of Victoria as Empress of India.	
1877	Hopkins's 'God's Grandeur' written.
1884 Third Reform Act passed, enfranchising working classes.	
1888	Death of Arnold; T. S. Eliot born.
1889	Publication of Tennyson's 'Crossing the Bar'; deaths of Browning and Hopkins.
1891	Publication of Hardy's *Tess of the d'Urbervilles*.
1892	Death of Tennyson.
1893	Owen born.
1896	Wilde imprisoned.
1897 Victoria's Diamond Jubilee.	
1899 Boer War in South Africa (until 1902).	
1900 Foundation of Labour Party.	Hardy's 'The Darkling Thrush' written; Freud's *Interpretation of Dreams* published.
1901 Reign of Edward VII (until 1910); Commonwealth of Australia established.	
1902	Publication of Conrad's *Heart of Darkness*.
1904 *Entente cordiale* between Britain and France.	
1905 Rise to prominence of Mrs Pankhurst's Suffragette movement.	Einstein's Theory of Relativity propounded.
1906 Liberals in power (until 1915), laying foundations of Welfare State.	
1907 Anglo-Russian *Entente*.	Auden born.

	Historical and political events	*Literary and cultural events*
1910	Reign of George V (until 1936); Union of South Africa set up.	
1913		Publication of Lawrence's *Sons and Lovers*.
1914	Start of First World War.	
1916		Dadaism launched in Zurich.
1917	Russian Revolution.	Publication of Eliot's 'Prufrock'.
1918	Universal franchise enacted; November Armistice signed, ending First World War.	Owen killed in France.
1919	Treaty of Versailles signed, demanding heavy war reparations from Germany.	
1920	League of Nations founded.	Publication of Owen's *Collected Poems*.
1921		Eliot's *The Waste Land* written.
1922	Partition of Ireland effected; rise to power of Mussolini in Italy.	Joyce's *Ulysses* published; regular broadcasts on BBC begun.
1924	First Labour government (under Ramsay MacDonald); death of Lenin.	Publication of Forster's *Passage to India* and André Breton's 'Manifeste du surréalisme'.
1926	General Strike.	Yeats's 'Sailing to Byzantium' written and *A Vision* published.
1927		Publication of Virginia Woolf's *To the Lighthouse*.
1928		Death of Hardy.
1929	Collapse of New York Stock Exchange.	
1930		Ted Hughes born.
1931	Start of Great Depression; 'National' coalition government formed.	
1933	Hitler's rise to Chancellorship of Germany.	
1936	Accession of Edward VIII followed by his abdication; reign of George VI (until 1952); start of Spanish Civil War (until 1939).	
1938	Germany's invasion of Austria; Chamberlain's 'agreement' with Hitler at Munich.	Auden's 'Musée des Beaux Arts' written.
1939	Nazi-Soviet Pact; Hitler's invasion of Poland, initiating Second World War (until 1945).	Death of Yeats.

	Historical and political events	*Literary and cultural events*
1940	Frustration of Hitler's invasion plans by Battle of Britain.	
1942	Beveridge Report produced, drawing blueprint for comprehensive National Insurance.	
1944	Butler's Education Act passed, expanding opportunities of secondary education.	
1945	Atom bombs dropped on Hiroshima and Nagasaki; commitment of Attlee's Labour government to widespread social welfare and nationalisation policies.	Publication of Orwell's *Animal Farm*.
1947	Independence granted to India.	
1948	Gandhi assassinated; blockade by Russia of West Berlin.	
1950	Start of Korean War (until 1953).	
1952	Start of reign of Elizabeth II.	
1953		Beckett's *Waiting for Godot* performed in Paris.
1956	Anglo-French invasion of Egypt aborted; Hungarian uprising crushed by Russian troops.	Osborne's *Look Back in Anger* performed in London.
1957	Replacement of Eden by Macmillan as leader of Tory government.	
1958	Race riots in Notting Hill, London.	
1961	Departure of South Africa from Commonwealth.	
1963	Assassination of President Kennedy.	
1964	Election victory of Wilson's Labour government.	Publication of Larkin's *Whitsun Weddings*.
1965		Death of Eliot.
1968		Theatre censorship abolished.
1969	Start of 'troubles' in Northern Ireland; landing of Americans on the Moon.	
1970	Heath's Conservative government elected; death of de Gaulle.	
1971		Publication of Hughes's *Crow*.

	Historical and political events	*Literary and cultural events*
1973	Entry of Britain into Common Market.	Death of Auden.
1974	Heath government brought down by miner's strike; resignation of President Nixon after Watergate.	
1979	Election victory for Conservatives under Margaret Thatcher; 'intervention' of Russia in Afghanistan.	
1984	Miner's strike (defeated after one year).	
1985		Hughes nominated Poet Laureate. Death of Larkin.

Select Bibliography

The works of the major British poets are available in complete standard editions or comprehensive selections, such as Oxford Standard Authors (Oxford University Press) and Penguin English Poets (Penguin Books). The following is a list of background and critical material for suggested further reading. Most of these books contain bibliographies useful for those who wish to extend their studies.

I. GENERAL BOOKS ON POETRY AND POETIC TECHNIQUES

BARBER, CHARLES, *Poetry in English* (Macmillan, 1983).
BATESON, F. W., *English Poetry* (Longmans, 1950).
BOULTON, MARJORIE, *Anatomy of Poetry* (Routledge & Kegan Paul, 1953).
BROOKS, C. and WARREN, R.P., *Understanding Poetry* (Henry Holt, 1938).

All of these books offer useful introductory guidance in poetry analysis. Barber combines a study of technique and genres with a historical perspective.

II. GENERAL HISTORICAL BACKGROUND

TREVELYAN, G. M., *A Shortened History of England* (Penguin, 1959).

Trevelyan's book is a useful chronological account but necessarily summary. For more detailed information in specific areas *The Oxford History of England* (15 vols, Clarendon, 1936–65), editor Sir George Clark, is authoritative.

III GENERAL HISTORIES OF LITERATURE

FORD, BORIS (ed.), *The New Pelican Guide to English Literature*, 8 vols (Penguin, 1983).

240

JEFFARES, A. NORMAN (ed.), *The Macmillan History of Literature*, 13 vols (Macmillan, 1982–85). Titles as follows:

MICHAEL ALEXANDER, *Old English Literature*
HARRY BLAMIRES, *Twentieth-Century English Literature*
DEREK BREWER, *English Gothic Literature*
KEN GOODWIN, *A History of Australian Literature*
A. NORMAN JEFFARES, *Anglo-Irish Literature*
DECLAN KIBERD, *A History of Literature in the Irish Language*
BRUCE KING, *Seventeenth-Century English Literature*
ALISTAIR NIVEN, *Commonwealth Literature*
MAXIMILIAN NOVAK, *Eighteenth-Century English Literature*
MURRAY ROTSON, *Sixteenth-Century English Literature*
MARGARET STONYK, *Nineteenth-Century English Literature*
MARSHALL WALKER, *The Literature of the United States*
RORY WATSON, *The Literature of Scotland*

Each of these series offers comprehensive coverage of the major writers in the various epochs, together with studies of the cultural and intellectual backgrounds. The recently produced Macmillan series includes volumes on American, Anglo-Irish, Scottish and Commonwealth literatures; the Pelican has been recently updated and incorporates essays on children's literature, Commonwealth writers and British opera.

IV. THE ELIZABETHANS AND SHAKESPEARE

BOOTH, STEPHEN, *An Essay on Shakespeare's Sonnets* (Yale U.P., 1969).
FULLER, JOHN, *The Sonnet*, No. 26 of *The Critical Idiom* (former editor John D. Jump) (Methuen, 1972).
KALSTONE, DAVID, *Sidney's Poetry: Contexts and Interpretations* (Harvard U.P., 1965).
LEVER, J. W., *The Elizabethan Love Sonnet* (Methuen, 1966).
LEWIS, C. S., *English Literature in the Sixteenth-Century, excluding Drama* (Oxford U.P., 1954).
LOVEJOY, ARTHUR O., *The Great Chain of Being* (Harvard U.P., 1936).
TILLYARD, E. M. W., *The Elizabethan World Picture* (Chatto & Windus, 1943).

Lewis, Lovejoy and Tillyard, though somewhat 'ancient' now, offer insights into the period that continue to be of value.

V. THE 17TH CENTURY

ALVAREZ, ALFRED, *The School of Donne* (Chatto & Windus, 1961).
BENNETT, JOAN, *Five Metaphysical Poets* (Cambridge U.P., 1963).
ELIOT, T. S., *Selected Essays* (Faber, 1932).
LEISHMAN, J. B., *The Monarch of Wit* (Hutchinson, 1951).

242 BRITISH POETRY SINCE THE SIXTEENTH CENTURY

POLLARD, ARTHUR (ed.), *Andrew Marvell: Poems. A Casebook* (Macmillan, 1980).
SUMMERS, JOSEPH H., *George Herbert: His Religion and Art* (Chatto & Windus, 1954).
TUVE, ROSAMUND, *Elizabethan and Metaphysical Imagery* (University of Chicago Press, 1947).
WILLEY, BASIL, *The Seventeenth Century Background* (Chatto & Windus, 1934).

Willey's book is a basic background study; Eliot's and Bennett's appraisals of metaphysical poetry have been influential; Summers provides a conscientious study of Herbert; Leishman examines cerebral qualities in Donne; Pollard covers Marvell comprehensively.

VI. THE AUGUSTANS AND THE 18TH CENTURY

BROWER, REUBEN A., *Alexander Pope: The Poetry of Allusion* (Oxford U.P., 1959).
CLIFFORD, JAMES L. (ed.), *Eighteenth Century English Literature: Modern Essays in Criticism* (Oxford U.P., 1959).
DOBRÉE, BONAMY, *English Literature in the Early Eighteenth Century, 1700–1740* (Clarendon, 1959).
HILLES, F. W. and BLOOM, HAROLD, (eds.), *From Sensibility to Romanticism* (Yale U.P., 1965).
HUMPHREYS, A. R., *The Augustan World: Life and Letters in Eighteenth-Century England* (Methuen, 1954).
MINER, EARL, *Dryden's Poetry* (Indiana U.P., 1967).
POLLARD, ARTHUR, *Satire.* No. 7 of *The Critical Idiom* (former editor John D. Jump) (Methuen, 1970).
WILLEY, BASIL, *The Eighteenth Century Background* (Chatto & Windus, 1940).

Again, Willey supplies fundamental material on the spirit of the age. Clifford's essay collection examines various aspects of the time through its main literary figures; Humphreys explores the cross-fertilisation of literature and society.

VII. THE ROMANTICS

ABRAMS, M. H., *Natural Supernaturalism: Tradition and Revolution in Romantic Literature* (Oxford U.P., 1971).
BLACKSTONE, BERNARD, *English Blake* (Archon, 1966).
BLUNDEN, EDMUND, *Shelley: A Life Story* (Collins, 1946).
BOWRA, C. M., *The Romantic Imagination* (Oxford U.P., 1950).
BROOKS, CLEANTH, *The Well Wrought Urn* (Dobson, 1949).
FRYE, NORTHROP (ed.), *Romanticism Reconsidered* (Columbia U.P., 1963).
FURST, LILIAN R., *Romanticism.* No. 2 of *The Critical Idiom*, (former editor John D. Jump) (Methuen, 1969).
JONES, JOHN, *The Egotistical Sublime: A History of Wordsworth's Imagination* (Chatto & Windus, 1954).
KNIGHT, G. WILSON, *Lord Byron: Christian Virtues* (Oxford U.P., 1953).

WARD, AILEEN, *John Keats: The Making of a Poet* (Secker & Warburg, 1963).

Furst outlines the contours of a rich terrain; Bowra and Brooks explore deeper. The books by Blackstone, Blunden, Jones, Knight and Ward are examples among the many hundreds of studies on the individual poets.

VIII. THE VICTORIANS

BLOOM, HAROLD and MUNICH, ADRIENNE (eds.), *Robert Browning* (Prentice Hall, 1981).

BUCKLEY, J. H., *Tennyson: The Growth of a Poet* (Harvard U.P., 1961).

———— *The Victorian Temper: A Study in Literary Culture* (Allen & Unwin, 1952).

DAVIE, DONALD, *Thomas Hardy and British Poetry* (Routledge & Kegan Paul, 1973).

JOHNSON, E. D. H., *The Alien Vision of Victorian Poetry: Sources of the Poetic Imagination in Tennyson, Browning and Arnold* (Archon, 1952).

LANGBAUM, ROBERT, *The Poetry of Experience: The Dramatic Monologue in Modern Literary Tradition* (Chatto & Windus, 1957).

PEARSALL, RONALD, *The Worm in the Bud: The World of Victorian Sexuality* (Penguin, 1971).

PICK, JOHN, *Gerard Manley Hopkins, Priest and Poet* (Oxford U.P., 1949).

TRILLING, LIONEL, *Matthew Arnold* (Allen & Unwin, 1949).

WILLEY, BASIL, *Nineteenth Century Studies* (Chatto & Windus, 1949).

WILLIAMS, RAYMOND, *Culture and Society, 1780–1950* (Penguin, 1961).

Pearsall exposes some of the repressions in Victorian society and their diversion into literature; Williams concentrates on the economic factors behind literary creation. Langbaum examines Browning's perfection of the dramatic monologue, and Davie considers Hardy's contribution to modernism.

IX. THE 20TH CENTURY

BERGONZI, BERNARD (ed.), *The Twentieth Century*, Vol. 7 of *Sphere History of Literature in the English Language* (Sphere, 1970).

GARDNER, HELEN, *The Art of T. S. Eliot* (Cresset, 1949).

GIFFORD, TERRY and ROBERTS, NEIL, *Ted Hughes: A Critical Study* (Faber, 1981).

JEFFARES, A. NORMAN, *W. B. Yeats: Man and Poet* (Routledge & Kegan Paul, 1949; rev. ed. 1962).

SILKIN, JON, *Out of Battle: The Poetry of the Great War* (Oxford U.P., 1972).

SISSON, C. H., *English Poetry 1900–1950: An Assessment* (Methuen, 1981).

SPEARS, MONROE K., *The Poetry of W. H. Auden: The Disenchanted Island* (Oxford U.P., 1963).

STEAD, C. K., *The New Poetic* (Hutchinson, 1964).

WELLAND, D. S. R., *Wilfred Owen: A Critical Study* (Chatto & Windus, 1960).

Jeffares' and Gardner's studies of Yeats and Eliot are seminal; Bergonzi provides a brisk sweep through all the literary fields of the period; Sisson traces the germination of modern poetry from some 19th-century seeds.

Index